MEN
BEHIND THE
MEDALS

MEN
BEHIND THE
MEDALS

A NEW SELECTION

AIR COMMODORE
GRAHAM PITCHFORK

First published in 2003
This edition first published in 2009

The History Press
The Mill, Brimscombe Port
Stroud, Gloucestershire, GL5 2QG
www.thehistorypress.co.uk

British Library Cataloguing in Publication Data.
A catalogue record for this book is available from the British Library.

ISBN 978 0 7524 5027 8

Typesetting and origination by The History Press
Printed in Great Britain

Contents

Air Chief Marshal Sir 'Sandy' Wilson KCB, AFC

If I were asked what characteristics most personified the generation that fought in the Second World War, like many others, I am sure, I would have to say that bravery and modesty were uppermost. Certainly, these characteristics are to be found in ample measure in this fascinating book.

Those of us who served in the Armed Forces in the aftermath of that war were privileged to know and fly with many gallant aircrew who had served with such distinction during those times. Although we thought we knew them well, and notwithstanding how distinguished they were, it was often not until we read their obituaries in our national newspapers that we gained any real appreciation of their service and heroism. Even then, one is often left wondering how much more could have been said. This was brought home to me when I was asked by the family of one of the most famous of all wartime aircrew, Flight Lieutenant Bill Reid VC, to give an address at his funeral. Whilst the epic story of how he won his supreme award has been widely told, it was only when I began to research the rest of his wartime service that I realised how much more there was to record.

As President of the Aircrew Association, I have been privileged to meet many of that modest wartime generation, and to hear at first hand their truly amazing untold stories. I have often asked them why they had not recorded their experiences for the benefit of future generations. Almost always, they reply, 'But I did no more than countless others – and would anyone be interested in my experiences anyway?' My instant reply has always been an emphatic 'Of course they would!'

Having said that, it has to be added that it takes the professional skill of an airmen with an acute eye for history to bring such stories properly to life. In this, his second volume of *Men Behind the Medals*, Air Commodore Graham Pitchfork has done just that and, once again, has brought these incredible stories to light before it is too late. In this volume he has gone further by including many roles and theatres not covered in his previous book, and it is particularly appropriate that he has included aircrew who served in the Fleet Air Arm and the Army, as well as one story featuring that loyal and dedicated band of RAF ground crew.

As we have come to expect, Air Commodore Pitchfork has researched this book meticulously, and it is enhanced by the many illustrations and photographs never before published – many provided by the individuals and their families. The book makes a very valuable and important contribution to our aviation history. Above all, these stories, which personify the grit, gallantry and sense of duty of this modest era of aircrew, should serve as an example to both present and future generations.

Sandy Wilson
Stow-on-the-Wold

Acknowledgements

Writing this book about gallant aircrew has been a particularly rewarding task, but it could not have been completed without a great deal of help from many people. Their patience, support, expert advice and friendship have allowed me to complete this second volume; I am extremely grateful and wish to thank all of them. I would particularly like to thank my friend of over forty years, Air Chief Marshal Sir 'Sandy' Wilson for his support and for his generous Foreword. As the President of the Aircrew Association, no one is more qualified to appreciate the exploits of the men whose stories appear in this book.

The Director of the Air Historical Branch, Sebastian Cox, and his excellent staff have given me a great deal of assistance, none more so than Graham Day. The staffs of the Public Record Office have also been most helpful. Ken Delve of Key Publishing and Ken Ellis, the editor of *Flypast* magazine, have given a great deal of advice, and I am grateful to both for their continued support of my series 'Men Behind the Medals' in their excellent magazine. I am very grateful that they have agreed to continue with the series after the publication of this book. Group Captain Chris Morris has proofread every chapter as it has been completed, and his expert advice has been invaluable. Wing Commander Jim Routledge has, once again, given his expert advice on medals. Paul Baillie, John Foreman and Mike King have given me valuable assistance, and I thank Jimmie Taylor for allowing me to use some of his research material for the Arnhem operation.

Photographs are a key component of this book and I want to thank my old friends Peter Green, Andy Thomas and Chris Ashworth for the loan of photographs, and for their advice and help on many aspects. I thank Paul Johnson at the Public Record Office, Flight Lieutenant Mary Hudson at the Air Historical Branch, and the staff of the Imperial War Museum for their help and for permission to use copyright photographs. Many others helped with individual photographs, and I hope they will accept the individual acknowledgements as my thanks for their help.

I am particularly grateful to Lady Lawrence, Mrs Ann Evans, Mrs Irene Neale and Mrs Estelle Wright for allowing me access to their late husbands' logbooks, papers and photograph albums. Also Nicholas Webb who loaned

me a great deal of material relating to his late grandfather, and to Jennie
McIntosh for help with material relating to her late father, John Neale,
who died during the preparation of this book. I reserve a very special
thank-you to members of the Aircrew Association, other former aircrew
who have given valuable advice, and to some of the 'Men' who appear in
this book. In particular, I want to single out the following who entertained
me in their homes, gave valuable information and advice and could not
have been more helpful and kind: Frank Bayliss AFM, the late Ken Brain
DFC, Dudley Burnside DSO, OBE, DFC and Bar, John Cruikshank VC,
Derek Smith DFC and Bar, Freddie Deeks DFC, Lionel Daffurn DFC,
David Ellis DFC, Guy Fazan DFC, Terry Goodwin DFC, DFM, Arthur
Hall DFC and Bar, Bob Large DFC, Derek Manley, Roy Marlow MM,
the late John Neale DSC, DFC, Doug Nicholls DFC, Charles Patterson
DSO, DFC, Tom Pratt DFC, Joe Reed DFC, the late Bill Reid VC, Denys
Stanley MBE, DFC, Jack Strain DFM, Joe Townshend DFM, David Urry,
the late Aubrey Young DFC.

Finally, I want to thank the staff of Sutton Publishing for all their
support, in particular Jonathan Falconer, Nick Reynolds, Elizabeth Stone
and Bow Watkinson.

Preface

The chapters that follow relate the stories of twenty gallant young men who flew on operations during the Second World War. Their particular stories have been selected in order to embrace a wide cross-section of the flying operations conducted, in the main, by the Royal Air Force. However, in recognition of the significant contributions made by aircrew serving in the Fleet Air Arm and the British Army, I have included a chapter devoted to a man from each of these services. I have tried to embrace as many different roles and theatres of operations as possible, but not all can be included. Some were covered in volume one of *Men Behind the Medals*, and some omitted from the earlier book have been included in this volume, making, I trust, a very wide and comprehensive range across the two volumes.

I have endeavoured to include as many different aircrew categories as possible, and also to include a wide example of the decorations awarded for gallantry in the air. Inevitably in a book limited to twenty accounts, there are a number of omissions, and I consciously decided not to include accounts of Victoria Cross holders since their amazing experiences have been covered in numerous other publications. I have not included the Conspicuous Gallantry Medal, although the story of Sergeant Stuart Sloan CGM is covered in volume one. As in that volume, it has been my intention that each story stands on its own as a comprehensive account of an individual's flying career, and this has caused a certain degree of overlap. For example, two of the 'Men behind the Medals' took part in bombing operations over North Africa, and two others took part in the first One Thousand Bomber Raid on Cologne. In other respects their stories are very different, and they would have been incomplete if I had abbreviated them on the basis that details had appeared in an earlier chapter.

Despite many years researching the history of the air war of 1939 to 1945, I continue to be amazed at the variety of roles, activities and the sheer scale of the air operations. One thing, however, remains constant, and transcends every other aspect – the determination, comradeship, gallantry and raw courage of a generation of young men who fought for our freedom. Sadly, they are now fading into history, but their exploits need to live on forever as a stimulus and example for future generations. They should never be forgotten, and, as in Volume One, I dedicate this book to 'the Many.'

Chapter One

The Medals

Introduction

This book tells the story of the exploits and service of gallant aircrew from all three British services whose courage was recognised by the award of medals for service during the Second World War. Some general knowledge of the medals referred to in the chapters that follow would, I believe, provide some useful and interesting background. However, it is not the intention to treat the reader to a detailed study of British medals. This is a vast and fascinating topic and there are some outstanding works that the enthusiast can study; none more so than *British Gallantry Awards* by Abbott and Tamplin and *British Battles and Medals* by Gordon, both of which are strongly recommended.

The medals that appear in this book can be split into four categories: gallantry, campaign service, long service and commemorative. This chapter will concentrate on the background to the medals awarded to British and Commonwealth aircrew for gallantry and for service in the Second World War.

Readers should be aware that major changes were made to the Honours system in 1993, and some well-known gallantry medals have disappeared – for example, the Distinguished Flying Medal. Others, such as the Conspicuous Gallantry Cross, have been introduced. Since all the stories covered in this book relate to the Second World War, these changes will not be discussed in this chapter, and all reference to medals will be based on the pre-1993 changes.

The exploits of those awarded the Victoria Cross, the nation's ultimate award for gallantry, have been researched and related in great detail and thus, I have chosen not to include a story of one of the recipients. To those with a specific interest in this award to airmen, I strongly recommend they read the eminent air historian Chaz Bowyer's *For Valour. The Air VCs.*

The descriptions outlined below are general and do not go into the numerous warrants, minor changes and styles of naming that have been made over the years. Clearly, all the awards reflect the appropriate cypher and crown, but this book is concerned only with those awarded during the reigns of His Majesty King George VI and Queen Elizabeth II. The gallantry medals that appear in the following chapters are listed in order of precedence.

The Most Excellent Order of the British Empire

This order was founded by King George V in June 1917 for services to the Empire. A military division was created in December 1918 with awards made to commissioned and warrant officers for distinguished services of a non-combatant character. The order consists of five classes and a medal. The insignia of the civil and military divisions is identical, but distinguished by their respective ribbons. In both cases, the ribbon is rose pink edged with pearl grey; the military division has a narrow central stripe, also in pearl grey. An example of the fourth order (officer) is included in this book.

Distinguished Service Order

The Distinguished Service Order (DSO) was instituted in 1886 and is only awarded to commissioned officers. It is available to members of all three services for 'distinguished services under fire', which might include a specific act of gallantry or distinguished service over a period of time. A good example of the former was the immediate award made to the then Pilot Officer Leonard Cheshire for safely bringing back to base his Whitley bomber of 102 Squadron, which had been severely damaged by enemy fire over Cologne.

The silver-gilt and white enamelled cross with the crown on the obverse and the cypher on the reverse hangs from a laurelled suspender and a red ribbon with narrow blue borders, which is attached to a similar laurelled bar and brooch. The year of award is engraved on the back of the suspender. Bars are awarded for subsequent acts of distinguished service or gallantry and these are similar in design to the brooch and suspender bars.

Some 870 orders and 72 bars were awarded to members of the Royal Air Force during the Second World War. A further 217 orders and 13 bars were awarded to members of the Commonwealth Air Forces and a further 38 Honorary Awards to foreign (non-Commonwealth) officers.

Distinguished Service Cross

The Conspicuous Service Cross, later to become the Distinguished Service Cross (DSC), was instituted in June 1901, primarily to be awarded to warrant officers or subordinate officers of the Royal Navy for meritorious or distinguished service in action. On 14 October 1914 it was re-designated the 'Distinguished Service Cross' when the eligibility was extended to officers below the rank of Lieutenant Commander. Subsequently, further Orders in Council were made, which extended the eligibility to other forces. This included, from 17 April 1940, officers and warrant officers of the Royal Air Force serving with the Fleet.

The plain cross with rounded ends has the crowned royal cypher on the obverse, and the plain reverse is hallmarked with the date of issue engraved on the lower limb. The cross is attached to the ribbon, of three equal parts of dark blue, white and dark blue, by a silver ring passing through a smaller ring fixed to the top of the cross. Bars are awarded for further acts of gallantry and the year of award is engraved on the reverse.

Distinguished Flying Cross

Following the formation of an independent Royal Air Force on 1 April 1918, specific awards for gallantry in the air were instituted on 3 June 1918. This included the Distinguished Flying Cross (DFC) awarded to officers and warrant officers 'for exceptional valour, courage and devotion to duty while flying in active operations against the enemy'. The award was extended to equivalent ranks in the Royal Navy on 11 March 1941.

The silver cross flory is surmounted by another cross of aeroplane propellers with a centre roundel within a wreath of laurels with an imperial crown and the letters RAF. The reverse is plain with the royal cypher above the date 1918. The cross is attached to the ribbon by a clasp adorned with two sprigs of laurel. Since July 1919 the ribbon has been violet and white alternate stripes running at an angle of forty-five degrees from left to right. The year of award is engraved on the reverse. Bars are awarded for further acts of gallantry and the year of award is engraved in a similar fashion.

During the Second World War just over 20,000 awards were made with a further 1,592 bars. Among the latter were forty-two second bars. Officers of the Royal Artillery engaged in flying duties during 1944 and 1945 were awarded eighty-seven crosses: the exploits of one of these officers, Captain A. Young, are described in a later chapter.

Air Force Cross

The Air Force Cross (AFC) was introduced at the same time as the DFC. It too is awarded to officers and warrant officers for an act or acts of valour, courage and devotion to duty while flying, though not in active service against the enemy.

The cross is silver and consists of a thunderbolt in the form of a cross, the arms conjoined by wings, the base bar terminating with a bomb surmounted by another cross composed of aeroplane propellers, the four ends inscribed with the letters GVRI. The roundel in the centre represents Hermes mounted on a hawk in flight bestowing a wreath. The reverse is plain with the royal cypher above the date 1918. The date of the award is engraved on the reverse. The suspension is a straight silver bar ornamented with sprigs of laurel. The ribbon is in the same style as the DFC with red and white diagonal stripes. Bars are awarded for further acts of gallantry or duty.

Distinguished Service Medal

The Distinguished Service Medal (DSM) was instituted in October 1914 for 'courageous service in war' by chief petty officers, petty officers and men of the Royal Navy, and non-commissioned officers and men of the Royal Marines. An additional Order in Council on 17 April 1940 made provision for the DSM to be awarded to NCOs and men of the Royal Air Force serving with the Fleet. On 13 January 1943, this was further extended to include service afloat yet not with the Fleet, such as air-sea rescue. Just twenty-three were awarded to members of the Royal Air Force during the Second World War. This Royal Navy medal is included here because a later chapter will relate the career of Flight Sergeant A.J. Brett RAF who was awarded the medal at the end of the Second World War.

The obverse of the circular silver medal carries the Sovereign's effigy. The reverse carries a crowned wreath inscribed 'FOR DISTINGUISHED SERVICE'. The medal is suspended from a straight suspender hanging from a ribbon of dark blue with two white stripes towards the centre. The medal is named on the edge. Bars are awarded for subsequent acts of valour.

Military Medal

Although the Military Medal (MM) is not awarded for flying operations, a number of awards have been made for gallantry to members of the Royal Air Force and the Women's Auxiliary Air Force. A brief description is included here since a later chapter will relate the story of Warrant Officer R. Marlow, who was awarded the medal in 1945.

The medal is awarded to non-commissioned officers and men of the British Army for bravery in the field. It was instituted in 1916 and extended by a 1920 warrant to include other ranks of 'any of Our Military Forces'. A warrant in 1931 refined this statement further with a new provision that it could be given to other ranks of 'Our Air Forces' for services on the ground.

The silver medal carries the sovereign's effigy on the obverse and the words 'For Bravery in the Field' surrounded by a laurel wreath surmounted by the royal cypher and a crown on the reverse. The medal is suspended by an ornate scroll bar suspender hanging from a dark blue ribbon with three white and two crimson narrow stripes down the centre. The medal is named on the edge with the recipient's number, rank, name and unit.

During the Second World War 129 medals were awarded to the Air Forces including six to members of the Women's Auxiliary Air Force. Surprisingly, some medals were awarded to Royal Air Force personnel for engagements at sea.

Distinguished Flying Medal

The Distinguished Flying Medal (DFM) was instituted at the same time as the DFC and is awarded to non-commissioned officers and other ranks for 'an act or acts of valour, courage or devotion to duty performed while flying in operations against the enemy'.

The silver medal is oval shaped and carries the sovereign's effigy. The reverse is more ornate showing Athena Nike seated on an aeroplane with a hawk rising from her right hand. Below are the words FOR COURAGE and the George VI issue contain the date 1918 in the top left-hand segment. The medal is suspended by a straight silver suspender fashioned in the form of two wings, all hanging from a ribbon of very narrow violet and white stripes at an angle of 45° from left to right. The medal is named on the edge. Bars are awarded for subsequent acts of valour and the date is engraved on the reverse.

During the Second World War 6,637 medals were awarded with just 60 bars and one second bar (the latter to Flight Sergeant Don Kingaby, who was later commissioned and awarded the DSO and AFC also). The small number of awards of the bar is explained since many recipients of the DFM were subsequently commissioned. Many were decorated again as officers.

Air Force Medal

The Air Force Medal (AFM) was the fourth of the 'flying' medals to be instituted by the Warrant on 3 June 1918 following the formation of the Royal Air Force. As with the AFC, the AFM is awarded for 'valour, courage, or devotion to duty performed while flying not in active operations against the enemy'. The medal is awarded to non-commissioned officers and other ranks.

The silver medal is very similar to the DFM with the exception of the reverse and the ribbon. The reverse shows Hermes mounted on a hawk and bestowing a wreath. The George VI issue has the date 1918 placed at the centre left. The ribbon is the same design as the DFM but with the colours of red and white. The medals are named on the edge. Bars are awarded for additional acts of valour or duty.

There have been about 850 awards of the AFM since the award was instituted almost eighty years ago. Of these, 259 were awarded in the Second World War including two to the Army Air Corps. The AFM is the second most rare of the awards for flying.

Mention in Despatches

The practice of mentioning subordinates in despatches is of long standing. During the Second World War, and in recent years, a Mention in Despatches was normally awarded only for acts of gallantry or distinguished services in operations against the enemy for services that fell just short of the award of a gallantry medal. Until recently, the only medal to be awarded posthumously was the Victoria Cross. Posthumous 'Mentions' invariably indicated that the recipient would have earned a gallantry award had he survived, but, with the exception of the Victoria Cross, the statutes of the day denied posthumous recognition.

The emblem is single-leaved being approximately three-quarters of an inch long. For the Second World War the emblem is worn on the ribbon of the War Medal and for other actions it is worn on the appropriate campaign medal ribbon. Recommendations are submitted for the sovereign's approval and a certificate is issued.

Air Efficiency Award

The Air Efficiency Award is not a gallantry award but is included here because it is an award made specifically to members of the Royal Air Force's Auxiliary and Volunteer Reserve Forces. It was instituted in 1942 and can be awarded to all ranks who have completed ten years of service. War service reduced the qualifying period depending on the type of service.

The silver medal is oval with the sovereign's effigy on the obverse. The reverse is plain with the words 'AIR EFFICIENCY AWARD'. The suspender is an eagle with wings outspread and the medal hangs from a green ribbon with two pale blue central stripes. Bars can be awarded for additional service. The medal is named on the edge.

Efficiency Medal (Territorial)

The Efficiency Medal is similar to the Air Efficiency Award described above, but was awarded to other ranks of Army volunteer forces for twelve years' service. Wartime service was counted as double value. A brief description is given because a later chapter includes the details of the service of Squadron Leader J. Harris, who commenced his military service in the Territorial Army before joining the Royal Air Force.

The oval silver medal has the monarch's effigy on the obverse and the plain reverse is inscribed 'FOR EFFICIENT SERVICE'. There is a fixed suspender bar decorated with a pair of silver palm leaves surmounted by a scroll inscribed 'TERRITORIAL'. The ribbon is green with yellow edges. The medal is named on the edge.

Second World War Campaign Stars and Medals

Eight campaign stars were awarded for services during the Second World War. The six-pointed stars were made of a copper zinc alloy and were identical except for the name of the campaign in an outer circle surrounding the royal cypher and crown. All the medals were issued un-named. The maximum number of stars that could be awarded to one individual was five. Nine clasps were issued but only one could be worn with each star.

The qualifying periods for the campaign stars vary greatly and the reader who wishes to verify specific awards should consult one of the authoritative books mentioned in the introduction to this chapter.

The 1939–45 Star. This star was awarded for service in an operational area between 3 September 1939 and 2 September 1945. The colours of the ribbon represents the three services with the navy blue of the Senior Service on the left, the red of the Army in the centre and the pale blue of the RAF on the right. Fighter aircrew that took part in the Battle of Britain between 10 July and 31 October 1940 were awarded the clasp 'Battle of Britain'.

The Atlantic Star. The Atlantic Star was awarded to those involved in operations during the Battle of the Atlantic from 3 September 1940 to 8 May 1945. The watered ribbon of blue, white and green represents the mood of the Atlantic. The clasps 'Aircrew Europe' and 'France and Germany' can be worn with this star.

The Air Crew Europe Star. The Aircrew Europe Star was awarded for operational flying over Europe from airfields in the United Kingdom between the outbreak of war and the invasion of Normandy on 6 June 1944. The ribbon of 'Air Force' blue, with black edges and two yellow stripes represents continuous operations by day and night. The clasps 'Atlantic' and 'France and Germany' were awarded with this star.

The Africa Star. This star was awarded for one or more day's service in numerous areas of Africa, primarily North Africa, between the entry of Italy in the war on 10 June 1940 and 12 May 1943. Other qualifying areas included Abyssinia, Somaliland, Sudan and Malta. The ribbon is a pale buff representing the desert with a central red stripe flanked by a single navy blue and light blue stripe. These represent the three services. The clasp 'North Africa 1942–43' was awarded to qualifying members of the RAF.

The Pacific Star. The Pacific Star was awarded for service in the Pacific area of operations between 8 December 1941 and 2 September 1945. These areas included those invaded by the enemy, Malaya and the Pacific Ocean. The ribbon is dark green with red edges with a central yellow stripe flanked by thin lines of dark and light blue. These colours represent the jungle and desert and the involvement of all three services. The clasp 'Burma' was issued with this star.

The Burma Star. This star was awarded for service in the Burma Campaign between 11 December 1941 and 2 September 1945 and for service in parts of India, China and Malaya over certain periods. The ribbon is dark blue with a wide red stripe down the middle. The latter represents the Commonwealth forces. The blue edges each have a central orange stripe representing the sun. Those eligible for both wore a clasp 'Pacific' with this star.

The Italy Star. This star was awarded from the beginning of the Italian campaign for operational service in Sicily or Italy from 11 June 1943 to 8 May 1945. Aircrew service between these dates over Yugoslavia, Greece, the Dodecanese, Sardinia and Corsica also qualified for this star. The ribbon represents the Italian colours of green, white and red in equal stripes with the green on the outside and the red in the middle of the white centre. There are no clasps with this star.

The France and Germany Star. This star was awarded for service in France, Belgium, Holland and Germany after D-Day on 6 June 1944 to VE Day on 8 May 1945. Operations mounted from Italy did not qualify for this star. The ribbon is red, white and blue representing the national flags of Great Britain, France and Holland. The colours are in equal stripes with the blue on the outside and the red in the centre. The clasp 'Atlantic' can be awarded with this star.

The Defence Medal. The Defence Medal is made of cupro-nickel and shows the uncrowned head of King George VI on the obverse. The reverse has the royal crown resting on the stump of an oak tree with the years 1939 and 1945 at the top left and right. The words 'THE DEFENCE MEDAL' are at the base. The ribbon is flame coloured with green edges and two thin black stripes down the centre of the green ones. These colours represent our green land and the fires during the night blitz. Qualification for this medal is complex but it was basically issued to reward those in a non-operational but threatened area and the qualifying period was three years at home and one year in certain areas overseas. The medal was issued un-named.

The War Medal. The medal is also made of cupro-nickel but the obverse has the crowned head of King George VI. The obverse shows a lion standing on a dragon with two heads with the years 1939 and 1945 above. The colours are symbolic of the Union Jack. All personnel with a minimum of twenty-eight day' service were eligible for the award. The War Medal was also issued un-named.

Campaign Medals

Since the early nineteenth century medals have been awarded to those who have taken part in the countless campaigns that have involved British forces overseas. Where there may have been numerous actions within a campaign, individual clasps have been awarded which are attached to the ribbon of the campaign medal. For example, during the early part of the twentieth century there were numerous actions in the North of India and a total of twelve clasps were awarded for the Indian General Service Medal. There are very many British campaign medals, but the reader will only encounter the General Service Medal in the chapters below, and so a brief description follows.

General Service Medal. To commemorate other 'minor' wars following the end of the First World War a General Service Medal was instituted in 1923, and by the time it was replaced in 1962 sixteen clasps had been authorised. Some will be covered in the stories that follow. The medal has been issued with three different obverse effigies and several different legends. The crowned head of the sovereign appears on the obverse. On the reverse is the standing winged figure of Victory holding a trident and who is placing a wreath on the emblems of the two services. The ornamental suspender and the medal hang from a purple ribbon with a central green stripe. The recipient's name is impressed on the edge. Recipients of a Mention in Despatches wear a bronze oak leaf emblem on the ribbon.

Royal Air Force Long Service & Good Conduct Medal

The RAF's Long Service and Good Conduct Medal (LS&GC) was instituted on 1 July 1919, and awarded to non-commissioned officers and other ranks of the RAF for eighteen years' exemplary service. (This was reduced to fifteen years in 1977.) In 1947 officers who had served for twelve years in the ranks became eligible for the medal. A bar is awarded for further similar periods of service.

The obverse of the silver medal carries the effigy of the sovereign, and the reverse has the RAF eagle and crown insignia surrounded by the words 'FOR LONG SERVICE AND GOOD CONDUCT'. The medal is named on the edge.

Chapter Two

Daylight Attacker – Charles Patterson

With war imminent, nineteen-year-old Charles Patterson returned from his farming studies in Ireland to join the Royal Air Force as a pilot. He commenced his training in November 1939 and was soon offered a commission. On completion of a basic aircrew course at 5 Initial Training Wing, based in a Hastings hotel, he left to begin pilot training on Tiger Moths at 12 Elementary Flying Training School at Prestwick. Patterson was allocated to nineteen-year-old instructor Sergeant Elder, and made his first flight in N 9430 on 18 June 1940 and completed his first solo after ten hours of dual instruction. Barely six weeks later he had completed the elementary course with forty-six hours recorded in his logbook and an above average assessment.

The next stage of training was at 2 Flying Training School at Brize Norton, and Patterson flew his first sortie in an Oxford (R 6317) with Flight Lieutenant de Sarigny on 6 August 1940. The young trainee pilots were suddenly introduced to the reality of war on 16 August when two Junkers 88 bombers wrought tremendous havoc on the airfield over a period of a few minutes. Two hangars full of Oxford aircraft were hit, and no less than forty-six aircraft were destroyed in one of the most successful attacks against any British airfield throughout the war. After seventy-five hours of instruction on the Oxford, Patterson was posted to Kinloss to learn to fly the Whitley at 19 Operational Training Unit (OTU). After a few sorties it was clear that the 5ft 6in Patterson was having difficulties with the rudder pedals, and he was 'taken off Whitleys due to shortage of stature'. This pleased him a great deal since he had always wanted to fly the Blenheim, and he was promptly sent to Upwood in Cambridgeshire and to 17 OTU to convert to the twin-engine bomber. He flew his first sortie with Flight Lieutenant Derek Rowe DFC, 'a 21-year-old veteran', and soon afterwards formed his own crew with Sergeant Shaddick as navigator and Sergeant Griffiths as air gunner. The latter would fly all his operational hours with Patterson. After some seventy hours' flying, he completed the course, was commissioned as a Pilot Officer, and posted with his crew to 114 Squadron equipped with the Blenheim IV at Thornaby on Teesside.

Charles Patterson as a very
youthful 21-year old Acting
Squadron Leader. (*Charles
Patterson*)

By the time Patterson finished his training at the OTU in April 1941, the fear of a German invasion had abated, but the threat from the U-boat menace in the Atlantic was increasing. The aircraft of Coastal Command needed to be relieved of the onerous task of patrolling the North Sea in order to concentrate their operations against the U-boats, and a number of 2 Group Blenheim Squadrons were detached to the Command to take on the patrols over the North Sea. These included 114 Squadron, and Patterson flew his first war sortie, a convoy escort, on 28 April 1941 from Thornaby in V 5888, an aircraft he would fly throughout his tour on the Squadron.

Orders were given to the AOC 2 Group, Air Vice-Marshal Stevenson, to halt the movement of all enemy shipping between Brittany and southern Norway 'whatever the cost'. To avoid detection by radar, aircraft had to attack at very low level and make the maximum tactical use of cloud. The North Sea was divided into a series of 'beats', which had to be patrolled constantly by groups of aircraft flying in line abreast so that any ship sighted would come under a concentrated attack. The weather had an impact on tactics and determined the number of aircraft allocated to a 'beat'. Patterson flew a number of these patrols off the Norwegian coast and, on one occasion, attacked a ship from fifty feet during a patrol from Leuchars.

All anti-shipping operations had proved extremely dangerous in the face of the increasingly powerful flak, and the Blenheims were gradually withdrawn and returned to 2 Group. Patterson had flown twenty-six patrols by the time his Squadron flew in formation to West Raynham on 19 July to recommence 'Circus' operations against targets in northern France. He also found himself appointed as a Flight Commander and promoted to the rank of Acting Flight Lieutenant, just three months after joining the Squadron.

The Squadron flew its first Circus within three days of returning from Scotland. The basic formation used was a close box of six Blenheims comprising two sections flying in vic, with the second slightly stepped down. Fighters provided close escort with others flying on the flanks, and a further Squadron giving top cover. Up to twenty-four Blenheims, armed with four 250-lb GP bombs, formed the bomber force operating at 12,000 to 14,000 feet, placing them above the light flak. Patterson led the second vic of three against the sheds and slipways at Le Trait, and the following day, the ammunition dumps near St Omer were bombed from 12,000 feet. Flying in the formation was Sergeant Ivor Broom on one of his first operations. Many years later he retired as an Air Marshal and a much decorated bomber pilot.

On 24 July the Blenheims of 2 Group were used to mount a major attack against Cherbourg in support of a large force of heavy bombers attacking the battleships *Scharnhorst* and *Gneisenau* at La Pallice and Brest. No. 114 Squadron provided twelve Blenheims and attacked after three other Squadrons had already bombed – Patterson was leading the second section in V 5888. The flak was intense, and four aircraft were damaged as they bombed from 12,000 feet. Air gunners reported hits and heavy black smoke in the vicinity of the target.

A 114 Squadron Blenheim IV at West Raynham. (*Andy Thomas*)

Early in August the 2 Group Blenheim Squadrons carried out a period of intensive low-level flying training in preparation for one of the most spectacular operations it ever mounted. The aircrew were not aware of the purpose for such activity but, as one of the Flight Commanders, Charles Patterson, was told confidentially of the target in the afternoon of 10 August, two days before the attack. He hardly slept that night. 'Operation 77' was mounted to fulfil a number of requirements of the current bombing campaign. It was a deep penetration, in daylight, into Germany with the aim of hitting a major target and drawing fighters from the Russian Front in the expectation that other similar attacks would follow. The targets chosen were the main power stations at Knapsack and Quadrath Fortuna near Cologne. Knapsack had the largest steam generators in Europe and was capable of producing 600,000 kilowatts. Quadrath could generate 200,000 kilowatts, and together they produced much of the electricity needed by the industries of the Ruhr.

A force of fifty-four Blenheims, drawn from six Squadrons, provided the main attacking force, with eighteen aircraft attacking Quadrath and thirty-six tasked to bomb Knapsack. Leading the Knapsack force was 114 Squadron with its new Commanding Officer, Wing Commander John Nichol, and each of the aircraft carried two 500-lb GP bombs with an eleven-second-delay fuse. Patterson was appointed deputy to the leader. A Circus operation of eighty-four fighters escorting six Hampdens also took

Blenheims of 114 Squadron at low level over Holland returning from the raid on the Knapsack power stations. (*Public Record Office*)

off to attack targets in northern France, and to act as a diversionary force to attract the St Omer-based Messchersmitt Bf 109s away from the Blenheim force, a tactic that worked well. Four of the RAF's new B-17 Flying Fortress bombers of 90 Squadron also flew diversionary raids at almost 30,000 feet with the aim of drawing off the fighters from the low-flying Blenheims.

Shortly after 0900 the Blenheims took off to head for Orfordness, and the rendezvous with the escorting force of Whirlwind fighters of 263 Squadron. The large force set course over the North Sea for Holland flying at low level in loose formation. As it penetrated through the mouth of the Scheldt estuary to Antwerp, the Whirlwinds had to return, and the Blenheims pressed on alone over the flat Dutch countryside to Cologne. The visibility was good and the prominent tall chimneys of the Knapsack power station could be seen clearly as the formation split to attack their targets. Nichol made a gentle turn to starboard to line up on the primary target, flying between the chimneys as he released his bombs with Patterson still formating on his wing. The flak batteries opened up, but the 114 Squadron aircraft emerged unscathed to join up for the return flight.

Everyone had anticipated that the return flight would be the most hazardous, but enemy fighters failed to appear as the Blenheims raced on to make their rendezvous with a Spitfire Wing. But, just as the Blenheims thought they were clear, the Messerschmitt Bf 109s of *JG 1* and *JG 26* found the returning bombers. The Spitfires entered the fray when numerous air battles took place, but some of the enemy fighters got through to the low-flying bombers. Nichol called his crews to tighten formation as he descended even lower, with his gunner, Pilot Officer J. Morton, calling evasive tactics as the formation flew down the Scheldt and out to sea where the enemy fighters finally broke off their attack.

With a great sense of relief, the Blenheim crews climbed to 500 feet as a further Wing of Spitfires arrived to escort the bombers home. The raid had been a great success and made headline news, but it had been achieved at a loss. Twelve of the fifty-four Blenheims failed to return and many others returned damaged. In recognition of his outstanding leadership, Wing Commander Nichol was awarded the Distinguished Service Order. Many, including his station commander, the Earl of Bandon, and Charles Patterson felt that he deserved the Victoria Cross. Tragically, he was lost a week later and never learnt of his award.

Two days later Circus operations were resumed when Patterson led six aircraft to Boulogne to attack the docks, and this was followed by more of the feared shipping beats during which he attacked a 300-ton trawler. With mounting losses among the Blenheim crews, the 21-year-old 'veteran' Charles Patterson was promoted to Acting Squadron Leader just five months after joining the Squadron as a Pilot Officer.

On 4 September Patterson led six aircraft, with a Spitfire and Whirlwind escort, against a whale oil ship at Cherbourg. The formation was met by intense flak during the bombing run at 8,000 feet, and the Whirlwinds broke off to drive away a formation of approaching Bf 109s.

As the Blenheims departed, the Exeter Spitfire Wing arrived to escort them home.

By mid-September Patterson's tour with 114 Squadron was drawing to a close. On 27 September he led twelve aircraft on Circus 103, an attack against the power station at Mazingarbe in France. Fighters of the Hornchurch Wing escorted the aircraft as they bombed with 500-lb bombs and 40-lb incendiaries from 15,000 feet. At 1600 he landed back at West Raynham and climbed out of V 5888 for the last time at the end of his fortieth operation. Shortly afterwards it was announced that he had been awarded the Distinguished Flying Cross. The citation, endorsed by Group Captain the Earl of Bandon, drew attention to his role as a section leader on the Knapsack raid and concluded 'He has shown great zeal and devotion to duty and his work has always been a fine example to his Flight.' Patterson was particularly delighted when his long-standing air gunner, who had been with him on every operation, Sergeant Alan Griffiths, was awarded the Distinguished Flying Medal.

For the next ten months Patterson instructed on the Blenheim Conversion Flight of 17 OTU at Upwood before returning to operational flying. After a brief spell flying Bostons with 88 Squadron, he transferred to 105 Squadron – the first to be equipped with the Mosquito, and commanded by Wing Commander Hughie Edwards VC, DFC. The superior performance of the Mosquito soon became apparent. Whereas a training navigation exercise in a Blenheim was a triangular route round the centre of England, the route in a Mosquito was a triangle around the British Isles – and completed in a similar time.

After just three sorties on the Mosquito, Patterson and his navigator, Sergeant Egan, found themselves flying DK 338 on their first operation. Led by the legendary crew of Roy Ralston and Syd Clayton, they took off on 22 September 1942 for a low-level daylight attack against the coke ovens at Ijmuiden, dropping four 500-lb GP delay-fused bombs in the face of intense light flak. Four days later, Patterson flew his second operation, a daylight weather reconnaissance sortie requested by Air Marshal Harris who intended to mount a large raid with his heavy bombers that night. Flying at 25,000 feet over Germany, the route took him to Magdeburg, Rostock, Kiel and Esjberg – a sortie completed in just over four hours and covering 1,200-miles, the absolute maximum range for a Mosquito IV. On landing, the crew were met by Hughie Edwards who explained that he was both delighted and surprised to see them back. Throughout the afternoon, the RAF listening posts had intercepted numerous German broadcasts scrambling fighters to engage the high-flying Mosquito – the only RAF aircraft over Germany that day – and Patterson and his navigator had been given up as lost. Throughout the Flight they had not seen a single fighter!

By early October the second Mosquito Squadron, 139 Squadron, had become operational and revised battle orders were issued for the two Mosquito Squadrons. Their primary role was to attack industrial targets deep in Germany, not only to destroy factories but also to act as nuisance raids to affect the morale of the civilian population. After night-time raids by the heavy bomber force, Mosquitoes would return the following night. The aircraft's secondary role was the attack against specific industries by small formations. Patterson flew a number of sorties deep into Germany, but by the middle of November the two Squadrons found themselves conducting a concentrated series of low-level exercises. Unknown to the crews, HQ 2 Group was planning the most ambitious low-level daylight operation of the war: Operation 'Oyster', the attack against the Philips radio and valve works at Eindhoven.

During the training period Wing Commander Edwards took Patterson on one side and told him that he had been 'selected' to fly a specialist reconnaissance task using a cine-camera mounted in the nose of his Mosquito. He was to fly down the Scheldt estuary to the German fighter airfield at Woensdrecht taking films that would be used to brief the crews taking part in the forthcoming attack. However, to create the correct perspective, he would have to fly at 400 feet, and this would give the German radars ample warning of his approach. In his unarmed Mosquito he would have to rely on surprise and the aircraft's speed to avoid being intercepted. On 20 November he took off in DK 338 to fly the sortie. His arrival took the Germans by surprise and they failed to intercept him, and he was back at Marham with his film two hours later. It was the beginning of an exceptional chapter in the remarkable operational career of Charles Patterson.

The plan for the Eindhoven attack was complex. The Bostons, Venturas and Mosquitoes of 2 Group had very different performances, yet the aim was to condense the raid into the shortest possible time. As a result, the Bostons were selected to lead the attack followed by the Mosquitoes with the slow Venturas bringing up the rear. Ninety medium bombers were assigned to the task with Spitfire and Mustang Wings tasked to provide escorts. The raid was planned to take place early during the morning of 6 December – a Sunday was chosen to minimise casualties among the Dutch work force, who would be at home.

Wing Commander Hughie Edwards led the twelve Mosquitoes, with Patterson flying at the rear of the second section. The cine-camera had been fitted in the nose of his aircraft, and he was to film the attack as he dropped his 500-lb bombs. As the formation passed Woensdrecht, Bf 109s rose to intercept, and two Mosquitoes broke formation to draw the enemy fighters from the rest of the formation leaving Patterson to lead the second section. The heroic gamble worked, allowing the Mosquitoes to attack the northerly target unmolested. Three miles short of the target they pulled up to 1,500 feet to commence their shallow dive-bombing attack with their delay-fused bombs. Immediately after releasing his bombs and running his camera, Patterson broke to the north at treetop height to make his way home at low level. To avoid the enemy defences, he flew north to the Zuider Zee and into the North Sea near the island of Vliehors – a tactic he would use on many more occasions.

Although the losses were high, the raid was a great success, and the factory did not return to full production for almost six months. For his leadership of the Mosquito formation, Hughie Edwards added a Distinguished Service Order to his VC and DFC.

Shortly after the raid on Eindhoven, Patterson was told that he would be the RAF Film Unit's pilot, and he was sent to Hatfield to select a Mosquito IV to use for all his future sorties. He selected DZ 414, which became 'O for Orange' and he would fly the rest of his many operations in this aircraft. On 13 February 1943 he took it to Lorient on its first operation following behind the main attack force. It was the beginning of a remarkable career for the aircraft, which flew 24,000 operational miles during the war. Patterson flew virtually all the sorties in the aircraft amassing 20,000 miles. It was always armed with four 500-lb bombs, and Patterson flew a few minutes behind the main formation – by which time all the enemy defences were alerted – dropping his bombs as the cine-camera recorded the results of the raid.

The regular low-level raids were sometimes interspersed with high-level nuisance raids, and Patterson took DZ 414 to Berlin to disrupt Hitler's birthday party celebrations on 20 April. At 20,000 feet the aircraft was jolted by a flak burst. On return, it was discovered that the tail had been hit, and just one strand of the elevator control remained intact! May saw the return to low-level operations, and Patterson took part in a particularly successful attack on the rail yards at Thionville near Metz. The formation was led by one of the RAF's outstanding low-level crews, Reggie Reynolds and Ted Sismore, with Patterson bringing up the rear with his camera-equipped Mosquito. It was a clear spring day as the Mosquitoes flew low over the English Channel and, after clearing the flak batteries on the coast, a long low-level route was flown over France to the target, dog-legging every few minutes to confuse the German radar and tracking system. The aircraft reached the target unscathed and pulled up to 300 feet to drop their bombs and for Patterson to run his camera. Instead of turning north-west to retrace their steps, the Mosquitoes headed due north to fly through Luxembourg, Belgium and Holland before exiting at the Zuider Zee and turning for home. The attack had been timed for early evening, and much of the route home was flown in darkness. After a four-hour flight, and over 1,000 miles, all the Mosquitoes returned safely.

By the end of May 1943 the Mosquitoes had been operating for a year, and they rounded off their campaign with the deepest-ever daylight penetration of Germany, with an attack against the Schott glass works and Zeiss optical works at Jena near Leipzig. Fourteen aircraft, led by Reynolds and Sismore, took part with Patterson occupying his usual role as Film Unit pilot at the rear. The sortie involved almost three hours of daylight flying over Germany, covering a distance of 1,000 miles. The Mosquitoes routed across the Zuider Zee and to the east of the Ruhr when they saw plenty of evidence of the Dam Busters' attack that had taken place a few days earlier. As the aircraft crested a hill near the Eder Dam, they encountered flak followed by a huge fireball as two Mosquitoes collided. The weather soon deteriorated, forcing the aircraft to split up in cloud. Patterson pressed on according to his flight plan, and descended when he should have been approaching the target. He broke cloud in very poor visibility to find a town, which he soon realised was not Jena: it turned out to be Weimar, and two long goods trains were stationary in its large railway station. He turned to attack them, and scored direct hits, when 'all hell let loose' as he encountered intense small calibre flak. He descended even lower to fly down valleys until he broke clear before heading west for the long flight home through darkening skies, and the welcoming flashing lights as the Dutch people opened and shut their house doors as a signal of friendship.

Some of the Mosquitoes attacked the primary target in very poor weather and against heavy flak. Two more were lost and others damaged with some crews wounded, including the leader Wing Commander Reynolds. It was the last raid flown by 105 Squadron before it was transferred to the Light Night Striking Force. As the Film Unit pilot, Patterson no longer had a role, so throughout June and July he flew a number of night nuisance raids against Berlin, Hamburg and Düsseldorf bombing from 25,000 feet.

Although 2 Group had lost its Mosquitoes, it gained a new Air Officer Commanding, the legendary and much revered Air Vice-Marshal Basil Embry. He was a great advocate of low-level operations, and he soon arranged for Patterson, and his 'O for Orange', to be returned to the Group to continue with his film work. His was the only Mosquito in the Group at the time and Patterson was attached to Swanton Morley, the home of two Boston Squadrons. He was sent for by the AOC when he explained how the Mosquito could be used, receiving the AOC's agreement that he could plan his own routes and timings.

Patterson flew his first raid under the new arrangements on 16 August when he followed forty Bostons attacking the large steel works at Denain in northern France. He arrived twenty minutes after the Bostons, dropped his bombs, all with varying time-delay fuses to create maximum disruption, flew between the chimneys as he took his cine-film, and returned by a devious route through Belgium. His films showed spectacular damage, and were used widely by the newsreels. More importantly, it convinced Basil Embry of the value of the cine-camera-equipped Mosquito, and Patterson was to spend much of the rest of his operational career in the same role. The AOC also recognised that the Ventura-equipped Squadrons were incapable of carrying out his low-level tactics, and they started to convert to the Mosquito VI. As the most experienced Mosquito pilot in the Group, Patterson found himself attached to the Mosquito Training Flight at Sculthorpe where he was heavily involved in converting the pilots of 21, 464 (RAAF) and 487 (RNZAF) Squadrons to the Mosquito.

During this training period, Patterson was tasked with flying on two raids, the first mounted by the newly converted 464 and 487 Squadrons on which the AOC took part as Wing Commander Smith – he was wanted by the Gestapo for the murder of a sentry during his escape after being shot down over France in May 1940. Patterson followed 464 to their target,

Patterson's spectacular photograph of the Denain steel works taken 20 minutes after an attack by 40 Bostons. (*Author's Collection*)

a power station in Brittany. After the Australians had attacked, he dived on the target, with cameras on, and dropped two of his bombs. He then headed off to film the New Zealanders' target some miles south. As he dropped the remaining bombs he heard a tremendous bang as a flak shell exploded and shattered the rear of the cockpit, the radio and the Gee navigation equipment. Worse still, it shredded his best officer's hat! The armour plating behind his seat had saved Patterson who was able to fly back and make an emergency landing at Sculthorpe.

The second sortie was to take film after a Mosquito attack against a large petrol refinery at Paimboeuf on the River Loire near St Nazaire. Again, Patterson planned his own route to arrive ten minutes after the Mosquito attack. He approached from the north at very low level when he could see the refinery on the southern bank . . . untouched! He continued, with cameras on, and dropped his four bombs on the target. On return, the AOC called for the film, which showed clearly that the Mosquito Squadron had missed the target. The inexperience of the newly converted Squadrons had been graphically demonstrated. Shortly afterwards, one of the Flight Commanders on 487 Squadron was lost on operations, so Patterson found himself promoted and posted as a Flight Commander to the Squadron where his experience was invaluable.

Although the Squadron was equipped with the Mk VI, Patterson continued to fly his Mk IV, DZ 414 on all his filming sorties.

Reconnaissance over northern France during late 1943 indicated that the Germans were preparing launching sites for pilotless aircraft – the V-1. Instructions were given to 2 Group to concentrate on these new targets, and almost 5,000 sorties were flown during the next six months. Patterson flew his first sortie on 21 December. He went ahead of the main formation, which, once again, included 'Wing Commander Smith', to a site near Dieppe, but the weather thwarted the Mosquitoes. The following day he set off ahead of the Squadron to film a site in the Pas de Calais, which he bombed and then returned before it was attacked by the rest of the Squadron. Two days later he was filming a site at Pommerval when he saw a flak position engaging the main bomber force, and he immediately attacked it with his bombs putting it out of action. Over the next few weeks Patterson attacked another eight rocket sites, often leading the Squadron. He flew additional sorties with his Film Unit aircraft.

Patterson was at home in February 1944 when he received a telegram informing him that he had been awarded the Distinguished Service Order, a rare distinction for a junior officer. Group Captain Pickard, his Station Commander, wrote: I can think of no more deserving case for the award of the DSO.' Air Vice-Marshal Embry wrote:

Patterson's cine-camera records the lack of damage on the Paimboeuf petrol refinery on the River Loire as he runs in to attack the target. (*Author's Collection*)

Flight Lieutenant Patterson has shown outstanding devotion to duty and a complete disregard for his personal safety in his keenness to complete his allotted missions successfully. He has flown sixty-nine sorties; many of these have been carried out at low level in the face of heavy opposition. I consider he well deserves immediate recognition and the award of the Distinguished Service Order.

He received a number of telegrams of congratulation but none pleased him more than the one from his old boss, Group Captain Hughie Edwards, who wrote, 'Well deserved. I am more than pleased.'

While on leave, his Flight of 487 Squadron breached the walls of Amiens jail, and a colleague flew his 'O for Orange' to capture on film the famous results of this unique raid. Sadly, his Station Commander, Group Captain Charles Pickard, who had so recently recommended him for the DSO, failed to return. Patterson returned from leave to find that he was to be rested after almost three years of continuous operations, and he was posted to the staff of 2 Group. However, his appetite for operations did not diminish and he managed to fly three more.

After an 'unofficial' sortie, with a former student, just after D-Day in a Mitchell to bomb the Headquarters of the Germans' 21st Panzer Division, Patterson flew down to Northolt to be re-united with his 'O for Orange'. On 10 June he flew across the Channel to take film of the first Spitfire Squadron to land in Normandy, before flying round the battle area at 500 feet. On 25 June he was tasked to obtain cine-film of Cherbourg just before the American Army entered the city. The weather prevented him taking film, but

Patterson is introduced to His Majesty The King at Northolt in May 1944. He had just been awarded the Distinguished Service Order. Others in the party are ACM Sir Trafford Leigh-Mallory, AM Sir Arthur Coningham, AVM Basil Embry. (*Charles Patterson*)

Patterson takes off for a reconnaissance of Cherbourg in his regular Mosquito IV, DZ 414 'O for Orange'. (*Author's Collection*)

Photograph taken by Patterson of Cherbourg docks after retreating German forces had supposedly departed. He was engaged by *flak!* (*Charles Patterson*)

R.A.F. Form 683.

SECRET.
CYPHER MESSAGE.

(L 12849-10348). Wt. 24387-1348. 346M. 8/40 T.S. 700

WARNING. This cypher message must first be paraphrased if it is necessary to publish its text or to communicate it to persons outside British Government Services and Departments. Messages marked "O.T.P." are excepted from this rule.

FROM— *REAR H.Q. 2ⁿᵈ TAF*

Date

To— *487 SQUADRON*

Time of / Receipt / Despatch

Reputed—

P302 20 FEB.

System

Personal from Air Marshal Commanding to S/L C.C.S. Patterson.
My congratulations on your fine record.
Well rewarded with a D.S.O.

Serial No. **68**

Charges to pay

s. .... d.

RECEIVED

POST OFFICE

TELEGRAM

No. **276**

OFFICE STAMP

1035

Prefix   Time handed in.   Office of Origin and Service Instructions.   Words.

From *BK*   *9.50 R/T*   12.

To

S/L Patterson
Raf. Hunsdon

Well deserved I am more
than pleased   Edwards

91-8536 MP

For free repetition of doubtful words telephone "TELEGRAMS ENQUIRY" or call, with this form 8 or C at office of delivery. Other enquiries should be accompanied by this form and if possible, the envelope

---

he returned two days later during the final mopping-up operations when he made a number of photographic runs at 300 feet. At briefing before the Flight he had been told that there would be no opposition so was flying slowly. After his third run he came under fire from a light flak battery. He opened up to full power and headed out to sea and back to Hunsdon where he landed after a two-hour flight, thus ending his seventy-second and final operational sortie.

Soon after this sortie he returned to instructing on the Mosquito with 13 OTU at Bicester, Finmere and Harwell before joining the air staff of Allied Command South-East Asia in June 1945, where he remained until his demobilisation in January 1946.

Charles Patterson left the RAF at twenty-five years of age having flown on some of the most hazardous operations of the war. He had survived a full tour on a low-level daylight Blenheim Squadron becoming a Flight Commander and Acting Squadron Leader at the age of twenty-one. He took part in three of the great daylight low-level operations, Knapsack, Eindhoven and Jena, and achieved outstanding results as the Film Unit pilot flying his Mosquito. He was one of the very few pilots to complete three tours on low-level daylight operations, and his superb skill and outstanding gallantry were recognised with the award of the DSO to add to his earlier DFC. Few junior pilots received the DSO, and the great majority of those that did received it for a single specific act of supreme gallantry. A 'non-immediate' award for continuous and sustained gallantry was extremely rare to a junior officer. Few served their country better or more gallantly than Charles Patterson.

Chapter Three

Taranto Observer – John Neale

During the autumn of 1938 John Neale was working in a London bank when the Royal Navy regained control of the Fleet Air Arm, a move that led the Admiralty to mount a strong advertising campaign seeking volunteers for aircrew training. He had a keen interest in radio, and could already read and send Morse, so he applied to be an observer. After a series of tests and interviews he was accepted as a midshipman and started his training early in 1939. As a potential officer in the Royal Navy he first had to train as a seaman officer and he was posted to the training aircraft carrier HMS *Hermes* in Plymouth for an intensive course in seamanship followed by instruction on the many subjects associated with being a Fleet Air Arm observer.

A detailed knowledge of wireless communication, photography, armaments, signalling, air gunnery and, of course, navigation was expected. There can have been few aircrew duties that embraced so many roles as that of an observer. After completion of this initial training, Neale and his twenty-six colleagues proceeded to the Royal Naval Air Station at Ford in Sussex, the home of the RN Observer School, to commence flying training with 750 Squadron. The unit was equipped with the Blackburn Shark III, a biplane torpedo-spotter-reconnaissance aircraft that had a brief operational career before being superseded by the Fairey Swordfish. Over the next few months Neale flew daily as he practised DR navigation, photography, wireless communication, bombing and gunnery. With just over 100 hours in his flying logbook, he completed the course and he was able to sew the coveted observer wings on the left sleeve of his midshipman's uniform. He was posted to 815 Squadron equipped with the Fairey Swordfish and operating from the Coastal Command airfield at Bircham Newton in Norfolk.

The Swordfish, officially described as a 'torpedo, spotter, reconnaissance' (TSR) aircraft, but affectionately known as 'the Stringbag', was one of the most unique aircraft to fly during the Second World War. A surprisingly large, rugged single-engine biplane, more reminiscent of First World War days, it was designed in 1934 yet served throughout the duration of the war, and was the only biplane to continue in an operational role in any country. It flew at less than 100 knots but was capable of carrying a war load of almost a ton, which included six 250-lb bombs and eight more 40-lb incendiaries, an eighteen-inch torpedo weighing 1,640 lb, rockets, mines or four 430-lb depth charges. It had a crew of three, seated in open cockpits, although there was no room for the gunner when a long-range fuel tank was carried in the observer's cockpit.

Neale joined his new Squadron on 29 May 1940 as a midshipman, a week before his twenty-first birthday, and he was immediately introduced to his pilot, Sub-Lieutenant 'Spike' Sparke DSC, a year older but already with a number of night operations completed. The Squadron had been tasked to fly a mine-laying operation that night and, to his great surprise, Neale discovered that he would be taking part. He had yet to fly in a Swordfish! At the afternoon briefing nine aircraft were tasked to fly to Texel, in the Frisian Islands, to drop magnetic mines in the approaches to the harbour. Neale spent the rest of the afternoon familiarising himself with the Swordfish cockpit, the instruments and the gun, which he would have to operate since the overload fuel tank was fitted and there was no air gunner. At 2000 he took off in the all-black Swordfish, L4C, as the number three in the Commanding Officer's sub-flight – less than twelve hours after he had joined the Squadron!

The nine aircraft climbed steadily outbound over the North Sea keeping in a loose formation, eventually reaching 8,000 feet. Once Texel appeared the CO started his steep dive and the rest followed in line astern to be met by anti-aircraft fire and streams of tracer. The mine was released at 500 feet, and the pilot immediately turned onto a westerly heading for the return flight. After a five-hour flight, Neale and his pilot landed back at Bircham Newton. It had been an interesting way to spend a first day on one's first Squadron. Two nights later, he went to Texel again, this time armed with six 250-lb bombs to attack the gun positions as other Swordfish dropped mines in the harbour entrance.

HMS *Illustrious* was launched in the late spring of 1940, and was one of the first of the Royal Navy's new fleet carriers with an armoured flight deck and capable of over 30 knots. 815 Squadron was one of two Swordfish Squadrons (819 was the other) assigned to the carrier, and they embarked on 11 June 1940 off Land's End. As they approached the carrier Neale's pilot noticed the rapidly rising oil pressure of the Pegasus engine of his Swordfish, and he instructed Neale to fire a red Very flare, a signal indicating that he needed to land immediately. Thus, a Sub-Lieutenant and a Midshipman had the honour of landing the first aircraft on the new aircraft carrier. Once the Air Group had been embarked, the carrier sailed for Bermuda to conduct an intensive work-up programme for the new ship and its Squadrons. This allowed Neale to build up his experience, and he achieved over eighty hours' flying in the next two months. Navigation was almost entirely by dead reckoning (DR), and observers soon became skilled at 'reading' the wind lanes and assessing the wind and drift of the aircraft. Accurate winds were found by dropping smoke floats. After an intensive work-up period, the carrier received a Squadron of Fulmar fighters and prepared to sail for Gibraltar.

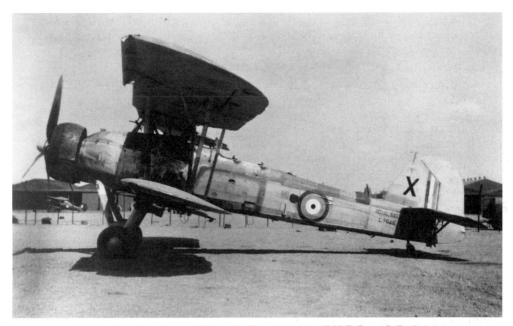

A Swordfish I of 815 Squadron at Heliopolis, Egypt in 1941. (*P.H.T. Green Collection*)

Early in August HMS *Illustrious* entered the Mediterranean to escort a convoy to Alexandria. Once established in the eastern Mediterranean, *Illustrious* accompanied westbound convoys to Malta as HMS *Ark Royal* escorted convoys from Gibraltar to Malta. In addition, Admiral Cunningham took every opportunity to sail his powerful fleet in a provocative and aggressive manner in an attempt to entice the Italian Navy and Air Force to mount attacks. The Italians were aware that Cunningham had numerous torpedo-carrying Squadrons, so the Italian Fleet spent much of its time in port, although there was always the submarine threat. However, the powerful Italian Air Force mounted many attacks against the British Fleet.

The autumn of 1940 was a very busy period for HMS *Illustrious* and Neale found himself flying anti-submarine patrols, convoy protection sorties and night attacks with 250-lb bombs against shore targets and the docks at Benghazi, the terminus for much of the supplies to support the Italians in their desert campaign. On the latter sorties, the Swordfish carried six bombs in addition to incendiaries and these were delivered in a near-vertical dive. On 17 October, an attack was launched against Benghazi. Nine Swordfish from 815 Squadron carried six 250-lb bombs each with aircraft from 819 Squadron dropping mines. By the time Sparke and Neale arrived at the port it was well illuminated by fires and flares, and they soon picked out a destroyer before starting their dive attack. They released the bombs at 2,000 feet causing violent explosions and fires. During a serious of violent evasive manoeuvres, Neale lost most of his navigation kit over the side of the aircraft, but they successfully recovered to the carrier. Reconnaissance the next day confirmed that an ammunition supply ship had blown up, and a destroyer had been badly damaged.

In October, Mussolini invaded Greece and this added to Admiral Cunningham's problems. With just one carrier, his resources were stretched to the limit. To retain maximum flexibility, the Swordfish were once again fitted with the auxiliary fuel tank giving a range of over 750 miles, and this allowed targets at longer range to be attacked. As a result, attacks were mounted against the islands in the Dodecanese and, in late October, another Squadron attack was mounted, this time against the island of Rhodes. Climbing through 5,000 feet, the Squadron encountered bad weather and soon split up. Neale and his pilot pressed on and descended below cloud when they thought they were over the target, but they found themselves over an empty sea. In the driving rain and poor visibility, Neale was able to pinpoint the aircraft's position, and they set off for the northern tip of Rhodes where they were able to start a timed bombing run for the target. Bombs were dropped blind and Neale heaved some leaflets over the side. They started their return and, as dawn broke, they found the carrier and landed. It transpired that they were the only crew to drop bombs over the target. A few days later the Squadron carried out a night attack against barracks on Leros when they were heavily engaged by searchlights and anti-aircraft fire. During this attack the Squadron suffered its first loss when Lieutenant Hamilton and his crew failed to return. The only comfort was the knowledge that heavy casualties had been inflicted on the Italian garrison.

From the time that Italy entered the war in June 1940, the powerful Italian surface fleet had been conspicuous by its absence. Based in the southern Italian port of Taranto, it posed a very considerable threat to British operations in the Mediterranean and North Africa. In October 1940 Admiral Cunningham decided to mount an attack against the fleet using torpedo-carrying Swordfish aircraft. The origins of the attack went back five years to the time of the Italian invasion of Abyssinia when a contingency plan was drawn up for an attack. The plan was developed to the extent that two Squadrons of Baffin aircraft started weapons training, but the crisis passed. This plan was resurrected and used as the basis for the Fleet Air Arm's most famous action.

Only HMS *Illustrious* was available, and six aircraft and crews from HMS *Eagle* augmented her two Squadrons. The plan proposed a moonlight torpedo attack against the battleships and cruisers in the outer harbour (Mar Grande) with simultaneous dive-bombing attacks against the ships in the inner harbour (Mar Piccolo) augmented by flare-dropping aircraft. The attack was planned for the night of 11 November and *Illustrious* steamed to a position 170 miles to the south of Taranto. Meanwhile, Flight Lieutenant Adrian Warburton flying a 69 Squadron Maryland reconnaissance aircraft flew a daring, daylight sortie into the harbour area to obtain some invaluable photographs, which the Royal Navy used for the final briefing of the aircrew.

A painting by Rowland Langmaid (official Admiralty artist) showing HMS *Illustrious* parting company with the 3rd Cruiser Squadron for the attack on Taranto. (*IWM. A 9763*)

John Neale and his pilot, 'Spike' Sparke, were briefed to take off in their aircraft L4C in the first wave of torpedo-carrying aircraft. They spent the afternoon studying the air photographs and memorising the silhouettes of the enemy warships before changing into their best uniforms – they were convinced that they would not return, and intended to be well dressed should they end up in a prisoner-of-war camp. The first of 815 Squadron's twelve Swordfish took off at 2035 to start forming up before setting off for the Italian port. They had been briefed to attack from the south-west and to descend to low level as they crossed the outer harbour in order to surprise the formidable air defences protecting Taranto.

The flare-dropping aircraft timed their attack to the east of the port perfectly, providing both a decoy and excellent illumination of the Italian fleet. Sparke and Neale were flying in the first sub-section, led by the CO, Lieutenant Commander K. Williamson. Once inside the outer harbour, the torpedo aircraft acted independently, and Sparke took his Swordfish down to thirty feet with most of the anti-aircraft fire going overhead. Flying between the balloon cables to the south-west of the battleship anchorage, he released the torpedo at the battleship *Cavour*. They immediately turned through 180° to fly out to sea before climbing and returning to the *Illustrious* for a night landing, almost five hours after taking off. Two of the Swordfish failed to return including the CO of 815 Squadron who, with his observer, spent the rest of the war as a prisoner. Photographs the following morning highlighted the spectacular success of the twenty Swordfish. Three battleships had been put out of action, one never to return to operations; a cruiser had been damaged; and considerable damage had been sustained by shore installations.

The attack on Taranto had been a stunning success with damage caused out of all proportion to the force used. Admiral Cunningham justifiably claimed that the attack 'had a profound effect on the naval situation in the Mediterranean'. With the Japanese Navy studying the attack in detail, he might have added that it also had a profound effect

A reconnaissance photograph taken by 69 Squadron after the attack on the Italian Fleet at Taranto on the night of 11/12 November 1940. No 1 is the 23,622-ton 'Cavour' class battleship beached on the east shore. (*IWM. CM 162*)

on the Pacific war twelve months later when the Japanese attacked Pearl Harbor. Perhaps just as important, the attack was a great morale boost for the success-starved British population.

Leaders of the attack were decorated, but there was a great deal of displeasure and anger at the miserly number of awards. Once the full impact of the raid had registered with higher authority, the Admiralty reviewed the scale of awards. The Honours and Awards Committee 'carefully considered the claims to recognition of further Officers of the Fleet Air Arm for good services in the same [Taranto] action'. A further list was submitted, which included two Distinguished Service Orders, eight Distinguished Service Crosses and twenty-four Mentions in Despatches. On seeing the results of this review, an unidentified senior officer wrote:

> I would emphasise that this attack was carried out from HMS *Illustrious* at night. These young men took off in the dark in a young moon, flew approximately 180 miles, made their attack on the enemy in a harbour whose AA defences I believe to be as strong at least as those at Scapa Flow, achieved a victory which is unique in history, returned 180 miles in the dark to find and land on a darkened carrier.

This succinct and outstandingly clear resumé was quite obviously written by someone who understood the magnitude of the attack and the skill and courage needed to carry it out. As a result, a number of the Mentions in Despatches were upgraded to Distinguished Service Crosses, including John Neale, and his pilot, 'Spike' Sparke, received a Bar to his DSC. The Admiralty recommendation for John Neale read:

> This officer is strongly recommended for valour and exemplary conduct. He was observer of aircraft L4C and shared with his pilot the hazards met in the successful attack on the Italian Fleet at Taranto. After dispersal he was jointly responsible for the correct approach to and despatch from the target under intense A.A. fire and for the successful return to the carrier.

After a brief respite, HMS *Illustrious* continued intensive operations in the eastern Mediterranean and John Neale flew a wide variety of operations. On 17 December he attacked targets on Rhodes and flew a series of anti-submarine sorties in the following days. Four days later, ten Swordfish were tasked to attack a lightly defended Italian convoy off Tripoli in daylight. The aircraft attacked from different directions to confuse the air defences. The leader scored a direct hit on a large merchant vessel just as Neale and his pilot released their torpedo, which hit almost amidships. A third torpedo hit, and the 10,000-ton ship sank within a few minutes; this very successful operation was completed when a second merchant vessel also sank. The following day, Neale bombed Tripoli at dawn, and he flew a shipping sweep east of Malta in the afternoon. By the end of December, just six months after embarking, Neale and his pilot had made ninety operational sorties from the deck of HMS *Illustrious*, many at night.

In the first week of the New Year the Fleet put to sea again. The Germans had arrived in the Mediterranean to make the British aircraft carrier responsible for the attack on Taranto their priority target, and they soon mounted a coordinated attack against the carrier force. On 10 January 1941 disaster struck the *Illustrious* en-route to Malta with a convoy. Without any warning, one of the escorting destroyers, HMS *Gallant,* had her bows blown off and Commander (Air) immediately ordered off a Swordfish for an anti-submarine patrol. Neale and his pilot were closest to hand and they rushed for their aircraft, which was already being started by the ground crew. As the pilot prepared to launch there was a deafening explosion as the carrier's main gun armament opened fire, and Neale looked up to see over twenty Stuka dive-bombers of *Fliegercorps X* rolling over into their dives. The ship fired all her guns and commenced a hard avoiding turn, yet Spence managed to get the Swordfish airborne. As the aircraft climbed away, the carrier received a direct hit on the Flight deck centre line causing a major fire. Over eighty of the ship's company were killed, among them a number of 815 Squadron aircrew who had flown on the Taranto raid. Neale circled the ship and received a signal lamp message to 'proceed to Malta, course 095'. Two Swordfish returning from patrols joined up with Neale's aircraft and they departed, landing very short of fuel on the island at Halfar airfield two hours later.

HMS *Illustrious* was badly damaged and out of action, but managed to make Valletta harbour in Malta where it continued to come under attack. After initial repairs it sailed for Alexandria and through the Suez Canal en route to the United States for repairs. In due course, it returned to action. In the meantime, the surviving members of 815 Squadron flew the remaining Swordfish to Dekheila near Alexandria where the Squadron reformed before moving into the desert to help in convoy protection, and to provide support for the army advancing towards Bardia.

Neale and his colleagues lived the spartan life that was typical of a desert existence while constantly on the move. Night bombing raids were mounted against Benghazi and convoy patrols were flown. After a few weeks of this nomadic, and unfamiliar, existence, the Squadron was ordered back to Dekheila to prepare to go to Crete to assist in the Greek campaign. On 6 March the single-engine Swordfish took off on the 400-mile sea crossing to Crete, landing at Maleme after a five-hour flight.

Anti-shipping and anti-submarine patrols were flown during March as the Squadron prepared to move to Greece. As night fell on 26 March Neale's aircraft was one of three sent to bomb an enemy airbase on Stampalia Island in appalling weather. The sortie had to be abandoned and Neale's aircraft crashed on landing – he and his pilot were uninjured. Over the next fourteen days they flew fifteen operational sorties including a daring torpedo attack against Italian cruisers during the Battle of Matapan, the Italian Navy's final major excursion to sea. By early April the Squadron had flown to an advanced airfield at Paramythia in the northern part of Greece to join the RAF's 211 Squadron equipped with

John Neale by his Swordfish at Dekheila in Cyprus. An oil fire burns in the background. (*Mrs I. Neale*)

Blenheims. Three days later, Germany declared war on Greece and Yugoslavia. The Swordfish were tasked with night attacks against the Albanian ports of Valona and Durazzo, but the high mountains and poor weather often defeated their efforts, and a number of aircraft were lost.

With the arrival of the *Luftwaffe*, the campaign in Greece took a major turn for the worse, and 815 Squadron with its antiquated Swordfish was no match for the Messerschmitt fighters. The depleted Squadrons soon started to withdraw and, on 18 April, the few remaining aircraft of 815 Squadron were ordered to return to Crete. Neale took charge of the ground party and left aboard the Greek coaster *Destro* arriving in Souda Bay three days later where they were promptly bombed. After a further two days it was apparent that there was no longer a job for the Swordfish, and the few serviceable aircraft left for Dekheila. Neale continued aboard the *Destro*, arriving in Alexandria on 27 April.

After a period of re-equipment with new Swordfish, and some rest for the air and ground crews, the Squadron received orders to proceed to Cyprus where it was 'to patrol the straights between Cyprus and Turkey and sink any unidentified shipping outside terri-torial waters'. It was also to 'arrange a line of retreat by sea from Famagusta or Limassol in the event of a German invasion'. Armed with a torpedo and with a long-range tank fitted, the Swordfish took off at 1400 on 29 May, arriving in Nicosia four hours later. By this time, Neale had been promoted to Lieutenant and made the Senior Observer of the Squadron.

There was a small Vichy naval force, La Division Navale du Levant, based at Beirut. With the onset of operations in Syria in early June, 815 Squadron flew shipping patrols searching for Vichy French re-supply ships en route to Syria. Neale located a small convoy, but it sought shelter in Turkish waters before an attack could be mounted. Night bombing operations against shipping in Beirut harbour were mounted, but Neale found the well-lit town and port distracting and this, allied to a low cloud base, made dive bombing difficult.

Neale and his pilot, Sub-Lieutenant D. Wise, took off on the night of 15 June in their Swordfish L 2818 on a shipping search. They spotted a large wake and turned to identify the ship. It was a fast-moving, four-funnelled cruiser later identified as the *Chevalier Paul* on its way from Toulon to Beirut to reinforce the Division Navale. In turning to attack, Neale and his pilot lost sight of the ship on the moonless night. Despite dropping flame floats and flares, they were unable to relocate the ship so they hurried back to Nicosia to refuel and gather reinforcements. Two more aircraft were quickly prepared, and with Wise and Neale in the lead they took off to fly a parallel track search 10 miles apart along the ship's estimated line of advance. At 0330, with a half moon rising, Neale spotted a wide wake of a fast moving ship, which they identified as the Vichy cruiser. Determined not to lose the ship again, Neale plotted a course to intercept it so that his pilot could make an attack from the port bow. He estimated that the ship was travelling at 35 knots, and Wise put this on the crude torpedo-dropping sight. The attack was perfect with the torpedo striking the fast-moving cruiser near the forward engine room. The Swordfish came under intense anti-aircraft fire, but emerged unscathed. Wise climbed the aircraft to allow Neale to drop flares to attract the other aircraft, which closed rapidly as the other two aircraft mounted individual attacks. One Swordfish was shot down, but the crew were rescued.

As Neale and his pilot left the scene, the cruiser had stopped and was listing badly. After a very brief rest at Nicosia, they returned to the scene at first light when they discovered that the *Chevalier Paul* had sunk. A destroyer had rushed out from Beirut to pick up survivors, including the 815 Squadron crew. Having achieved the unique distinction of sinking a heavily armed warship travelling at high speed at night, Wise and Neale were feted as heroes by their colleagues. Wise was immediately awarded the DSC, but for the hard-working and skilful observer there was just a Mention in Despatches.

More bombing sorties against Beirut and shipping searches followed. Neale flew over fifty hours during June, but a rest was imminent. After twelve months of continuous operations, 815 Squadron was withdrawn from the front line and flew to Alexandria prior to embarking on HMS *Formidable* before sailing to the United States for a refit. Neale was one of the few survivors of the original Squadron, and he had flown continuously on a wide range of dangerous operations, which included some of the most dramatic in the Fleet Air Arm's history. He more than deserved his rest.

On his return to Britain in October 1941, John Neale completed a radio course where he was introduced to the new air-to-surface vessel (ASV) radar. With a range of just over 20 miles, ASV gave the Fleet Air Arm's Swordfish and Albacore Squadrons a significant new capability in their role attacking ships. Neale joined 823 Squadron at Crail in Fife shortly after the Squadron had been re-equipped with the Albacore, another biplane, but with a more powerful engine, greater weapon load and much better conditions for the crew, including a closed cockpit. On 25 November, Neale travelled to Buckingham Palace with his proud parents to be invested with his Distinguished Service Cross by HM The King.

By mid-1942 there was an urgent need to send reinforcement fighters to the besieged island of Malta. Plans were made for Spitfires to be embarked on a number of Royal Navy aircraft carriers and taken to the western Mediterranean before the fighters took off for Malta. Neale flew on board the old carrier HMS *Furious* with four other Albacore crews. Thirty-eight Spitfires had been loaded, and the carrier sailed to rendezvous with the rest of the force off Gibraltar. Five aircraft carriers formed part of the huge convoy – the famous 'Pedestal' convoy – and sailed into the Mediterranean ready to launch their precious Spitfire reinforcements on 11 August. The Albacores flew anti-submarine patrols as the Spitfires were ranged on the Flight deck prior to take off. Just as *Furious* was about to launch her Spitfires, HMS *Eagle* was torpedoed by *U-73*, and she sank within ten minutes taking almost all her Spitfires with her. *Furious* had already turned into wind and launched the first eleven aircraft, but the launch was stopped until the threat of attack was over. Eventually, the launch recommenced and the remaining Spitfires took off, although one, flown by Sergeant Stead, developed problems soon after take-off. To everyone's admiration, he successfully landed the aircraft on the larger carrier HMS *Indomitable*. With her task completed, *Furious* returned with a destroyer escort to Gibraltar to pick up Spitfires for a further delivery.

A bombed-up, all-black Albacore of 841 Squadron in a dispersal at RAF Manston. (*Public Record Office. ADM 207/30*)

On the second delivery, Neale was kept busy flying patrols as the thirty-two Spitfires launched for Malta on 17 August. After this important operation, *Furious* sailed back to Greenock and Neale and his colleagues disembarked back to Crail. Within a few weeks Neale was posted as the Senior Observer to the newly formed 841 Squadron based at RAF Tangmere.

The matt-black Albacores of 841 Squadron were attached to No 11 Group, Fighter Command and soon moved to Manston. Their task was to operate at night against the enemy's coastal convoys sailing behind minefields and hugging the French and Belgian coasts. The Fighter Command radars had a low-level capability to see surface targets as far south as Etaples to the south of Boulogne. They also had the first four-channel push-button crystal controlled VHF radio, which speeded up communication dramatically. The two capabilities allowed the controllers to direct attacking aircraft with considerable precision. The Albacore had also been equipped with a four-channel VHF radio – a major improvement from the Swordfish days. Ground controllers based at Manston and Hornchurch in a collection of trailers and caravans directed them to likely targets when the ASV would be switched on and an attack mounted. The Albacores were loaded with twelve 100-lb HE bombs or a mixture of 100 and 250-lb bombs together with flares to illuminate the target. Once a contact was made, the sleeve-valve engine Albacores approached in a shallow dive to straddle the target with a stick of bombs.

As the Senior Observer, Neale flew with the CO, Lieutenant Commander Bill Garthwaite DSC. They flew their first operation together on 11 January 1943 when 'Swingate Control' directed them to a small convoy heading east off Cap Gris Nez. Neale quickly obtained a contact on his ASV radar and an attack profile was set up. The contacts were visually sighted up moon just one and a half miles off the French coast. Turning in at 4,000 feet, Garthwaite attacked the rear ship fine on its starboard quarter, but this placed the aircraft almost up moon of the target, which immediately subjected the Albacore to intense flak. The shore batteries also opened fire, and the bombs were released as a full salvo at 2,000 feet before the pilot took violent evasive action to escape. The crew were unable to observe their attack, but the radar units ashore confirmed that the convoy stopped immediately after the attack and was stationary for a number of hours afterwards.

Throughout the hours of darkness, the crews of 841 Squadron maintained two aircraft at thirty minutes readiness with two more at sixty minutes. Whenever the ground control units detected any convoys or German naval patrol boats, aircraft were scrambled to investigate and attack. The naval operations staff at Nore Command at Dover, responsible for operations in the English Channel, maintained a very close liaison, and would often request Albacore sorties in support of operations by the Royal Navy's coastal forces. Such a sortie occurred in the early hours of 11 March when a single merchant vessel with five escorts was plotted moving from Calais towards Ostend. The naval coastal forces were lying in wait for the target somewhere off Dunkirk so the five Albacores which were scrambled to attack had just fifteen minutes in which to deliver an attack. Four aircraft took off at 0400 and were directed to the target. Neale and his pilot found the target and were starting their dive-bombing attack when the ground controller called them to abort the attack, afraid that the target was friendly. The second aircraft found the target, but was not allowed to attack as the others were ordered to orbit off Dunkirk. A few moments later, a fierce naval engagement started, which finished with one of the Motor Torpedo Boats (MTBs) torpedoing the merchant vessel. The Squadron diarist recorded, 'the MV was filled with iron-ore so it didn't stop to argue but went straight to the bottom.'

During the daylight hours, Neale spent many hours training the new observers on the use of the ASV. He made regular visits to discuss tactics with supporting units, including the radar controllers at Hornchurch and the crews of the MTBs at Ramsgate. The Albacores were also regular visitors to the bombing range at Pegwell Bay where dive bombing was practised.

On the night of 28/29 April the Squadron was ordered to patrol near Berck off the Belgian coast. The first aircraft patrolled without incident and landed at 0100. The patrol was continued by a second aircraft, which sighted blue lights in the water. These turned out to be the phosphorescent wakes of twelve E/R-boats steaming at 15 knots in two columns of six, but with considerable distance between them – a lesson learned from earlier

John Neale and his WAAF bride. (*Mrs I. Neale*)

enemy attacks. As soon as the crew had called up for reinforcements they attacked at 0127, scoring a near miss on one of the boats. They immediately returned to Manston to refuel and rearm. In the meantime, two more Albacores arrived on the scene and Sub-Lieutenant Rutherford attacked three boats, which were in a vic formation at 20 knots. His bombs missed by a few yards, and one of the boats immediately slowed. During the attack, his observer dropped a flame float, allowing the second Albacore to make contact and also attack. A third aircraft arrived on the scene to deliver a dive-bombing attack on a further three boats. Finally, Neale and his pilot arrived on the scene 'to find the enemy in a state of chaos' with eight or nine boats steering in various directions. At 0352 they attacked two boats steering 080/15 knots. Although their bombs narrowly missed, they were able to observe that one boat was belching smoke. They landed just before dawn when the Squadron was stood down. Although only modest damage was achieved, the disruption of such a large force undoubtedly stopped a major attack developing against the crucial coastal convoys sailing to the Thames Estuary.

More patrols followed when it soon became clear that the Germans appreciated the significance of the Albacore harassing attacks and their nuisance value. Observers had noticed an increasing amount of interference on their ASV radars, as the enemy made concerted attempts to jam the aircrafts' attack radars.

Just after midnight on 6 June, Garthwaite and Neale led three Albacores to attach a convoy picked up by Swingate Control. The aircraft headed for Berck and were vectored to the target by Swingate. Despite severe jamming, Neale gained radar contact at 7 miles followed by a visual sighting on the wakes of two merchant vessels of approximately 800 tons escorted by six E-boats in vic formations ahead and astern. Garthwaite bombed the main ship in a sixty-degree dive from 3,300 feet releasing his six 250-lb AS bombs at 1,800 feet. Neale released a flame float for the second aircraft, which dropped four bombs as the convoy started to turn. Despite heavy flak from ships and shore, the third also attacked, pulling out of the dive at 700 feet. The formation claimed one of the ships as damaged.

After a number of scrambles during the short summer nights of June and early July, Neale flew his last operation on the night of 8 July, this time with one of the Squadron's new pilots, Sub-Lieutenant Wilson. They were scrambled to patrol Calais–Dunkirk just after midnight with a second Albacore flown by Lieutenant Fisher. They soon spotted six E/R-boats 3 miles west of Gravelines, and they mounted a dive-bombing attack, both achieving a good straddle and claiming Cat III damage. A third Albacore appeared on the scene and attacked an E-boat, and also claimed Cat III damage. After refuelling and rearming, Wilson and Neale returned to the scene to find the target stationary and smoking. However, it was a mere 1,000 yards from the hostile shore and they decided not to re-attack the already disabled boat. They landed at 0300 at the end of John Neale's last wartime operation. A few days later he was suitably dined out by the officers at Manston when he was 'invited' to place the imprints of his blackened feet on the 14-foot-high ceiling of the bar.

On 3 September an announcement appeared in the *London Gazette* that Lieutenant John Neale DSC had been awarded the Distinguished Flying Cross. The recommendation highlighted his service and achievements with 841 Squadron:

Operating from Manston and Tangmere during the past seven months, he has completed 25 operational armed searches as Senior Observer of the Squadron flying throughout with the Squadron Commander, their aircraft sometimes acting as pathfinder for the squadron. In addition he has carried out nine Air Sea Rescue searches at night under conditions generally unfavourable to A.S.R. Squadrons. His aircraft credited with 1 x 4,000 ton M/V Cat.1 in a combined operation with Navy; 2 M/Vs Cat IV and 2 E/R boats Cat IV.

The RAF Station Commander drew attention to Neale's role in the Battle of Cape Matapan, in operations in Greece, Crete, Cyprus and the Western Desert, as well as operations in the English Channel. He 'strongly recommended' Neale for the award of the DFC.

Neale's departure from 841 Squadron might have signalled the end of his operational flying career, but there was to be no rest from the dangers of war. Indeed, he was about to embark on some of the most hazardous activities of the war. He was promoted to Acting Lieutenant Commander and posted to be the air staff officer of the Merchant Aircraft Carrier (MAC) *Empire Maccoll* fitting out at Camel Laird's Shipyard in Liverpool. During 1942 and early 1943, U-boats had take a heavy toll on the convoys sailing the North Atlantic, particularly in mid-ocean, or the Atlantic Gap, where shore-based air support was not available. The 'Gap' was the U-boats' favourite hunting ground. To provide some air cover in this critical region, the MAC ship concept was introduced.

The MAC ship design was quite brilliant in its simplicity. It was a relatively cheap conversion of a merchant ship of around 10,000 tons. Tankers were chosen because it was easy to put a flight deck on top of their long, uncluttered decks. Their cargoes of grain or fuel could be pumped out, making the need for hatches and derricks unnecessary, and also making for a quick turn round in port. Four arrestor wires and a barrier were added, and the bridge made smaller and moved to the starboard side amidships. There were no hangars or lifts, so the four Swordfish were stored in the open on deck, anchored down by wires behind heavy metal windshields slotted into the deck. All servicing of the aircraft was carried out on deck in the face of the North Atlantic weather. Below decks the only changes were a special tank to store 5,000 gallons of aviation fuel, a magazine for depth charges and rockets, and accommodation for the extra 100 officers and ratings.

As air staff officer, Neale was responsible for all flying operations from *Maccoll*, a British Tanker Company ship capable of carrying 10,000 tons of oil. He had to become proficient at aircraft direction with radar in addition to supervising all flying operations from the deck, and coordinating anti-submarine patrols and tactics. After a concentrated work-up, culminating in an operational inspection by Flag Officer Carrier Training, the *Maccoll* sailed for Halifax in Canada with its first convoy in late 1943. The Swordfish flew patrols throughout the voyage and augmented patrols flown by long-range aircraft of Coastal Command and the US Navy.

Neale completed seventeen round trips across the Atlantic before sailing into Gourock for the final time on 8 May 1945. It was the culmination of five consecutive, unbroken years of operational service that had seen him take part in the Fleet Air Arm's most famous battle – Taranto – followed by many daring night attacks, and all in a biplane. Few can have given longer or more courageous service than John Neale, one of the Fleet Air Arm's most decorated observers.

Chapter Four

Millennium Evader – Bernard Evans

Manchester-born Bernard 'Bunny' Evans enlisted in the Royal Air Force Volunteer Reserve in July 1939 and volunteered for aircrew duties. At thirty-two years of age he was considered too old to be a pilot, but was selected for training as an air gunner. First he completed a basic wireless course at No 2 Electrical and Wireless School at Yatesbury before commencing his air gunnery training with 9 Bombing & Gunnery School at Penrhos in North Wales. The unit was equipped with Hawker Demons and Fairey Battles. After completing his gunnery training on 20 April 1940, he qualified for his aircrew brevet as a Wireless Operator/Air Gunner (WOP/AG).

Evans attended a course at the School of Army Co-operation at Old Sarum, but after flying just ten photographic and reconnaissance exercises his course was cut short as the German Blitzkreig tore through the Low Countries and Northern France. Urgent reinforcements were required for the Squadrons of the Advanced Air Striking Force, and on 15 May 1940 Evans flew to Amiens to join 4 Squadron equipped with the Lysander aircraft, and based near Lille. The Squadron operated in the Army Co-operation role carrying out reconnaissance and artillery spotting duties. Throughout the following seven days the Squadron flew many sorties to identify the main German lines of advance. This was dangerous work, and a number of the slow and vulnerable Lysanders and their crews were lost. Half the Squadron moved to Boulogne on the 20th as the remainder fell back to rudimentary advanced landing grounds in the face of the German advance. Tactical reconnaissance sorties by eight aircraft were ordered on the 21st, and a large armoured force was found in the forest north of Hesdin. Two more aircraft and their crews were lost, and the adjutant made the decision to retreat to Dunkirk whence one Flight was evacuated to England late on the 22nd. The remainder of the Squadron, with seven aircraft, moved to Clairmarais near St Omer to conduct reconnaissance sorties. However, a further retreat was soon ordered, and stores and vehicles had to be destroyed. The remaining aircraft continued to fly sorties from Dunkirk, but the advance of the German armoured forces was relentless,

Lysanders of 4 Squadron over England just before the outbreak of war. (*Via Andy Thomas*)

and the Squadron was ordered to evacuate to Hawkinge in Kent with the ground party leaving for Dover on HMS *Wild Swan*. On 25 May 1940 the Squadron moved to Ringway to reorganise and lick its wounds.

Throughout this hectic and, at times, chaotic first week in his operational flying career, Bunny Evans had flown five daylight reconnaissance and photographic sorties seeking enemy lines of advance and tank positions. During these flights his aircraft was subject to frequent attacks by fighter aircraft, and he had seen many of his new colleagues shot down in the fierce air fighting. It was a true baptism of fire.

In contrast, the remainder of his time on 4 Squadron was relatively peaceful and lacked major incident. The Squadron moved to Linton-on-Ouse in June 1940 to carry out reconnaissance sorties over the coastal waters bordering the East Coast. Evans had flown ten such sorties before being posted to the Middle East in September.

After arriving in Egypt, Evans spent six weeks with 70 OTU at Ismailia being acquainted with the 'conditions to be encountered in the Middle East'. He was then posted to 70 Squadron equipped with Wellington Ic aircraft, and based at Kabrit in the Canal Zone. The Squadron had a distinguished record of service in the Middle East, and formed one of the heavy bomber Squadrons of 257 Wing. Towards the end of 1940, the Squadron sent a detachment of aircraft to Menidi and Eleusis in Greece to bolster the limited RAF forces facing the Italian invasion. Within days of joining the Squadron, Evans took off for Greece in Wellington Ic, T 2732, with an experienced pilot, Flying Officer Ridgeway, at the controls.

The Greek campaign had grown in intensity over the previous two months, so the Wellingtons were introduced to supplement the Blenheim

Squadrons that had borne the brunt of the bombing offensive against the Albanian ports and the build up of Italian reinforcements. Evans flew on the early sorties but, within a few weeks, the Squadron was able to operate from the less vulnerable airfields in North Africa. The rapid advance of General Wavell's army through Cyrenaica had allowed the Squadron to be based at the advanced landing grounds at El Adem, which were well within range of Greece, and also allowed the Wellingtons the flexibility to support the Army in North Africa.

The end of March 1941 marked major changes to the situation in the Middle East. The arrival of General Rommel in North Africa, coinciding with the beginning of the German offensive to capture Greece, created major problems for Wavell. The Wellingtons were tasked in support of both areas, and Evans flew on bombing sorties to Greece interspersed with seven-hour sorties to bomb Tripoli in North Africa. Rommel's rapid advance to regain the ground recently lost by the Italians saw 70 Squadron falling back to Fuka, and on 14 April Evans took off in his regular Wellington Ic (N 2739) to bomb El Adem, the airfield that the Squadron had vacated only days before.

Suddenly, another flash point occurred to cause further problems for the Middle East commanders. Raschid Ali, who was in the pay of the Germans, had seized power in Iraq, and by the end of April he had begun to lay siege to the RAF's major base at Habbaniya. The RAF immediately reinforced the area, and nine Wellingtons of 70 Squadron flew to the RAF's other main airfield in Iraq at Shaibah: Evans and his regular pilot Flight Lieutenant Ridgeway arrived in T 2739 on 30 April. At 0200 on

A Wellington Ic arrives at a desert Advanced Landing Ground. (*Author's Collection*)

the morning of 2 May eight Wellingtons took off to bomb Iraqi troops positioned in a commanding position on the escarpment to the south of Habbaniya. Bombing with 250-lb general-purpose (GP) bombs was carried out from 2,000 feet, and direct hits were achieved against a gun position and transports.

Over the next ten days Evans flew eight more sorties, including attacks against the Iraqi Air Force airfields at Rachid and Washash. He also flew numerous low-level strafing attacks during which he was kept very busy in the rear turret of his Wellington shooting up Iraqi columns and transports that were threatening Habbaniya.

Due to the demands of the Western Desert campaign, and the reduction of the direct threat to RAF Habbaniya, the Wellingtons were recalled to Kabrit on 12 May, and they were in action almost immediately. The bombers were badly needed to support operations in Cyrenaica, in particular, to attack the Libyan ports being used to bring in reinforcements for the *Afrika Korps*. At the same time, attacks were needed against newly acquired German airfields in Greece following the final withdrawal of British forces. The crisis deepened a few days later when the Germans launched an airborne assault, with gliders and parachute troops, against the beleaguered forces on Crete.

Evans and his fellow crews on 70 Squadron now found themselves in constant demand on three fronts with sorties being flown daily. On 12 and 13 May, airfields in Greece and the Dodecanese Islands were bombed, and the Wellingtons returned to targets in Southern Greece a few days later. With the German grip on Crete tightening, 70 Squadron dropped urgently needed supplies of ammunition and medical supplies to the defenders from the very low height of 200 feet. In between these sorties, Evans and his crew bombed targets in Libya, including advanced landing grounds. However, most effort was directed to assisting the forces trying to evacuate Crete, and airfields on the islands of Scarpanto and Rhodes were bombed at night. As the evacuation gathered pace, Evans returned to Crete on 1 June when he and his crew bombed the airfield at Heraklion, which was being used by Junkers 52 transports of the *Luftwaffe*.

The British Army mounted a counter-attack in Cyrenaica in early June supported by the Wellingtons of 257 Wing, but it soon petered out. Evans and his fellow crews had been flying at intensive rates, but all their efforts had come to nought; Cyrenaica, Greece and Crete had been lost. With Rommel's army at the gates of Egypt, the Wellingtons concentrated on bombing attacks against the German-held ports of Benghazi and Bardia. To attack Benghazi the aircraft flew forward to the advanced landing ground at Fuka in order to extend their range. Evans was still crewed with Flight Lieutenant Ridgeway, and they flew almost all their sorties in aircraft T 2739. By mid-July they had attacked the two ports on six occasions, but these were to be their last operational sorties with 70 Squadron.

To supplement the Middle East bomber force a fifth Squadron, 108, was formed on 1 August. The nucleus of the new Squadron came from the other Wellington Squadrons, and Evans and his crew were among those

'Bunny' Evans in the rear turret of his 108 Squadron Wellington. (*Mrs A. Evans*)

transferred from 70 Squadron – Evans was appointed as assistant gunnery leader. This cadre of experienced crews would prove invaluable, but the Squadron was not without its problems. The Squadron Commander commented that the accommodation for the airmen was 'appalling'. The 108 Squadron Operations Record Book pulled no punches when describing the condition of the aircraft:

> The folly of equipping newly formed Squadrons with old aircraft has now become apparent. The Squadron holds eighteen aircraft on charge. Six are on major inspections, one requires a complete fabric recovery, two others require both engines to be changed and three are awaiting a Board to declare them unserviceable for operations. This leaves six only for operations.

For the inexperienced ground crew, with a lack of equipment, this situation presented major challenges, but the Squadron flew its first sorties within six weeks. The pattern of attacks had changed little with the majority of bombing raids against shipping and harbour facilities at Bardia and Benghazi. Evans was now crewed with Flying Officer V. Harcourt, and they were kept busy during September. After night bombing attacks, his pilot descended to low level over the desert allowing his gunners to strafe enemy transports along the Benghazi to Derna road 'seriously damaging a large number and silencing enemy opposition'.

By November the Squadron's scale of effort had built up with as many as sixteen aircraft taking off on each raid. The German-held airfields and landing grounds at Maturba West, Derna and Gazala received the attention of Evans and his crew. Bombing heights were round 8,000 feet with the Squadron dropping 40,000 lb of HE bombs and 2,000 lb of incendiaries on each target. Enemy fighters were encountered over some targets, and the Squadron started to lose aircraft. Some of the aircraft returned at low level, machine-gunning any transports found. To assist with the identification of some targets, Albacore aircraft of the Fleet Air Arm dropped flares, and this tactic became more effective as the techniques were perfected.

December brought a return to bombing sorties to Maleme in Crete, and a raid was flown on 30 December 1941 to Salamis near Athens. Finally, on 13 January 1942 Bunny Evans took off in Wellington Z 8783 to bomb El Agheila with the aid of the Albacores on his forty-ninth and last operational sortie in the Middle East. On 16 February 1942 he boarded a Pan American Airways Douglas DC-3 to return to England via Lagos where he boarded the SS *Batory* for the final stage of his journey home. While on leave it was announced that he had been awarded the Distinguished Flying Medal. The citation mentioned his long service and drew attention to his skill during the ground-strafing sorties. It concluded with the comment '. . . by his leadership he has been an inspiration both in the air and on the ground to all air gunners with whom he has come in contact.'

After his return from the Middle East, and a spell of leave, Bunny Evans reported on 11 April 1942 to RAF Harwell, the home of 15 OTU, to commence a tour of duty as an air gunnery instructor teaching and flying with the trainee air gunners. This period coincided with the rapid build-up of Bomber Command and the four-engine bomber force. However, shortly after his arrival all training was suspended for a short time in preparation for one of the most significant events in the history of Bomber Command.

The recently arrived Commander-in-Chief, Air Marshal Arthur Harris, had intensified the bomber offensive, and the results had all pointed to the need for concentration in time and space along the route and over the target. He had also been subjected to considerable pressure and criticism from the Army and the Navy, with the latter suggesting that the bomber effort could be better employed against maritime targets including the U-boat ports and shipyards. Harris decided to mount a spectacular operation to strike a heavy blow against a German city in the hope that he might win over his critics or at least silence them. He was also determined that the theory of mass concentration should be tested, and when asked by his Senior Air Staff Officer how many bombers would he require for such a raid, Harris answered 'a thousand'. And so the famous 'Thousand Plan' started to take shape.

One of the most remarkable aspects of the plan was the extremely short time between conception and execution. Harris alerted the Chief of Air Staff on 18 May 1942 that he intended to launch 1,000 bombers against a single target in a single night. He decided that he must attack during the full-moon period, which was a mere ten days away. His operational Squadrons could generate just over 600 bombers only, and he sought the cooperation of the other Commands. After receiving their initial approval, the Admiralty refused to allow the Coastal Command Squadrons to participate, so Harris turned to the OTUs in his own Command. By stopping all training and utilising the instructor crews he was taking great risks with his training capabilities, but he was able to generate 1,046 bombers. And so frantic work commenced with the planning of Operation 'Millennium'.

The Bomber Command OTUs provided no less than 367 bombers for the operation, the majority being old and worn-out Wellingtons. Among these were twenty Wellington aircraft from Harwell, with the 15 OTU satellite airfield at Hampstead Norris generating a further ten. To crew this large element of the force there was a requirement for 150 aircrew, involving all the instructors and a number of the students who were close to completing their courses. All the crews were called to the briefing room on the 25th and told that 'there was something big on requiring a maximum effort'. The unit's Flight Commander devised a scheme with playing cards to allocate aircraft and to create crews. Bernard Evans was crewed with Warrant Officer John Paul DFM, a veteran of over thirty operations, and who had returned from a week's leave and his honeymoon just the day before. It was the first time that the two Middle East veterans had met! Two other instructors and a student gunner made up the rest of the crew, which was to operate with a single pilot instead of the normal complement of two. It was to be Bunny Evans's fiftieth operational sortie.

The attack was scheduled for 27 May, but weather interfered with plans and the raid had to be delayed each night until the night of 30 May. The primary target was to be Hamburg, but the weather forecast remained poor and Harris decided to launch 'Millennium' against Cologne.

The Harwell crews were driven to their aircraft at 2000 ready for a take-off one hour later. Evans and his crew had been allocated one of the better Wellingtons, but a serious magneto drop on one engine sent them rushing to the spare aircraft. Not surprisingly, this was one of the oldest and worst aircraft on the Unit, with numerous items missing. The crew settled in to the aircraft (R 1791), and took their position for take-off at the end of the stream finally getting airborne at 2314. John Paul described the aircraft as 'a bit of a heap and we were so slow that we must have been one of the last to arrive over the target, which was a mass of flames that I could see for miles'.

The observer, Warrant Officer S. Green, dropped the 500-lb GP bombs and incendiaries, and Paul turned the Wellington for home. Flying over Belgium one hour later at 14,000 feet, Evans saw a Messerschmitt Bf 110 night fighter approaching from below on the port quarter and shouted a warning, which was drowned out by another crew member. With the night fighter at a range of 300 yards, the two aircraft opened fire simultaneously, and the Wellington was hit. The intercom was rendered useless, and Evans's rear turret was badly damaged. The turret could not be turned fully and one of the guns was useless. The pilot pulled the bomber into a hard turn, and the fighter overshot allowing the student front gunner, Sergeant J. McCormick, to open fire. The Bf 110 returned for a second attack, and Evans opened fire with his one serviceable gun, but he was wounded in the hand. The Wellington suffered further damage, with fire breaking out near the port engine, and this quickly spread. Without the intercom, further instructions could not be passed so Paul shouted to the wireless operator, Flight Sergeant T. Lyon, to tell the crew to bale out. Shortly afterwards Paul passed out and he did not regain consciousness until he was on the ground.

After the second attack Evans realised that the aircraft was severely damaged. He opened his turret door and could see flames in the fuselage, but no sign of the rest of the crew. Without communication he assumed that the rest of the crew had baled out, so he clipped on his parachute and jumped from the rear turret as the aircraft passed through 2,000 feet. In the descent he saw part of the aircraft explode on the ground, and shortly afterwards he landed in a plum tree near the village of Mont-sur-Marchienne near Charleroi.

Leutnant Helmut Niklas and his radar operator *Unteroffizier* Wenning of *II/NJG 1* based at St Trond in Belgium had attacked the Wellington. After this engagement Niklas went on to shoot down another Wellington, but his aircraft was damaged by return fire and he was wounded. As he was losing consciousness he made a wheels-up crash landing with the aid of his radar operator. He recovered from his wounds, but was killed in January 1944 after an engagement with USAAF bombers on a daylight raid.

The Bf 110 night fighter flown by Leutnant Niklas after crash landing near St Trond following his success in shooting down Evans' Wellington. (*Via Alfred Price*)

After landing in the tree, Evans quickly disentangled himself and immediately set off to get clear of the immediate area. Ever since that night, the tree has been known as 'The Tommy Tree'. In the meantime, the Wellington had broken into a number of pieces just before hitting the ground. The only other survivor was the pilot John Paul, who had a miraculous escape as the cockpit section broke clear before hitting a house. The occupants were asleep, but soon rescued the badly injured Paul. After a visit from a doctor, he was transferred to a German hospital where he had an operation on his broken legs and where an English woman, Ruby Dondeyne, who had married a Belgian, nursed him. Within a few days he received a short written message which read, 'Baled out. Am in good hands, Yours, Bunny.' He promptly swallowed the paper, delighted that one of his colleagues was safe. Sadly, the other three members of the crew had died in the aircraft, and they were subsequently buried with full military honours in Charleroi cemetery. John Paul spent the rest of the war as a prisoner of war.

The plum tree in the garden at Mont-sur-Marchienne that arrested Evans' parachute descent, and forever known as 'The Tommy Tree.' (*Andre Sevrin*)

After landing, Evans heard windows opening and voices, so he decided to get clear of the area. He eventually came to a house with a light on and knocked at the door and, after explaining that he was a British aviator, he was welcomed inside. He was given a drink, and his wounded hand was dressed before he was moved to another house where he was fed and hidden in an attic. During the day, the Germans searched all the houses with the exception of his hiding place. Later that evening he was collected and transferred to Charleroi. Although he was not aware of the fact, members of the Belgian Resistance movement had seen his parachute descent in the bright moonlight, and he was soon in the hands of the Comet Escape Line.

Over the next few days he was moved to various houses, living as a Belgian. He had a reasonable knowledge of French, which allowed him to visit, with friends, various cafés and shops, and he was able to stroll along the streets. During one walk with two Belgian friends, a street photographer suddenly appeared and took their photograph. This alarmed Evans, but his two friends were amused and ordered a copy. Planning started for his return to England and, after a few days he was moved to

A photograph taken in Brussels of 'Bunny' Evans and two of his helpers of the 'Comet' escape line. (*Andre Sevrin*)

Brussels dressed as a worker. Three other evading aircrew joined him, and they were all provided with the necessary papers and identity cards.

The next stage of the journey took them by train to Paris. They were instructed to follow a young girl, but to move separately. They stood in the corridor of the train to be less conspicuous, but Evans had a severe fright when an officious French ticket inspector made numerous inspections of his forged documents as the train passed into France. Once in Paris, the evading airmen were kept in separate 'safe houses' while plans were made for their onward journey. During the enforced wait they were subjected to a rigorous physical training programme in preparation for their journey across the Pyrenees into Spain.

Once preparations had been completed, the party were escorted on the night train to Biarritz before moving to a safe house in the small town of St-Jean-de-Luz close to the Spanish border. With French guides, the party set off for the mountains to cross into Spain. After eight hours of steady climbing they ran into a German patrol, forcing the party to scatter. Evans hid in a tree-lined hollow, and buried his wallet in a scrape. It contained potentially incriminating evidence, including his Brussels photograph, which would have placed the lives of his helpers at risk. Some of his French guides and a Canadian airman were captured, and he was unable to relocate his other colleagues so he set off to return to his safe house. Tired and weary, he hit the coast 10 miles south of his destination, and arrived a few hundred yards away from a submarine base at Hendye, an unwelcome surprise. Without adequate identification and authorisation papers for the area, he was in a difficult and dangerous situation, so he decided to bluff his way through the checks: his boldness paid off.

His French helpers immediately arranged a new guide, and within twenty-four hours he crossed the Pyrenees safely and was taken to San Sebastian, where he reported to the British Consul. He was moved to Madrid, but he had no means of identifying himself so he reported the loss of his wallet. Unknown to him, the authorities sent a Basque to search the area and his wallet, with the photograph, was returned to him nine months later!

Evans finally arrived in Gibraltar on 18 August, and within twenty-four hours he was flown to Whitchurch airfield in a Whitley. He was debriefed by officers of MI 9 to whom he reported the loss of his Wellington colleagues. He was also able to give valuable information about the German gun defences on the road between St-Jean-de-Luz and Hendye. The Deputy Director of the MI 9 Prisoner of War Section recommended that Evans be awarded a Mention in Despatches for his successful and resourceful evasion. He commented on the file, 'His good luck was the result of a good effort to get going.' His award was gazetted on 1 January 1943.

Bernard Evans returned to Harwell to continue his tour as an air gunnery instructor. No doubt his unique experiences as an evader would have involved him in many lectures to the trainee aircrew. Like the great majority of successful evaders, Evans did not return to operational flying for fear of further capture, and risk to the safety of the gallant resistance workers and 'helpers' in Belgium and France. He was commissioned in January 1943 and visited Buckingham Palace on 23 December to receive his Distinguished Flying Medal. He continued as an instructor at various OTUs, eventually becoming the gunnery leader at 20 OTU based at Lossiemouth. On 21 October 1945 he left the Service having participated in some of the most difficult and dangerous bombing operations of the war, culminating in a successful evasion from deep in enemy territory.

Chapter Five

Bomber Squadron Commander – Guy Lawrence

The excitement and romance of flying in the early 1930s caught the imagination of Guy Lawrence, and, as soon as was practical, he persuaded his elder brother to teach him to fly. By the time he was eighteen years old he saw an opportunity to gain more flying experience, and he joined the Reserve of Royal Air Force Officers (RAFO) as a direct entrant. He was accepted and appointed to the Reserve as an acting Pilot Officer, reporting to the Bristol Flying School at Filton on 9 July 1934. A few days later, with Mr Kerr as his instructor, he took off in one of the school's Tiger Moth aircraft G-ABSX – ten days later he completed his first solo after just six and a half hours' flying time. By early September he had completed the *ab-initio* course, having achieved fifty hours' flying time with almost half as solo time.

Each pilot in the RAFO was required to devote two weeks each year to continuation flying, twenty hours being allocated for the purpose. Lawrence was assessed as 'above average' at the end of his third summer training period, was promoted to flying officer, and was selected to attend a course for instructors. In 1938 he transferred to the De Havilland School of Flying at Hatfield where he continued with his instructor's course. He had just completed his annual training in 1939 when war was declared, and he was immediately mobilised for active service. After attending the Initial Training Wing (ITW) at Cambridge he was sent to 12 Elementary Flying Training School at Prestwick to complete his training to be an instructor. However, he was keen to fly operationally and he persuaded the authorities to release him from his instructor's course. Thus, he reported to the Flying Training School at RAF Cranwell where he completed multi-engine training on the Oxford in June 1940.

Assessed as above average at the end of his advanced training course, Guy Lawrence was posted to the heavy bomber force, and he reported to 10 OTU at Abingdon to commence his training as a bomber pilot flying the Whitley aircraft. On 17 June 1940 he took off with Flying Officer Strong in K 7229 for his first flight in a Whitley II. Once familiar with the Whitley, he converted to the more powerful Mark V powered by the

Rolls-Royce Merlin X engine. To complete the course, student crews were tasked to fly an operational sortie dropping propaganda leaflets over enemy territory, known as 'Nickel' sorties. Lawrence took off on 21 July with his crew in P 4940 to drop leaflets over Amiens, returning six hours later after a successful sortie.

On completion of the course, Lawrence remained with 10 OTU and was posted as a staff pilot to C Flight based at the satellite airfield at Stanton Harcourt. Over the next five months he flew many bomber-training sorties with student crews. He was also able to build up his night flying hours, which included his second operation when he took a student crew on a 'Nickel' raid to Abbeville. During this period as a staff pilot he amassed over 200 flying hours in the Whitley, and this additional experience stood him in great stead when he moved to a front-line Squadron.

The Whitley equipped the Squadrons of 4 Group based in Yorkshire, and Lawrence joined 78 Squadron at Dishforth in mid-December as a newly promoted flight lieutenant. On 19 December he flew his first bombing operation as second pilot to the Flight Commander, Squadron Leader R. Wildey DFC, on a raid to Duisberg, but complete cloud cover over the target prevented any bombing. A few days later he took his own crew in N 1490 to Boulogne but, once again, he was thwarted by cloud. He was

Bombing up a Whitley V bomber of 78 Squadron at Middleton St George. (*Author's Collection*)

experiencing the frustration that dogged the bomber crews during the early years of the war, and matters would not improve until new navigation and bombing aids were introduced.

The mainstays of the RAF's heavy bomber force at this time – the Hampden, Wellington and Whitley – were designed in the 1930s for daylight bombing, but the very heavy daylight losses in early operations, and the increasing capability of German air defences, dictated that the bombers should operate by night. However, they were ill equipped for long-range night bombing, lacking sophisticated navigation and bombing aids and bombsights, and bombing accuracy was very poor. During this early phase of the bomber campaign most operations were carried out during the moon period (this was to change with the advent of the new better-equipped heavy bombers), and small numbers of aircraft were allocated to four or five different targets. Crews were briefed on their particular target, the enemy defences and the weather, but individual crews planned their own routes and timings and attacked as single aircraft, thus giving enemy defences ample opportunity to engage the individual aircraft.

Numerous targets were attacked on a single night with the emphasis on the German transportation system, oil refineries and industrial areas. On New Year's Day 1941 Guy Lawrence took N 1490 to Bremen where the primary target was the Focke-Wulf aircraft factory. Conditions were good with excellent visibility, and the 141-aircraft raid was considered to be one of the most successful to date. The raids that followed to the oil refineries at Gelsenkirchen and the port facilities at Calais and Dunkirk were less so, almost entirely due to poor weather, and the difficulties encountered in trying to identify the target. A good attack was mounted against Cologne on 1 March, but fog over England caused problems as the bombers returned. Lawrence was unable to land at Dishforth so he headed south to find a suitable airfield, finally landing at Langham in north Norfolk almost ten hours after taking off. The physical demands on the aircrews flying for many hours in their unheated, noisy bombers was considerable, and this was recognised in setting the length of a tour on heavy bombers as thirty completed operations.

By early March German surface ships and U-boat successes against the convoys on the North Atlantic run reached dangerous levels, and Bomber Command received a new directive on 9 March, often described as the 'maritime diversion'. There were insufficient naval and maritime air forces available to hunt the German ships at sea, so Winston Churchill decreed that Bomber Command must attack associated land targets such as the U-boat building yards, the docking and port facilities, and factories making major components for ships and Germany's long-range bombers.

On 15 March Lawrence formed part of a small attack against the U-boat base at Lorient, but poor weather again interfered with bombing. Three days later, however, he flew as part of a 100-aircraft raid against the Deutsche Werke U-boat building yard at Kiel in what was later described as the 'heaviest raid so far'. On 23 March, Lawrence visited

Berlin for the first time, but cloud obscured the target, and it was a very tired crew that landed after a nine-hour flight. It is interesting to compare the capabilities of the slow Whitley with the fast-flying two-seat Mosquito, which was later able to fly to Berlin twice during a night bombing offensive – and carry the same bomb load.

After the Berlin interlude it was a return to attacks against the shipbuilding cities, and Lawrence attacked Kiel on successive nights on 7 and 8 April. 229 aircraft attacked on the first night and 160 returned the following night. Together, these raids caused considerable damage, with U-boat production halted for several days, and a naval armaments depot burned for two days. The raids were probably the most successful of the war on any target at that stage of the war.

Throughout May and June the 'maritime diversion' continued and Lawrence, flying his usual aircraft, Z 6466, attacked the German battle-cruisers *Scharnhorst* and *Gneisenau* in Brest, in addition to targets in Bremen, Hamburg, Mannheim and Cologne. During this period his tenacity and courage became increasingly noticed, and he was given the added responsibilities of being made a Flight Commander. His determination to bomb accurately is reflected in his sortie to Bremen on 5 May when he spent almost an hour in the target area before he was satisfied that he had properly identified the aiming point enabling him to mount a successful attack. He returned on one engine after attacking Schwerte, and shortly after completing a Lorenz beam approach course, he diverted to Linton-on-Ouse in very bad weather and successfully landed at night off a beam approach with a cloud base of 250 feet.

On 9 July, a new directive was received at Bomber Command ordering the resumption of the bombing campaign over Germany. It specifically identified the transportation system and 'destroying the morale of the civil population as a whole and of the industrial workers in particular' as targets. The era of 'area bombing' had arrived.

Guy Lawrence's outstanding tour of operations was recognised when it was announced on 31 July that he had been awarded the Distinguished Flying Cross. The recommendation stated that

> He has proved himself to be an operational pilot of outstanding ability. He has displayed the greatest courage and resourcefulness in successfully completing his missions, and the high standard of efficiency he has attained is a source of inspiration to all.

On 6 September Lawrence took off in Z 6948 for his thirtieth bombing operation, an attack against the chemical works at Huls when 'good results were obtained'. The six-hour flight was his final flight in a Whitley. His end-of-tour assessment was 'exceptional', and a few days later he was promoted to Squadron Leader and reported to Heslington Hall near York, the home of Headquarters 4 Group. He was appointed as the Group training officer on the staff of the Air Officer Commanding, Air Vice-Marshal C.R. Carr. With his considerable flying training experience, and the recent completion of a very successful operational tour in 4 Group, he was an ideal choice for the appointment. The four-engine Halifax had recently entered service with the Group, and he was made responsible for developing and monitoring the training at the Operational Training Units.

Guy Lawrence spent almost eighteen months on the staff of 4 Group, during which time he managed to achieve 250 hours flying time in the Group's communication aircraft as he visited the many operational and training units. At the end of his tour he was promoted to Wing Commander, and appointed to lead the Halifax II-equipped 78 Squadron based at Breighton, near York.

His arrival to command 78 Squadron in early August 1943 coincided with the time that Bomber Command was reaching peak efficiency, and a 'maximum effort' was routine. Enormous strides had been made during Lawrence's time away from operations. The Command had a new Commander-in-Chief, the dynamic and single-minded Air Marshal Arthur Harris. New navigation and bombing aids, such as Gee, H2S and Oboe, had been introduced, the Pathfinder Force was well established, and the Command's heavy-bomber force was exclusively a four-engine force with the Lancaster proving to be the outstanding bomber of the

Wing Commander Guy Lawrence DFC as Officer Commanding 78 Squadron in 1943. (*Lady Lawrence*)

Second World War. Many electronic counter-measures, including 'Window', had been introduced, and the addition of the Mosquito to the Pathfinder Force and the Light Night Striking Force had given the Command a new and unique capability.

Lawrence started his conversion to the Halifax with a brief one-hour sortie with an instructor before selecting his crew and personal aircraft, V for Victor, JD 173 (which was to survive the war). Six days later, on 10 August, he flew his first operational sortie with just six hours experience on the aircraft – a perfect example of a CO 'leading from the front'. During this first sortie he was to display this quality to an even greater extent.

He took off to bomb Nuremberg as part of a force of 653 bombers. Returning over France after a successful attack, he had to feather both engines on the port side due to overheating. This would have imposed a tremendous strain on the slightly built Lawrence, as he would have had to hold full starboard rudder. He coaxed the aircraft towards England where he elected to land immediately after crossing the south coast, so he headed for Ford in Sussex. On the final approach, he re-started the two port engines just for the landing, which he successfully completed after an eight-hour flight. With so few hours' experience on the Halifax, this was a remarkable achievement, instantly endearing him to his air and ground crews.

Armourers load 1,000-lb and incendiary bombs into the bomb bays of a Halifax. (*IWM. CH 6626*)

Two nights later he attacked Milan, a round trip of almost ten hours, and within a few days he flew on one of the most famous of all Bomber Command's operations – the attack on the experimental and research site at Peenemunde on the Baltic coast. Intelligence had indicated that the site was being used to test a new 'terror weapon', the *Vergeltungswaffe 2* – known throughout the war as the V-2. Mosquitoes flew regular photographic reconnaissance sorties over the site throughout the summer when a second weapon was identified – the V-1 pilotless aircraft or flying bomb. Churchill ordered Harris to bomb the site as soon as the conditions were right. Harris decided to bomb during the moon period to aid aiming, so the raid was planned for 17 August.

Three waves of heavy bombers were tasked to attack the pinpoint target under the direction of a master bomber, Group Captain John Searby of 83 Squadron. Three aiming points were selected, including the housing estate where the scientists lived, the rocket-production plant, and the main experimental works, the scientific heart of the complex. Two diversionary raids to keep the German night fighters occupied were planned with eight Mosquitoes of 139 Squadron attacking Berlin, and Mosquitoes and Beaufighters of Fighter Command flying intruder missions over the German night-fighter bases.

The Halifax Squadrons of 4 Group formed part of the first wave of 244 aircraft with twenty-one provided by 78 Squadron. Guy Lawrence rolled down the runway at Breighton at 2108 at the head of his Squadron before setting heading for the Danish coast as he climbed to 18,000 feet. After crossing Denmark, the bombers headed out over the Baltic to attack Peenemunde from the north. The Halifax force bombed from 8,000 feet on the Pathfinder's markers before turning for home. The second and third waves followed, and bombed their aiming points as Searby gave instructions and aiming corrections. By the time that the third wave arrived – mostly Lancasters of 5 Group – the German night fighters had regrouped after being lured to Berlin by the diversionary raid, and most of the night's bomber losses occurred in this last wave. Although some vital targets were missed, the raid was a success, setting back the programme by at least two months, and causing the Germans to relocate some crucial work to safer places. Most importantly, it delayed and reduced the scale of attack against London and the south of England, but it was achieved with the loss of 245 aircrew.

Six days after the Peenemunde raid, the 'Battle of Berlin' commenced. Berlin was an important target, being the administrative capital of the Reich, a major centre of industry, and a key point in the German road and rail communications network. However, it was at the maximum range of the RAF's bombers and, to increase their chances of survival, the city could not be attacked during the short summer nights. It also involved a long transit period over enemy territory giving the increasingly sophisticated German night-fighter organisation more opportunities to mount attacks against the bomber stream. The 'Big City' was a formidable target.

Aerial photograph taken of the V-2 rocket pre-launch assembly halls at Peenemunde before the attack on 17 August 1943. Several V-2s can be seen in the open. (*Aircrew Association Archives*)

Once again, Guy Lawrence was at the head of his Squadron for this major raid involving 719 bombers, and with HE bombs on board and maximum fuel, he lifted V for Victor off the runway at 2033. The bombers headed for the Zuider Zee before turning on an almost direct route to Berlin, with the first wave arriving just before midnight. On this long route, the German night fighters started their continuous attacks, and losses among the bombers mounted. South of Berlin, the bombers turned north to drop their bomb loads on the Pathfinder's green TIs before they continued north to the Baltic where they turned for home over Denmark. Guy Lawrence recorded 'fighters flares seen over target'. These were part of a new German tactic to drop high intensity flares falling very slowly from high level. The flak batteries were restricted to firing up to 15,000 feet, allowing single-engine fighters to operate over the target above this height to attack bombers silhouetted against the flares. Sixty-two bombers were lost, representing almost 8 per cent of the force – the heaviest losses in one night so far. Together with 158 Squadron, Guy Lawrence's 78 Squadron suffered the worst losses with five Halifaxes failing to return. It was a sad return for the popular and courageous Squadron Commander. Among those lost was his veteran Flight Commander, Squadron Leader P. Bunclark DFC, DFM. Eight nights later, he once again led his Squadron on the second Berlin raid when two more 78 Squadron crews were lost.

The role of a bomber CO was a very onerous one. As a result, in recognition of the arduous nature of the appointment, he was not expected to fly regularly on operations, perhaps just two or three each month. However, this was not Guy Lawrence's style, and he insisted on taking part with his crews on the most demanding operations.

On a typical day, his cheerful batman awakened the CO of a bomber Squadron at 0715 before meeting the Squadron adjutant for breakfast. This was often a sombre affair, particularly if there had been recent losses, but a compensating, refreshing air of normality was given by the smart, attractive and efficient WAAF waitresses. The adjutant reminded the CO that he needed to see young Smith who was asking for compassionate leave after his mother was killed during an air raid on Portsmouth. Then there were two new crews to see; they had arrived the previous night to replace the losses on the Peenemunde raid a week before. At 1000 Flight Sergeant Cook had to be interviewed regarding his suitability for a commission, followed by two airmen on a charge for breaking windows in the NAAFI. At 1045 'C' Flight's hangar and dispersal areas had to be inspected. He would then need to find time to make a number of telephone calls regarding the establishment of parachute packers, and to make a strong protest to Group Headquarters to support his engineering officer regarding his concern over the delay of vital aircraft spares. The padre and medical officer wanted to see him about their increasing concern over the stalwart Flight Lieutenant J****** DFC, DFM who had forty-five operations under his belt, but who was now showing extreme nervous tension and was developing the 'twitch'. After lunch he intended to visit the patients in sick quarters before fulfilling his promise to watch the inter-Flight football match between 'A' and 'C' Flights, and afterwards to join them in the 'Hare and Hounds' for a few pints.

Just as he entered his office, the scrambler telephone rang to alert him that operations were on again that night, and a maximum effort was required for a raid on Berlin. Briefing was arranged for 1830 with take-off two hours later. He decided that he must fly on the operation and warn his crew to be ready. He had to cancel most of the day's plans as details of the bomb and fuel loads, route, weather, enemy defences and aiming points came through from Group Headquarters. He left the three Flight Commanders to start selecting their crews as he left to speak to the ground crew working non-stop to get the fifteen aircraft serviceable. He went on to see the armourers preparing the bomb loads before driving back to the airmen's mess to speak with the catering staff preparing meals. All the station personnel were involved to ensure that the maximum effort called for would be met.

At 1500 the CO carried out a short air test on his Halifax before returning to the operations room to prepare for the main briefing of the 105 aircrew flying on the operation. At 1830 the crews assembled in the Nissen-hutted briefing room, and he addressed them and outlined the main plan of the raid on the large wall chart before the specialist officers gave more detailed information. Once the briefing was complete, and the crews dispersed, the CO waited to have a brief word with the Station Commander before joining his crew in the locker room with all the other crews. After dressing in his heavy clothing and flying boots, he collected his parachute and jumped on the crew bus to drive out to the dispersal where JD 173 and its ever faithful and diligent ground crew were waiting. After inspecting the aircraft he signed the aircraft documents and had a brief word with the sergeant before climbing into the pilot's seat. For the first time in the day, he was alone with his thoughts for a few brief moments. Then it was time to start up, taxi, and take off before setting course for Berlin.

Unlike some of his Squadron, he and his crew returned safely after an eight-hour flight. It was almost 0400, and other returning crews started to arrive in the debriefing room to report their account of the raid to the intelligence officers. They all reported heavy flak and plenty of night-fighter activity on the approach to and exit from the target area. As the crews drifted away, the CO remained with the Station Commander in the flying control tower waiting for five crews to return. They waited for news – silent except for a WAAF asking if they would like yet another cup of coffee. By 0600 it was clear that the five Halifaxes would not be returning.

Exhausted, he walked slowly to his room in the officers' mess where his batman was waiting. Soon he would have to get up, and he would need no reminding that he had thirty-five letters to write or that he would not have to interview Flight Sergeant Cook. Another day in Bomber Command's campaign had begun, and he wondered if he would be flying again that night.

Guy Lawrence chats to his crew at dispersal before they take off in their Halifax 'V for Victor', JD 173, to attack Berlin on 31 August 1943. (*Lady Lawrence*)

After the initial attacks on Berlin, Lawrence attacked Montlucon, and twice went to Hannover when good results were obtained. The single most destructive attack of this period, however, was on 22 October when 569 bombers attacked Kassel, the home of important fighter assembly plants. Lawrence was flying LW 295 as he took off at 1726 with a mixed HE and incendiary bomb load. The visual markers of the Pathfinders had identified the centre of the town and had placed their markers accurately as the main force approached. Lawrence arrived over the target five hours later at 17,500 feet, and bombed the centre of the markers. The attack was so accurate that a firestorm developed and damage was greater than any raid since the Hamburg firestorm raids in July. It was mid-1944 before another attack of similar devastation was achieved. The cost, however, was high, with forty-three aircraft missing; Guy Lawrence had another fourteen sad letters to write.

A raid against the marshalling yards at Cannes on 11 November achieved poor results, and Lawrence struggled back to land at Beaulieu after spending almost ten hours behind the controls of LV 271. On the same night, Leonard Cheshire and Mickey Martin were making their epic attempts to destroy the rail viaduct at Anthéor just down the coast. Two weeks later, while attacking Frankfurt, Lawrence had to exert all his skill as he 'corkscrewed' to the directions of his gunners as a night fighter attacked their Halifax.

On 19 November it was announced that Air Marshal Harris had approved the immediate award of the Distinguished Service Order to Guy Lawrence. The citation written by his Station Commander recorded his outstanding service and courage on operations:

> Wing Commander Lawrence is an excellent example of a most fearless and efficient Squadron Commander. His exceptional qualities of courage and leadership, and his scornful disregard for enemy opposition over Germany's most heavily defended targets has been an inspiration to his Squadron. His bombing results have always been of a very high standard, despite all opposition. When raiding Nuremberg, after pressing home his attack in face of fierce opposition, he managed, by superb captaincy and airmanship, to fly his Halifax a considerable way back from the target on two engines only – both the same side.

Air Vice-Marshal C.R. Carr, the Air Officer Commanding, endorsed the recommendation and added:

> I cannot speak too highly of this valuable officer's courage, skill and initiative on operations. His complete disregard for all opposition and determination to reach his objective sets a high standard to his Squadron. I most strongly

Crews wait for transport to take them to their aircraft dispersal at Breighton before taking off for Berlin. A number of them failed to return. (*Lady Lawrence*)

recommend that his fine record of constant endeavour, both in the air and on the ground, be recognised by the immediate award of the DSO.

The main Battle of Berlin reached a peak during the winter of 1943–4, and Guy Lawrence next attacked the city on 20 January 1944. The northerly route chosen took the 769 bombers close to Kiel before turning for Berlin. The crews took off in fine weather late in the afternoon, but ran into the cloud of a cold front over Germany where the night fighters had already been alerted. Berlin was completely covered by cloud, and the Pathfinders had to drop their sky markers blind. Lawrence's navigator had recognised the aiming point on his H2S radar, and the bomb load was dropped successfully. The bombers returned over Holland where they continued to be harried by the German fighters. Losses among the Halifax Squadrons were particularly heavy and Lawrence lost another crew.

During late January 78 Squadron converted to the higher-performance Halifax Mk III powered by the more powerful Bristol Hercules radial engine. The aircraft also embodied the new fin and rudder assembly giving the aircraft greater stability, which had been incorporated successfully into some of the later Mark II variants. The Squadron resumed operations in February, but Guy Lawrence was approaching the end of his tour. On 15 March he took off in LV 795 to attack Stuttgart when the results were assessed as poor due to adverse winds causing the Pathfinder markers to drift over open countryside. On the way home, Lawrence had to shut down the port inner engine when the oil pump failed, and he was forced to make an emergency landing at Odiham. His second tour was over.

Lawrence was promoted to Acting Group Captain on posting to the staff of Headquarters Bomber Command at High Wycombe, where he was responsible for training policy and standardisation, particularly at the Heavy Conversion Units. Not surprisingly for such a dedicated and energetic officer, he paid regular visits to the bomber-training units flying himself and staff officers in an Oxford or a Proctor from the nearby airfield at Halton. Towards the end of 1944 he converted to the Lancaster.

After fifteen months in the appointment, Lawrence was made an Officer of the Most Excellent Order of the British Empire in the 1945 King's Birthday Honours List for '. . . raising the standard of interest in the heavy conversion units by producing a new syllabus and coordinating and standardising methods of instruction. He is energetic and has great initiative.' He was posted to command the Pathfinder airfield at Warboys near Huntingdon, the home of the Pathfinder Force Navigation Training Unit. At the end of 1945 he left the RAF to return to civilian life.

In just five years Guy Lawrence rose from being a junior bomber pilot to a Station Commander of a Pathfinder station. Throughout this period he had displayed exceptional qualities of leadership, and he developed a reputation among his crews that was rarely surpassed. One of his pilots, who was himself decorated for gallantry, commented, 'Guy Lawrence was a superb Boss who never asked any of us to do anything that he wouldn't do himself. He led us from the front, and there was nothing that we wouldn't do for him.' These same qualities emerged in his highly successful postwar business career, and this was recognised by a knighthood for services to the food industry in 1976.

Chapter Six

Torpedo Attack Pilot – 'Del' Wright

The Second World War was six months old when nineteen-year-old Derrick Wright, known throughout his long RAF career as 'Del', reported to the Aircrew Selection Board where he was selected for pilot training. He reported to RAF Cardington in June 1940, his training starting a few days later at 1 Initial Training Wing at Babbacombe where he spent six weeks discovering the joys of drill, and the basic flying subjects such as the theory of flight, meteorology and navigation.

On 25 July 1940 he started pilot training at 3 Elementary Flying Training School at Watchfield near Swindon. Four days later he took off in an Avro Cadet (G-ADTN) for his first flight with his instructor Pilot Officer Wilson, and after ten hours' dual flying he flew his first solo. Just six weeks later, he finished this elementary phase of flying with sixty-two hours flying in no less than 112 flights. It is worth remembering that this was all completed as the Battle of Britain raged in the skies overhead. On 7 September he reported to RAF Spitalgate near Grantham to commence multi-engine training, and four days after completing his course on the Avro Cadet, he was airborne for his first sortie in an Avro Anson (N 5286). This phase of his flying training was just as intensive, and within ten weeks he had flown seventy-five hours in the Anson. On 27 November 1940 Del Wright was awarded his pilot's wings and promoted to sergeant, a mere four months to the day since commencing flying training – an indication of the urgency to replace those lost in France, the Battle of Britain and the early bomber operations, losses which had been greater than training plans had anticipated.

The final stages of Wright's training saw him at RAF Catfoss, the home of 2 (Coastal) OTU, where he converted to the Blenheim. The course was devoted almost entirely to basic aircraft handling sorties, navigation exercises and instrument flying practice. Just before completing the course in March he flew with the Flight Commander who demonstrated 'fighter tactics'. The sortie lasted one hour. With only 180 hours in his logbook, he reported to 254 Squadron at Sumburgh in the Shetlands on 2 April 1941 to start operational flying on the fighter version of the Blenheim IV.

A month after joining the Squadron, Wright flew his first operational sortie, a 'security patrol' in Blenheim V 5801. In effect, these flights were convoy support, and they became the standard task for the Squadron, although it also provided fighter escort for the Beauforts attacking shipping off the Norwegian coast. In May 1941, Wright flew eleven operational sorties before the Squadron flew to Aldergrove in Northern Ireland.

The collapse of France in June 1940, and the *Luftwaffe*'s occupation of airfields in northern France, rendered shipping routes in the Channel and South-Western Approaches extremely vulnerable to air attack. This resulted in drastic alterations to the routeing of convoys, and the main emphasis for Coastal Command moved to an area off the north-west coast of Northern Ireland where more airfields were constructed. Squadrons were transferred to the area to provide escorts for the increasing number of convoys using the port of Liverpool. For the next six months, five-hour patrols and convoy escorts provided the main bulk of 254 Squadron's task. The flying was tedious, but had the indirect benefit of giving the new crews experience of operating in all types of weather and practising maritime techniques – experience that proved invaluable later when the Squadron re-equipped with the Beaufighter.

A formation of Blenheim IV aircraft of 254 (F) Squadron over Northern Ireland with Lough Neagh in the background. (*Author's Collection*)

The Squadron moved to Carew Cheriton in Pembroke early in 1942, and within a few days, Del Wright was commissioned as a Pilot Officer. Convoy patrols and escorts were still the order of the day, but these were interrupted on 28 March when the Squadron provided air cover for a special operation described in the Squadron Operation Record Book as 'Secret Force, Chariot'.

Operation 'Chariot' was the bold commando raid on the dry docks at St Nazaire situated at the mouth of the River Loire. The convoy carrying the raiders sailed on the night of 27 March with an old, former US Navy, destroyer HMS *Campbeltown* in the lead. She was packed with six tonnes of explosives secured in the bow, and her job was to ram the gates of the main dry dock before time-delay fuzes set off the explosives. The ship succeeded in ramming the dock, but the commandos and the Royal Navy patrol boats suffered severe losses. From first light on the 28th, air cover was provided to assist their withdrawal.

Six Blenheims of 254 Squadron took off in two formations of three to refuel at Predannack in Cornwall before making the long flight around the Brest Peninsula. Wright was flying T 2131 with his crew of Sergeant K. Jones and Sergeant J. Blank. South-west of Brest they commenced a search for returning ships and survivors of the raid where they encountered a Heinkel 111 – Wright's gunner opened fire, but the German bomber disappeared in the haze. Shortly after making a landfall, his aircraft developed engine trouble forcing it down to 200 feet, and Wright prepared to make a crash landing as he followed the coastline. Fortunately, he was able to keep the aircraft level, so turned due north to try and make the long journey home. Near the town of Crozon he flew over a dummy airfield, with twenty-five wooden Heinkel 111 replica bombers supported by props, where he was engaged by anti-aircraft fire. He finally managed to clear the French coast at Ushant, and struggle across the Channel finally landing at St Eval in Cornwall after a six-hour forty-minute flight. His leader's aircraft was badly damaged by flak and the third aircraft failed to return.

The Squadron started to re-equip with Beaufighter VIc aircraft in June 1942, and Wright flew his first sortie on 11 July in T 5197. Torpedo training started in August when the Squadron was detached to Abbotsinch. Camera attacks were practised before dummy torpedoes were dropped against the training ship HMS *Mistral*. Intensive training continued throughout August culminating in Squadron formation attacks against the target ships. Returning to Dyce on 1 September flying X 8098, Wright crashed into the railway sidings close to the airport. He was injured and admitted to hospital, returning to flying duties six weeks later, just as the Squadron moved to North Coates to become part of the first Beaufighter Strike Wing.

The North Coates Strike Wing consisted of three Beaufighter-equipped Squadrons with 143 and 236 Squadrons flying armed with cannon and bombs for the anti-flak role, and 254 Squadron flying Torbeaus. The Wing carried out its first strike on 20 November when it attacked a southbound convoy off the Hook of Holland. Twenty-five aircraft, including nine

Torbeaus of 254 Squadron, took off but the attack went disastrously wrong from the outset. The fighter escort failed to make the rendezvous, and the difficulties were compounded by poor weather and inexperience. Three aircraft were lost and seven were damaged with two crash-landing at base. Although one pilot described the sortie as 'a shambles', valuable lessons were learned. The Wing was withdrawn from operations, and a comprehensive training programme was implemented to practise the complex procedures for a coordinated attack. Over the next three months, the Wing carried out intensive training under their new Wing Leader, Wing Commander H.N.G. Wheeler DFC (later Air Chief Marshal Sir Neil Wheeler). It soon became clear that the anti-flak sections had to attack just before the low-flying Torbeaus ran in to drop their torpedoes, and much of the training was built around this tactic until it was perfected.

Individual searches and reconnaissance sorties were flown during this period, and by mid-April, the Wing was declared available for strikes. On 18 April it had an opportunity to put its concentrated training into practice.

An important and large convoy had been spotted sailing north from the Hook of Holland, and had been shadowed by Mustangs and a 236

A Beaufighter VI armed with a torpedo. (*Author's Collection*)

Del Wright took this photograph as he released his torpedo against the *Hoegh Carrier* off the Frisian Islands. The Beaufighter on the left is turning away after releasing a torpedo. (*Author's Collection*)

Squadron Beaufighter. At 1320 nine Torbeaus of 254 Squadron and twelve anti-flak aircraft from 143 and 236 Squadrons took off under the leadership of Wing Commander Wheeler. Wright was flying JM 219 armed with a Mk XV torpedo and four cannons. The rendezvous with the fighter escort of twenty-two long-range Spitfire Vs and six Mustangs went perfectly. The convoy was found, and a coordinated attack was set up with the cannon-armed and bomb-carrying anti-flak Beaufighters going in first to attack the escort ships. Flying in pairs at 100 feet, the Torbeaus headed for the freighters, releasing their torpedoes at 800 yards range. It was estimated that three torpedoes hit the 4,900-ton ore carrier, the *Hoegh Carrier*. Although individual pilots did not observe their torpedoes as they took evasive action immediately after the drop, following crews saw definite hits on the main target, and other ships were left burning. Analysis indicated that Wright had scored one of the hits. It was later confirmed that the *Hoegh Carrier* had sunk, and other ships had been badly damaged. The attack was completed in four minutes without loss. The operation had been a resounding success, marking a turning-point in the fortunes of the strike Squadrons.

Throughout the intensive training period, Wing Commander Wheeler had insisted that fighter escort was essential. On 1 May thirty-one Beaufighters of the North Coates Strike Wing were sent on a sweep along the Norwegian coast to attack the cruiser *Nurnberg*. Wright was flying JL 953 armed with a torpedo. The target was outside the range of fighters, so the Beaufighters approached the Norwegian coast without an escort. The cruiser was sighted and the Wing had just turned in to attack when Focke-Wulf 190

A great mêlée of Beaufighters attacking a convoy while avoiding anti-aircraft balloons off the Dutch coast. (*Air Historical Branch*)

and Messerschmitt Bf 109 fighters intercepted the aircraft. In the mêlée that followed, torpedoes and bombs were jettisoned as the Beaufighters descended to sea level as they turned for home. Two Fw 190s closed in to attack Wright, but they sheered off to attack another Beaufighter. Wright landed at Skitten in the Orkneys with other aircraft landing at Wick. Three aircraft from 254 Squadron and two of 143 Squadron failed to return. It had been a costly operation, graphically confirming the Wing Commander's views about the need for a fighter escort.

The next Wing strike had the benefit of a strong fighter escort – no fewer than fifty-nine Spitfires. A Mustang of II (AC) Squadron had sighted a northbound convoy off Texel, and a strike was ordered. Twenty-six Beaufighters took off, with Wright flying JM 219 in the leading section of Torbeaus. The convoy was made up of six merchant vessels disposed in two lines, escorted by three 'M' class minesweepers sailing in front, with four armed trawlers on the flanks. All the merchant vessels were flying balloons on a 400-foot cable. Wright and two other aircraft attacked the leading merchant vessel in the starboard column. Others attacked the second vessel, and later reported seeing a torpedo hit followed by a fire on the 3,000-ton ship attacked by Wright. Some of the escorts were also hit and left blazing. Analysis showed that two of the merchant vessels had been seriously damaged, while another and three escorts were also damaged.

The Strike Wing tactics had been proved, and also highlighted that the Squadrons were capable of reacting quickly once a worthwhile convoy had been reported. Del Wright flew his next strike on 13 June in JL 950 when twelve Torbeaus took off accompanied by eighteen anti-flak Beaufighters and a strong fighter escort. One of the 254 Squadron aircraft returned early when the radio caught fire – it was extinguished with a tin of orange juice! The convoy was sighted a few miles south of Den Helder and included the 5,200-ton merchant vessel *Stadt Emden*. The Torbeaus encountered intense flak, and with some aircraft badly positioned or baulked on their attack runs, only seven torpedoes were dropped. Wright and the others released their torpedoes against the main target, which was hit and swung out of line listing heavily to port. Other ships were left blazing after being attacked with cannon fire and bombs. It was later confirmed that the *Stadt Emden* and another merchant vessel had been sunk, and a number of escorts seriously damaged.

On 22 June Wright took off at 0420 on a sweep heading for the Dutch coast where he sighted a large convoy of eight merchant vessels and six escorts off Vlieland. Having noted details of the convoy, he returned to North Coates. A Wing strike was ordered, and thirty-six aircraft took off with the 143 and 236 Squadron aircraft armed with cannons and, for the first time, with the rocket projectile (RP) with a 60-lb explosive head. Thirteen heavily armed escorts protected the convoy, and the attack achieved only modest results. Two Torbeaus were lost, three crash-landed on return, and others were damaged. It had not been an auspicious début for the rockets, but over the next two years, and after some early difficulties, it proved to be an outstanding success, becoming the major anti-shipping weapon, eventually replacing the torpedo.

A few days after this attack, it was announced that Del Wright had been awarded the Distinguished Flying Cross. The citation recorded that he had been on continuous operations for over two years and had flown seventy-four sorties. It concluded:

'He has shown himself to be a fearless pilot and his efficiency, keenness and devotion to duty has at all times been a great example to the Squadron.' The Air Officer Commanding commented, 'Flying Officer Wright has shown great determination and dash when carrying out shipping strikes off the Dutch coast. Very strongly recommended for an immediate award of the DFC.'

At the end of July 1943 Wright was rested from operations having completed seventy-five sorties, and accumulated almost 300 hundred flying hours on operations. His Squadron Commander assessed him as 'above average'. He had been involved from the outset in the development of Strike Wing operations and helped to pioneer the tactics. Other Strike Wings followed in the footsteps of the North Coates Wing, and became key elements in the RAF's anti-shipping capability, achieving great success, and making a major contribution to the winning of the war at sea.

Del Wright pictured with his observer just after receiving his DFC. (*Mrs E. Wright*)

After a short period as an instructor at 2 Torpedo Training Unit, Wright was posted to 23 Service Flying Training School based at Heaney in Southern Rhodesia where he was a flying instructor on Oxfords. He returned to the United Kingdom in November 1945, and was released from the service in 1946. Within a year, he had been recalled as a Flight Lieutenant, spending the next three years in various posts associated with the prevention of flying accidents.

Del Wright returned to flying duties in June 1950 when he attended the Flying Refresher School at Finningley before joining 120 Flying Instructor's Course at the Central Flying School at Little Rissington. On completion of the course flying Harvards, he was posted to 3 Flying Training School at Feltwell as a flying instructor. On promotion to Squadron Leader six months later, he became a Squadron commander at No 1 Flying Training School at Moreton-in-Marsh where he remained until October 1953. During this time, he completed almost 700 hours flying the Harvard before converting to jet aircraft for the first time.

After completing a jet familiarisation course on the Meteor and the Canberra conversion course at 231 Operational Conversion Unit at Bassingbourn, Wright was posted on 13 April 1954 to command 12 Squadron flying Canberra B2s from Binbrook. The previous Squadron Commander, Squadron Leader J.S. Millington DFC, had been killed in a flying accident a few days earlier, and Del Wright had the difficult job of restoring morale in the aftermath of this tragedy. However, he was kept busy as the Squadron made preparations for the presentation of the Squadron Standard, which took place on 23 June when the Squadron's first Commanding Officer, Marshal of the RAF Lord Newall, made the presentation. Within a few weeks, the new Standard was paraded through the streets of Grimsby on the occasion of the Squadron being granted the Freedom of the town.

The Canberra had entered service in May 1951 as a replacement for the Lincoln and B29 Washington and, by 1955, no less than twenty-four bomber Squadrons were equipped with the high-flying medium bomber. The B2 version was the standard bomber, carrying a crew of three including two navigators. It was steadily replaced by the more powerful B6 version, which 12 Squadron re-equipped with in June 1955. The primary blind-bombing aid was Gee-H, a development of the wartime Gee navigation system. It was easily jammed and the system was never very successful, so the reversionary backup of visual bombing using the T2 bombsight was frequently used.

In August 12 Squadron was warned to prepare to deploy to Malaya for Operation 'Mileage', a four-month detachment to relieve 617 Squadron operating against the communist guerrillas. The Squadron's Canberra B6 aircraft underwent a modification programme, including the installation of the radio compass navigation aid. The aircrews completed a concentrated training programme, including low flying and the dropping of 1,000-lb bombs at Luce Bay. On 10 October 1955 the first aircraft were ready to depart for the RAAF base at Butterworth in Malaya.

Watched by Air Vice-Marshal J.R. Whitley, Del Wright released the brakes of WH 968 at 1300, and took off on the first leg of the journey to Malaya. Three more aircraft immediately followed him, and they arrived at Idris in Libya four hours later. The ground crew followed behind in Hastings aircraft, and by 18 October all the aircraft and support had arrived at Butterworth. Four more Squadron aircraft arrived by the end of the month when a concentrated in-theatre training programme commenced, including the 'Austermark' technique. A low-flying Auster identified the target and marked it with smoke before calling in the bombers. The Canberras usually bombed as a vic of three to ensure a good distribution of bombs. The other main bombing technique, used mainly for area targets, was the 'Datum Point' method, which involved a timed run from a final pinpoint fix.

The Squadron commenced bombing operations on 22 November when Wright led three aircraft, each armed with three 500-lb bombs, on a strike in the Johore area. Following this first successful strike, the standard bomb load was increased to six 1,000-lb bombs, and operations were mounted on a daily basis. By the end of November, Wright had led another five strikes.

On 1 December Operation 'Saturation' commenced against key communist strongholds in the Pertang area of central Malaya. This was the most concentrated air offensive since the Emergency began in 1948. During the six-day operation, 12 Squadron's Canberras mounted a

Canberra B6 aircraft of 12 Squadron release 1,000-lb bombs on terrorist camps in the Cameron Highlands, Malaya. (*Author's Collection*)

maximum effort, and Wright led nine sorties in the period when 144 tons of bombs were dropped by 12 Squadron and the Lincolns of 1 (RAAF) Squadron. On 2 December alone, the Squadron dropped sixty 1,000-lb bombs. At the end of the Operation, congratulations flooded in to the Squadron, and the Commander-in-Chief signalled that '12 Squadron have upheld the highest traditions of the RAF in the skill with which you have conducted these intensive operations'. On 5 December Wright flew his fifteenth and final strike when he bombed the Triang area. A few days later he flew to Changi to collect Air Vice-Marshal Kyle, the Air Officer Commanding, who had arrived from England before setting off on a tour of Australia.

On return from Australia at the end of the year, 12 Squadron said good-bye to their Commanding Officer Del Wright. The Squadron Diary recorded, 'It is with great regret the Squadron said farewell to its Commander. As a gesture of loyalty and appreciation, the aircrew towed their retiring Squadron commander on a bomb trolley to the aircraft which flew him on the first leg of his return journey to the United Kingdom.' Wright was returning to convert to the RAF's first V-bomber, the Vickers Valiant.

After completing 4 Valiant Conversion Course at Gaydon, Wright was posted to Marham to join 207 Squadron as a Flight Commander on the re-formation of the Squadron. As the Squadron completed its initial work-up, it was ordered to carry out an intensive training programme of night flying and bombing from 40,000 feet – the blind bombing system was restricted to use below 25,000 feet, so the Valiants had to carry out visual bombing with the T2 sighting head. This training was in preparation for possible operations over Egypt. Two aircraft, one captained by Wright, flew to Luqa in Malta on 10 October 1956, but were soon joined by four other aircraft as it became clear that air attacks against Egypt were being planned following the nationalisation of the Suez Canal Company by the Egyptian President, Colonel Gamal Abdel Nasser.

On the night of 31 October Operation 'Musketeer' was ordered, with the initial aim being the neutralisation of the Egyptian Air Force within forty-eight hours as a prelude to the airborne and amphibious invasion to regain the canal. At 2000, five Valiants of 207 Squadron took off as part of a large air armada launched from Cyprus and Malta. The Squadron's target was the airfield at Kabrit, the home of a fighter wing equipped with the Soviet built MiG-15 aircraft – Wright was flying XD 813 as he set off for bombing operations in his third war. The bombing effort carried on for another three days, and once the Egyptian Air Force had been destroyed, military installations were targetted. Wright flew his second bombing sortie on the night of 4 November when he took off in XD 813, armed with twelve 1,000-lb bombs, to attack the fortifications at El Agami Island near Alexandria. Three other Squadron aircraft took part in the raid, which proved to be 207 Squadron's last contribution to the Suez operation. On the following morning, the airborne assault commenced, and there was no further requirement for the Valiants, which returned

A Valiant waits to be bombed up on the dispersal at Luqa, Malta. (*P.H.T. Green Collection*)

home a few days later. In December, Wright was promoted to Wing Commander, and he crossed the airfield at Marham to take command of 148 Squadron.

During his two years in command of 148 Squadron, Wright had some notable achievements. He gained a 'Select' rating shortly after taking command, and this was later upgraded to the highest category of 'Select Star'. In June 1957 he led the Queen's Birthday Flypast, and a few months later completed the first transatlantic 'Western Ranger' by a V-bomber when he flew to Winnipeg in November. During this detachment, he made the 1,100-mile flight from Ottawa to Winnipeg in one hour fifty-one minutes – seven minutes faster than the record set by a RCAF CF-100 fighter. On the return flight across the Atlantic, he landed at Aldergrove after a flight of four hours ten minutes – the fastest at the time. In September 1958 he flew XD 874 to March Air Force Base in California to participate in the Strategic Air Command Bombing Competition when he and his crew were placed seventeenth out of 164 crews. He finally handed over command of the Squadron in March 1958 having flown 806 hours in the Valiant.

He served in the RAF for a further five years before retiring after twenty-four years' service that had seen him delivering bombs on operations from 100 feet during the Second World War, and from heights in excess of 40,000 feet during the Suez campaign. In the space of those relatively few years, aerial bombing had progressed from modest anti-shipping bombs, with a 250-lb warhead dropped from obsolescent bombers, to the nuclear bomb age of the V-Force.

Chapter Seven

Jungle Hurricane Pilot – Doug Nicholls

Douglas Nicholls joined the RAF Volunteer Reserve in July 1938 to train as a pilot. On acceptance, he reported to 25 Elementary and Reserve Flying Training School at Waltham near his home town of Grimsby. The school was equipped with the Magister, and on completion of initial training student pilots graduated to the Hart and Hind. Nicholls completed his training in August 1939, and was immediately called up for full-time service. To his chagrin, he had to join new recruits at an Initial Training Wing at Downing College, Cambridge before completing refresher flying on Tiger Moths at Sywell.

After completing advanced training on Masters at Montrose, Sergeant Nicholls travelled to 7 OTU at Hawarden where he converted to the Spitfire. After short spells with 85 and 242 Squadrons, he joined 151 Squadron based at Digby equipped with Hurricanes. He was soon in action during the later stages of the Battle of Britain. On 30 September 1940 the Squadron was due to assume 'readiness' at 0800. The pilots were making towards the dining-room when the Tannoy broadcast system urgently announced 'all available pilots to report . . .'. Nicholls responded immediately, and he took off a few minutes later in P 5182 as Red 3, with Flight Lieutenant K. Blair DFC leading the three aircraft formation. Ninety miles off the east coast they intercepted a reconnaissance Junkers 88, and they succeeded in shooting down the German aircraft. Three members of the crew were seen to bale out and get into their life rafts, but a long search failed to locate them. Both Blair's and Nicholl's aircraft were hit by return fire, but landed safely. This engagement was the Squadron's first success since moving to Digby.

Within a month, 151 Squadron was designated as a night-fighter Squadron and, after moving to Wittering, one Flight was re-equipped with Defiants, but Nicholls remained with the Hurricane Flight. The black-painted single-seat fighters were hardly ideal as night fighters. They lacked radar, and the gyro compass, easily visible on the instrument panel, was always liable to 'topple' during an abrupt manoeuvre, leaving the pilot to peer down into the gloomy cockpit to read the magnetic compass. Not surprisingly, the night Hurricanes achieved very few successes. One notable exception was Pilot Officer R.M. Stevens, a former civil airline pilot. He established a unique record for a single-seat night-fighter pilot with fourteen aircraft destroyed in ten months, an extraordinary achievement that was never approached. After being awarded the DSO and the DFC and Bar, he was killed over Holland in December 1941.

Nicholls flew many night-fighter patrols during the German Blitz mounted against British cities in late 1940 and early 1941, but the nearest he came to meeting a German aircraft at night occurred on 21 December 1940, when he was approaching to land at Bramcote. He had been cleared to land, switched on his navigation lights, lowered the undercarriage and flaps, and was at 150 feet on final approach when tracer bullets flashed either side of the cockpit. He could not have been more vulnerable, but he applied full power, raised the undercarriage and flaps, and staggered away trying to gain height as he turned. He managed to evade the German night-fighter, returning to the airfield some time later to make a safe landing.

As 1941 progressed, 151 Squadron became an all-Defiant Squadron, and Nicholls converted to the aircraft. Like the Hurricane, the Defiant was not fitted with radar, and trials to develop night-fighting tactics were carried out with Turbinlite Havocs. The aim was for the Havoc to home in on an enemy aircraft with the aid of instructions from controllers at Ground Control Interception (GCI) units and, when within visual range, to switch on a powerful searchlight carried in the nose of the aircraft. Once the enemy was illuminated, a Defiant flying in close formation with the Havoc manoeuvred to engage the enemy. The technique was not successful, although the Squadron's Defiants did achieve a number of night successes when operating independently.

Flying in the early, ill-equipped night fighters was a frustrating business, and Doug Nicholls was pleased when he learnt that he was posted back to a day-fighter Squadron. After serving with 151 Squadron for twelve months, he joined 258 Squadron at Martlesham Heath on 9 September 1941. The Squadron was equipped with Hurricane IIB aircraft and, within four weeks, and after a move to Debden, it was ordered to prepare for service overseas. On 30 October, twenty-two pilots travelled to Greenock to board the aircraft transport ship, HMS *Athene*, where they joined the pilots of two other Squadrons (242 and 605). Seventy-two crated Hurricanes were loaded on to the converted 10,000-ton Clan Line fast steamer, which sailed for Gibraltar two days later.

It soon became clear that the three Squadrons were destined as reinforcements for the Middle East and, after arriving in Gibraltar, half the aircraft were transferred to HMS *Ark Royal*. The plan was for the aircraft carrier to sail towards Malta and launch the Hurricanes 600 miles from the island. After refuelling, the aircraft would continue on to Egypt. Thirty-six aircraft of 242 and 605 Squadrons were launched successfully before the aircraft carrier turned back to Gibraltar to collect 258 Squadron for a repeat of the operation. Unfortunately, a German submarine sank HMS *Ark Royal* on the return voyage leaving

258 stranded at Gibraltar where it was formed into a local air defence force. A few days later, Japan attacked Pearl Harbor and plans for the Squadron were revised. With 258 Squadron, and half of 605 Squadron on board, HMS *Athene* eventually sailed from Gibraltar on Christmas Eve arriving at Takoradi in the Gold Coast a week later. All the aircrew disembarked and the ship, together with its cargo of Hurricanes, sailed for an unknown destination. Within two days, the aircrew boarded a Pan American Airlines Douglas DC-3 to make the long journey through Central Africa to Khartoum before travelling on to Port Sudan on the Red Sea coast. On arrival, Doug Nicholls discovered that he had been commissioned as a Pilot Officer.

Within days of the attack on Pearl Harbor, the Japanese landed in the north of Malaya and, by mid-January, they had occupied most of the country. At the outbreak of war in the Far East, the Commonwealth Air Forces could muster just 181 serviceable aircraft in the region, the great majority being obsolete. The fighter force was made up entirely of Buffalo and Wirraway aircraft, which were totally outclassed by the Japanese fighters. Reinforcements were urgently needed.

As soon as the pilots arrived at Port Sudan, 258 Squadron received new tropicalised Hurricane IIBs, which were assembled and taken on board the new aircraft carrier HMS *Indomitable* when it became clear that the Squadron was heading for the Far East to face the Japanese. The carrier, and its precious cargo of forty-eight Hurricanes and pilots of 232 and 258 Squadrons, sailed on 9 January 1942 for a point south of Christmas Island in the eastern Indian Ocean.

At dawn on 28 January, the first sixteen Hurricanes were raised from the aircraft carrier's hangars and positioned at the rear of the deck to await the arrival overhead of two Blenheims that were to escort the fighters to Batavia. After some delays, Squadron Leader 'Jock' Thompson, the CO of 258 Squadron, led the way as he took off from the very short flight deck to be followed by fifteen more Hurricanes. The second element was delayed, but Doug Nicholls took off with the second group the following day. He landed safely at Batavia after a two-and-a-half hour flight, although others suffered various landing accidents. After refuelling, eleven Hurricanes flew to Palembang in Sumatra to join thirteen of the first group, ready to reinforce the Singapore garrison that was under heavy Japanese attack. During this hazardous ferry operation, the Squadron had already suffered a loss of 25 per cent since launching from HMS *Indomitable*, and they had yet to meet the enemy.

As 258 Squadron arrived in the Far East, the military situation had deteriorated badly, with the Japanese poised to land on Singapore. Fighter aircraft reinforcements were urgently needed, and the Hurricanes were rushed to the island. In the event they were not available for operations until the end of January, by which time it was virtually too late. The Squadron flew its first operational flight on 31 January, but lost two pilots. Japanese bombing attacks against Singapore increased, and the depleted fighter force was withdrawn to Palembang in Sumatra ten days

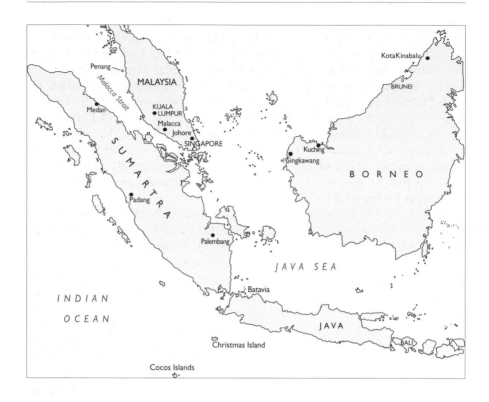

later. Within five days, the Singapore garrison surrendered, and the Japanese immediately turned their attention to Sumatra.

Flying operations from Palembang were fraught with difficulties. Spare parts for the diminishing number of Hurricanes were virtually non-existent, there was no accommodation, and there was a lack of transport and ground support equipment. More importantly, there was only a very crude early-warning system – there was no radio direction finding equipment to assist returning aircraft in poor weather, and the Hurricanes were not equipped with VHF radios. Most pilots felt that the lack of radios was the biggest obstacle to efficient fighter operations.

On 6 February the Japanese launched an attack against P1 airfield situated 10 miles north of Palembang. Six Hurricanes of 258 Squadron, including Doug Nicholls, were returning to the airfield from a patrol when they intercepted the attacking enemy bombers and their fighter escort. Other Hurricanes scrambled, but it was too late and they suffered badly. Five Hurricanes were lost and other aircraft were destroyed on the ground. Nicholls combined with three others in damaging a Navy Zero. The following day, the Japanese mounted more bombing attacks against the airfield, but the lack of an early-warning system meant that the enemy was virtually over the airfield before it was detected. Doug Nicholls was one of the few pilots who managed to scramble and, immediately after take-off, he pulled up beneath the attacking bombers and opened fire on one of the rear aircraft, which began to smoke and shed pieces, but he was driven off by fighters before he could complete the engagement. As he climbed away to gain height, Zero fighters attacked him, and his aircraft was badly damaged forcing him to bale out 30 miles from the airfield. He landed in a mangrove swamp, but managed to reach firm ground where he found himself cut off following a Japanese parachute assault near the airfield. Unable to reach P1 airfield, Nicholls headed for the town of Palembang. In the confusion following the Japanese airborne landings, he was unable to discover the location of his Squadron, so decided to head for Java. He commandeered a car and set off for the port of Oosthaven. When the car ran out of petrol, he traded it for a railway ticket, eventually reaching the small port where he boarded a ferry for Batavia.

During the hectic fighting in the days following Nicholl's bale out, the Squadron lost two more pilots, and the airfield at P1 had to be evacuated. The Squadron moved to a jungle airstrip, P2, 30 miles south of the town to continue the impossible fight. By 15 February the continuous heavy air attacks, followed by a sea borne invasion, forced the Squadron to evacuate to Java where Nicholls met up with the remnants, seven days after being shot down.

A few days later it was announced that 258 Squadron was to be withdrawn from Java, but six pilots had to stay behind to fly the remaining Hurricanes and reinforce 605 Squadron. Two pilots were detailed and one volunteered. The remainder gathered in a local hotel and it was decided to cut cards with the three drawing the lowest remaining behind. Doug Nicholls cut a jack, which was just high enough to allow him to join the party to be evacuated. Those who remained were either killed in action or spent almost four years as prisoners of the Japanese. 28 February was a sad day as the Squadron pilots bid each other good-bye. Just six of the original twenty-two sailed for Ceylon on the overcrowded SS *Kote Gede*.

The remnants of the Squadron arrived at Colombo on 7 March to become the nucleus of a new 258 Squadron, initially called 'K' Squadron, under the command of Squadron Leader Peter Fletcher (later Air Chief Marshal Sir Peter Fletcher). After a brief spell at Ratmanala, the Squadron moved from the overcrowded civil airport to the Colombo Racecourse where it remained for the next twelve months. The Squadron was equipped with Hurricane IIBs with seven Mark Is allocated to make up the numbers.

After four months of success, the seemingly invincible Japanese – mainly through their overwhelming naval air power – looked to the Indian Ocean and the destruction of the large British Fleet based in Ceylon. Within days of Admiral Sir James Somerville taking command of this Fleet, an intelligence report warned of a large-scale attack on Colombo planned for early April. The Fleet was dispersed, and the Ceylon air defences were placed on a high alert state, including Doug Nicholls and his fellow pilots of 258 Squadron. On the morning of 4 April, a searching Catalina of 413 (RCAF) Squadron located the Japanese Fleet, and a radio message was transmitted just as fighters shot down the Catalina. Squadron Leader L.J. Birchall and his surviving crew were captured and suffered great privations, but their vital message saved Colombo. On release from a POW camp, over three years later, Birchall was awarded the DFC.

Some Hurricanes were maintained at 'Readiness' through the night and, at 0400 thirty-six Hurricanes of 30 and 258 Squadrons were brought to immediate readiness. As no radar was working at Colombo that day, a dawn patrol was flown but nothing was seen. At 0740, with no warning, Japanese bombers, with a strong fighter escort, appeared over Colombo. The Hurricanes were scrambled and Nicholls took off in BD 881 (ZT-Q), but the lack of warning meant that there was no time to form up as a formation, so it was every man for himself. With the Japanese bombers heading for the harbour, the Hurricanes followed, but were subjected to heavy, friendly anti-aircraft fire in addition to attacks by Navy Zero fighters. Nine of the fourteen Hurricanes were shot down with the loss of five pilots; two others were seriously wounded, including the CO. The Squadron destroyed four dive bombers with Nicholls being credited with a 'damaged'. Twenty-one Hurricanes were lost, but the Japanese attacks were severely disrupted. Four days later, the Japanese attempted a second attack, this time against the naval base at Trincomalee, but radar warning allowed the British fighters to scramble in time, and the Japanese suffered heavy losses, although the aircraft carrier HMS *Hermes* was sunk. Ceylon was saved, but at a heavy cost.

For the next few months, Doug Nicholls and his colleagues on 258 Squadron remained in Ceylon providing air defence cover and flying convoy patrols. In the meantime, Japanese forces had swept north through Burma to the Indian border in Assam, but, as 1942 ended,

Monsoon weather grounds a Hurricane parked in a revetment on the Red Road airstrip near Calcutta in 1942. (*Author's Collection*)

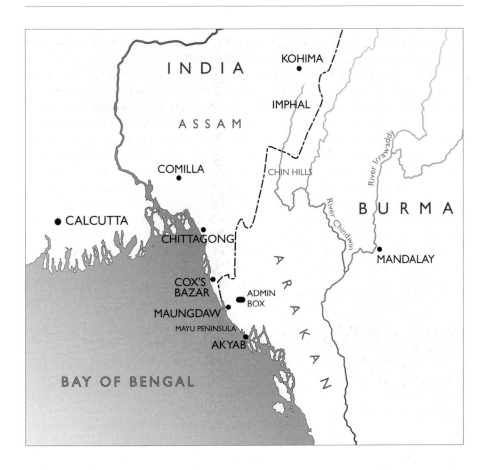

the British 14th Division commenced an offensive in the Arakan in an attempt to capture Akyab and its airfields. The threat to Ceylon had diminished, so 258 Squadron flew to Dum Dum airfield at Calcutta, and then on to Chittagong, to reinforce the Squadrons of 224 Group supporting the Army advance. They remained for three weeks, flying their Hurricane IIBs on 'Rhubarbs' with attacks mounted against Japanese lines of communications, barracks and radio facilities. These ground-attack sorties provided valuable experience that was put to great effect when the Squadron returned to the battle a few months later.

Within a few weeks, Nicholls returned to the front line in Bengal when he was attached to 79 Squadron flying from airfields around Cox's Bazaar. Despite the onset of the monsoon, and the inevitable slow down of army action, Nicholls and his colleagues continued to fly ground support sorties and to provide escorts for the Blenheim bombing sorties. On 17 May he flew his first night 'Rhubarb' sortie when he sought out targets on the Mayu Peninsula – a daunting task in a single-engine fighter with very limited navigation aids. Similar sorties followed before the Squadron left the flooded, temporary airfields for Comilla where bomber escort sorties continued to be flown. After six weeks, Nicholls returned to Colombo where 258 Squadron was working-up in preparation for a return to the battle in north Burma.

Throughout 1943 there was a steady build-up of ground and air forces in India. The Hurricanes of 258 Squadron started to move to the area at the end of July, and were operational at Comilla four weeks later. The Squadron formed part of 224 Group, which had six Hurricane ground-attack Squadrons by the end of the year. It flew its first operational sortie on 1 September. The Squadron was tasked to support XV Indian Corp's drive down the Mayu Peninsula as the dry season started. In addition to flying strafing sorties, the Hurricanes provided escort to the recently arrived Vengeance dive-bombers used in the close support role. The latter became a crucial element of the air support provided to the ground forces, and the Hurricanes of 258 Squadron became regular escorts.

During the Squadron's work-up period, the Hurricanes had been fitted with long-range under-wing fuel tanks, and these were soon needed. On 6 September, Nicholls flew on a strafing sortie to the River Irrawaddy where over 100 sampans were strafed, landing after a three-hour flight over the inhospitable jungle and mountains. A similar sortie was flown a few days later when the Hurricanes came under heavy anti-aircraft fire.

The Japanese Air Force continued to pose a serious threat to Calcutta and the port of Chittagong, and the Hurricanes were always available to act in the air defence role. On 20 October Nicholls had just landed from a long-range sortie escorting a Vengeance Squadron when a large Japanese bomber formation of Mitsubishi Ki-21 'Sally' bombers, with a fighter escort, was detected heading for Chittagong. He was immediately scrambled, and the raid was repulsed after a fierce fight in which two Hurricanes were lost. The Squadron re-equipped with the cannon-armed Hurricane IIC in late November, and Nicholls flew his first sortie on the type in LA 104 on 23 November.

Although primarily assigned to ground-attack operations, scrambles continued to be a feature of operations for all fighter Squadrons over the following weeks, with the most significant occurring on 5 December when a raid was detected approaching Calcutta. Ten aircraft were scrambled at 1000 and climbed to 30,000 feet over Cox's Bazaar where forty-plus aircraft were detected. Doug Nicholls was leading a section detailed to provide top cover to the formation leader, Flight Lieutenant Art Brown and his section. During the climb he noticed the leader's aircraft start to porpoise, and it was clear that Brown was in trouble. Radio contact with him was lost, so he detailed Warrant Officer 'Ginger' Hickes, the leader's No 2, to stay with him as the rest of the Squadron continued to climb. Brown's aircraft was seen to stall, and it dived towards the sea as Nicholls spotted an enemy formation through the thin haze. It was part of the fighter escort, but was too high, and it would have been unwise to approach it from below, so he broke off the interception. Meanwhile, Hickes had dived after his out-of-control leader, and found himself in the middle of a large enemy bomber formation. He succeeded in shooting down a 'Sally' bomber, but was immediately 'bounced' by an 'Oscar' fighter. He took immediate evasive action by diving to sea level where he succeeded in losing the Japanese fighter before having to return to base short of fuel. The Canadian, Brown, failed to return, and it was assumed that he had experienced an oxygen failure.

Three days later it was another night 'Rhubarb' for Nicholls who attacked some lights on the banks of a river. By this stage of the campaign, he was one of the most experienced pilots on the Squadron. He frequently led twelve aircraft escorting Vengeance formations from 82 Squadron as they attacked the airfields around Akyab, where they encountered heavy anti-aircraft fire. Nicholls also faced other dangers. Returning from an operation, he collided with a vulture, which badly damaged the windscreen and dislodged the hood from the canopy rails. He was unable to move the hood to bale out and, with a great deal of difficulty, he completed an emergency landing – his mechanics had to lever the hood away before he could climb from the aircraft. He was awarded a 'confirmed destroyed'!

A Hurricane attacks a bridge on the Tiddim road. The leader has just dropped his bombs on the target. (*IWM. CF 175*)

A Hurricane IIB carrying long-range fuel tanks under each wing escorts a 62 Squadron Dakota on a supply drop. (*Author's Collection*)

A few days later, ten Hurricanes took off to attack aircraft on a landing ground near Akyab. Five aircraft flew at 5,000 feet as top cover, and arrived at the target just ahead of the attacking force flying at 50 feet. Gun positions were attacked with cannon, and three aircraft were hit by return fire including Doug Nicholls. The oil tank of his aircraft (LB 784) was hit, but he just managed to get back to an advanced landing ground where he crash-landed successfully.

Crucial aspects of the war in Burma were the airborne resupply of the ground forces by the RAF's hardworking Dakota Squadrons, and close-support bombing sorties by Vengeance aircraft. During January, a strong Japanese counter-attack in the Maungdaw area isolated large elements of the 7th Division. As the fighting intensified it was vital to maintain control of the air in order to keep the beleaguered troops resupplied by the Dakotas of 31 Squadron, and supported by the Vengeance dive-bombers of 8 (RIAF) and 82 Squadrons. The latter maintained continuous bombing

Doug Nicholls poses by his Hurricane at an airstrip in Assam. (*Doug Nicholls*)

The Squadron Commander gives a final briefing to his pilots before they take off to attack a Japanese target. Most are wearing the 'Beadon' survival suit with kukri knives and revolvers. (*IWM. CF 175*)

operations on a daily basis. The Hurricanes of 258 Squadron acted as escorts for both types of operations, in addition to mounting many strafing sorties against the Japanese advances – some targets just a few hundred yards ahead of Allied troops. During February, Doug Nicholls flew twenty-seven operational sorties during the most intensive period of flying since the Squadron had arrived in Burma.

At the beginning of the month, Squadron Leader Neil Cameron (later Marshal of the RAF Lord Cameron) assumed command of 258 Squadron, and he quickly established himself as an outstanding and dynamic leader who led from the front. He was soon in action and, shortly after taking over command, his aircraft was hit by anti-aircraft fire, and he only just regained a friendly airfield. He was subsequently awarded the DSO for his outstanding leadership of the Squadron over a long period of successful operations.

The intense rate of flying continued during March 1944 as the Japanese continued to counter-attack. The West African Division in the Kaladan Valley, just to the east of the area known as the Admin Box, became isolated and was involved in bitter fighting. Resupply and close support operations were increased, and this placed heavy demands on the Hurricane escort and ground-strafing Squadrons. Nicholls flew another twenty-eight sorties during March, strafing enemy positions, escorting

Dakotas and Vengeances, and flying fighter sweeps. He led the Squadron on an attack against Japanese infantry and artillery positions near the village of Inbauk. After landing, he was met by the intelligence officer who had just received a long signal from the army sector commander. It was fulsome in its praise and offered congratulations for the attack, confirming that the Squadron's strafing attack had driven the enemy from their positions with many casualties together with the loss of artillery pieces. Such close support was a feature of the air war in Burma. At the end of the month, Nicholls was promoted to Flight Lieutenant and made a Flight Commander.

The intensity of air operations continued during April and May with 512 operational sorties flown in April when a record 94,024 rounds of 20 mm were fired. On 24 May, just as the monsoon broke, 258 Squadron was withdrawn from the front line to Arkonham, near Madras, after nine months of continuous and intensive operations. The Squadron diarist noted, 'Good billets, showers and a swimming pool. What a change from the Arakan.' On their departure from the front line, the General Officer Commanding XV Corps sent the following signal:

> Now that Squadrons are dispersing and advanced Group HQ is closing down, I would like them to know how much their efforts have been appreciated by front-line troops. It is difficult to exaggerate the heightening in morale which results from such good close support as we have had this season.

The Japanese advance had been held, and within a year the tide turned as the Army, supported by the Air Forces, steadily regained Burma until final victory.

On arrival at Arkonham Doug Nicholls received a signal informing him that he had been awarded the Distinguished Flying Cross. The citation drew attention to his 380 hours of operational flying in single-seat fighters and concluded:

> For the last 14 months he has been operating in the Arakan and has carried out many escort and strafing sorties against the Japanese. Flying Officer Nicholls has displayed great enthusiasm and determination at all times to engage the enemy.

The men of 'The Forgotten Air Force' earned their medals the hard way. Nicholls had flown 127 operations directly in the face of the enemy in the Far East, and there are many who feel he and his colleagues deserved far greater recognition for such courage and skill in the most adverse and difficult conditions. Shortly after the announcement of the award of his DFC, he left 258 Squadron on promotion to take up the post of Squadron Leader Tactics at Headquarters 224 Group, and almost immediately returned to the Arakan to plan and organise attack operations.

Doug Nicholls had completed almost three continuous years on the Squadron that had seen him flying convoy patrols off East Anglia, fighting desperate rearguard operations in Sumatra and Java, flying fighter sorties over Ceylon, and culminating in a long and intensive period of flying strafing and escort sorties over the inhospitable Burmese jungles. He continued to fly whenever possible and his last flight in the RAF took place on 17 July 1945 when he flew Spitfire Mk VIII, MT 839 on a one-hour local flight. With the war over in the Far East, he returned to England and left the service in December 1945, although he continued to give valuable service to the RAF as a gliding instructor with the Air Training Corps.

Chapter Eight

Malta Blenheim Navigator – Freddie Deeks

Like many of his generation, Woolwich-born Freddie Deeks joined the wartime RAFVR as soon as his age allowed. He enlisted as the last troops were evacuated from the beaches at Dunkirk in May 1940, just after his eighteenth birthday. After completing the traditional aircrew initial training courses he reported to Staverton airfield on the outskirts of Gloucester to start his air observer training with 6 Air Observer and Navigator School.

In the early years of the war, the air observer was a multi-talented individual trained as a navigator, bomb aimer and gunner. Deeks started his flying training on the Anson I with many sorties concentrating on map reading and basic navigation. After three months, he moved to Dumfries to continue his training with 10 Bombing and Gunnery School. Whitleys were used for air gunnery training with the students firing from the nose and tail turrets against a towed target. The Fairey Battle, equipped with the Mk 9 bombsight, was used for bombing training over the weapons ranges in the Solway Firth. On completion of the course at Dumfries in May 1941, Freddie Deeks was awarded his distinctive air observer brevet, promoted to sergeant, and posted to 17 OTU at Upwood to convert to the Blenheim.

As the pilots on the course were learning to fly the Blenheim, initial operational conversion training for the observers was carried out on the Anson. Once this phase was complete, the aircrew were invited to team up as crews, and Deeks and the Australian pilot Ray Noseda decided to fly together. They invited Doug Webber to be their gunner. This decision taken over a beer was to herald the start of a highly successful team. Having completed the conversion course they were posted to 110 (Hyderabad) Squadron at Wattisham.

Shortly after joining the Squadron, Deeks and his crew were detailed for their first operational sortie, an attack on the railway marshalling yards at Amiens on 22 September 1941. Flying a Blenheim IV (V 6523) they took off with 226 Squadron in the lead. Unfortunately, the formation leader's observer had left his TR 9 radio transmit switch permanently on, allowing the crew's conversation to be broadcast to the whole formation and, presumably, to the German air defence forces. They were heard discussing the target and the estimated time of arrival, so the controlling authority had no option but to broadcast a recall, and the formation returned to base. As Freddie Deeks remarked, 'the whole thing was a shambles and hardly the way to start an operational tour'. After the abortive Amiens raid, two successful raids against the town, and attacks on Boulogne soon followed. To their surprise, the crews saw no opposition over Amiens, but the following morning the newspapers reported 'a great air battle over the Channel'. The escorting fighters had intercepted a large force of Me 109 fighters and engaged them before they could attack the bomber formation. Due to the unacceptable casualty rate among the Blenheim force during the early part of the war, fighter escort eventually had to be provided, and this was one of the first occasions that they had been made available.

During the latter part of 1941 the inadequacies of the Blenheim as a daylight bomber over Europe were becoming increasingly apparent, and many of the aircraft and crews were reallocated to the overseas theatres. Being one of the junior crews, Freddie Deeks and his two colleagues were earmarked to join a Middle East Squadron where the Blenheim was still operating in large numbers. They were allocated a Blenheim IV (Z 7914) to ferry to the Middle East, setting off from Portreath on 3 November 1941. They flew at 10,000 feet and routed via the Scilly Isles, across the Bay of Biscay to Estaca Point on the north-west tip of Spain, and then round the Spanish and Portuguese coasts to Gibraltar before landing after a seven-hour flight.

The next stage of the transit flight was to Malta, a flight of seven and a half hours, with the final three hours flown at low level to avoid detection by the Axis radar sites along the Tunisian coast and on the islands approaching Malta. The Air Commander, Air Vice-Marshal Hugh Pughe-Lloyd, was

A Blenheim IV of 107 Squadron. (*P.H.T Green Collection*)

desperately short of bombers to attack the Axis convoys, and he regularly 'hi-jacked' crews and aircraft on their way to the Middle East. Within a few hours of arriving in Malta, it was apparent that Deeks and his crew would be going no further, since they were sent to the recently arrived 107 Squadron, which had already suffered some heavy losses.

In broad terms, the Blenheim crews were tasked with three types of sorties, all designed to interrupt the flow of crucial supplies from Italy to Rommel's *Afrika Korps* in the North African desert. A number of crews would fly reconnaissance sorties in search of Axis shipping. Others would remain on standby waiting for reports from 69 Squadron, the specialist reconnaissance Squadron equipped with Maryland aircraft. If enemy shipping were sighted, a formation of Blenheims would take off for a bombing attack. The third type of sortie was called a 'road beat' when individual aircraft would fly at very low level along the North African coastal roads bombing and strafing troop convoys, resupply vehicles, stores dumps, and any other valuable target on the 'Africa Road'.

A few days after their arrival on the besieged island of Malta, Deeks and his crew flew their first sortie, a shipping reconnaissance to the north of Tripoli that lasted over four hours. This was followed by their first visit to the 'Africa Road' where transport lorries, oil tankers and aircraft on landing grounds were machine-gunned and bombed. The whole flight was carried out below fifty feet, making the aircraft vulnerable to small-arms fire – most aircraft on this type of operation returned with damage.

The pressure on the Blenheim crews was immense, with operational flying on almost every day. As they took their toll of Axis shipping sailing from Sicily direct to Tripoli, the enemy was forced to seek longer routes sailing from Brindisi, through the Greek islands before crossing the Mediterranean to North Africa. The Blenheims, together with Malta-based Wellingtons, continued to seek out the ships carrying vital supplies, and this often required a 900-mile round trip to the Greek coast with accurate landfalls necessary, and all flown over the sea placing a tremendous burden on Freddie Deeks and his fellow navigators. Often the crews would return from these extremely long-range sorties to find that Malta was under attack, and they would have to orbit out to sea before being allowed to land with minimum fuel and, very often, with wounded crew members.

Deeks and his crew flew their first sortie to the Greek coast on 29 November 1941 when they joined five other Blenheims to carry out a high-level bombing attack against shipping in Navarino Bay. Despite heavy rain and intensive anti-aircraft fire from shore batteries and escorting destroyers, some of the formation were able to bomb, and hits were registered on a tanker. Deeks's aircraft suffered hits in the rudder and elevators, but the crew were able to return safely.

More success followed on 1 December when four aircraft of 107 Squadron were sent to intercept shipping off the Tunisian coast. Flying Blenheim Z 7619, Ray Noseda lifted off from the Luqa runway at 1520.

The 7,000-ton tanker, *Iridio Mantovani*, with a destroyer escort, was located 65 miles off Melita, and the four Blenheims attacked at mast height. A number of hits were registered, and as soon as Deeks had dropped his bombs, he sprayed the decks with the forward-firing machine-guns. Following a radio report by the formation, the Navy closed in and sank the severely damaged tanker. This spectacular success was featured on the front page of *The Sunday Times of Malta* with a dramatic photograph taken from one of the Blenheims. The Italian authorities stated, 'It cannot be denied that the blow was a hard one.'

The routine of searching for shipping off the Kerkenna Islands, Misurata, Lampadusa and Pantellaria continued on a daily basis during the early part of December. On 13 December, a reconnaissance sortie reported a build-up of shipping off the Greek coast. Six Blenheims of 107 Squadron, led by Pilot Officer Broom (later Air Marshal Sir Ivor Broom), took off at 0800 loaded with 500-lb bombs to attack shipping in Argostoli harbour. Noseda and Deeks in their Blenheim (Z 9741) took up station on the leader's aircraft for the long transit. Two hours later the formation made its landfall and turned south for the target area using the valleys to hide their approach. Under intense fire from the escorting destroyers and the shore batteries, the leader and Pilot Officer Williamson attacked a 4,000-ton merchant vessel as Noseda and Deeks attacked another of 8,000 tons from mast-top height. Taking violent evasive action after his attack, Noseda joined up with the other two aircraft just as a Macchi 200 fighter closed in to attack. Deeks opened fire with his rearwards-firing machine-gun forcing the fighter to break away. After the long return flight, two of the Blenheims were missing.

The pressure on the surviving crews increased, and Deeks and his crew were tasked, together with another aircraft, to fly a 'road beat' to the west of Tripoli. Shortly after crossing the coast, the two crews spotted a train with six coaches and a number of fuel tanks, which they bombed with 250-lb bombs before carrying out three machine-gun attacks. The train was completely wrecked, and more precious fuel failed to reach the Axis armies. As they left the target, a Fiat CR 42 fighter closed in on the two bombers, keeping up a continuous attack as the Blenheims escaped to sea, flying in close formation. After ten minutes the fighter broke away. The pilot of the second bomber radioed to say that his aircraft had been hit and his observer wounded, and Deeks navigated the pair back to Malta. Due to bad weather both aircraft had difficulty landing at Luqa where it was discovered that the second Blenheim had been badly damaged by a flock of wild ducks before the CR 42 inflicted further damage.

Despite poor weather, there was to be no let-up for the surviving Blenheim crews as Christmas approached. On Christmas Day 1941 Freddie Deeks and his crew flew a shipping reconnaissance off the west of Sicily, landing after a five-hour sortie. Before New Year a number of successful 'road beats' were flown against the retreating *Afrika Korps* with numerous vehicles and installations destroyed. In the six weeks

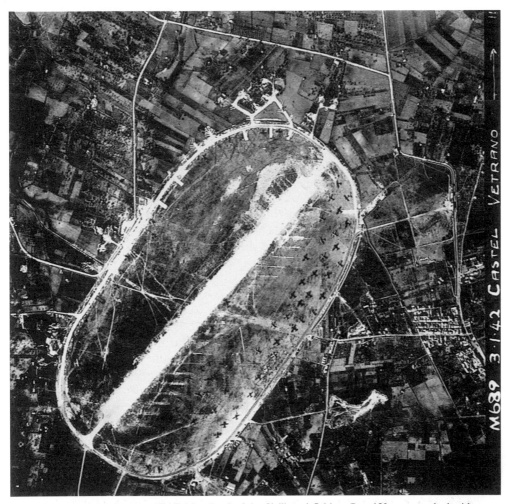

A photograph taken by a RAF Maryland of the Sicilian airfield at Castel Vetrano packed with German transport aircraft the day before the highly successful bombing attack on 4 January 1942. (*Author's Collection*)

since arriving in Malta, Freddie Deeks and his crew had flown seventeen hazardous operations as they celebrated the arrival of 1942.

Another means of denying supplies to Rommel's army was to attack transportation targets in Sicily and Italy. On 4 January 1942, reconnaissance Marylands of 69 Squadron had discovered over seventy large transport aircraft closely parked on the enemy airfield at Castel Vetrano on the western spur of Sicily. A mixed formation of Blenheims, drawn from 18 and 107 Squadrons, was tasked to mount an attack. Deeks and his crew in Z 7966 flew in the number two position of the 107 Squadron box. After crossing the coast at low level, the formation in three vics line abreast attacked the airfield from west to east at heights as low as 25 feet. The calm of the Sunday afternoon was shattered as the formation swept across the airfield taking the enemy gun crews by complete surprise. Deeks dropped a stick of four 250-lb time-delayed bombs across a group of transport aircraft, which were being serviced by ground crew, before opening up with the forward-firing VPO gun. As the formation departed, many of the transport aircraft could be seen on fire with rising smoke visible from 40 miles away. A follow-up attack by Wellingtons caused more damage. An RAF Middle East communiqué issued to Reuters a few days later reported that the attack had been 'a devastating and lightning' raid in which forty-four aircraft, mostly transports, had been destroyed. The *Malta Times* described it as 'one of the most successful raids ever carried out by Malta-based aircraft'.

The spectacular raid on Castel Vetrano signalled the end of a full tour for Deeks, his pilot Ray Noseda and gunner Doug Webber. Seven days after the raid, they delivered a Blenheim (Z 7534) to Helwan in Egypt from where they returned to England. They had been on Malta for just nine weeks during which time they had flown on thirty dangerous operations, many at maximum range and against intense opposition, and where the loss of crews had been among the highest sustained on any RAF operations. It is hard to believe that Freddie Deeks was not yet twenty, and had started his observer training just a year before the end of his tour on Malta.

After spending nine months at Bicester as an instructor with 13 OTU, during which time he was commissioned, Deeks returned to operations, but not before he had completed five dinghy search operations in support of the bomber crews returning from the night bomber offensive over Germany. Together with his pilot John Reeves and gunner Dinty Moore, Deeks joined 88 Squadron in October 1942. The Squadron was equipped with the Boston III light bomber and was in the process of moving to Oulton in Norfolk.

During 1942 much more capable, purpose-built aircraft, including the Boston, had replaced the slow and vulnerable Blenheims of 2 Group. The aircraft was well liked by the aircrew and it proved to be an excellent tactical bomber aircraft. Other changes in the RAF's tactical bomber Group saw the regular use of fighter escorts, and more innovative tactics under the leadership of the Group's dynamic leader, Air Vice-Marshal Basil Embry.

The first operations flown by Deeks and his crew were against port and oil installations, but extensive cloud cover forced the bomber formations to abort their attempts. November saw a temporary cessation of operations as the whole Squadron participated in large-scale exercises in preparation for one of the most spectacular low-level bombing raids of the war, Operation 'Oyster' the attack against the Philips radio and valve plant at Eindhoven. The factory was a major producer of specialist and valuable radio equipment with an output that met over a third of Germany's requirement.

The target was situated in a heavily built-up area, and it was paramount to make every attempt to avoid civilian casualties, so the raid was timed for a Sunday when the great majority of the work force would be at home. The raid took place on 6 December with the Bostons taking off from Oulton at 1115. Deeks and his crew, flying a Boston III (AL 693), were leading the second box of six, and the whole formation set

Bostons of 88 Squadron at low level over the North Sea en-route to a target in Holland. (*Author's Collection*)

heading for Southwold twenty minutes later. The Ventura and Mosquito formations followed closely behind. The whole formation crossed the North Sea at less than 100 feet to make an accurate landfall on the Dutch coast. Precise timing and accurate navigation was essential. Enemy defences were soon alerted, and the formation had to face a heavy barrage of flak together with the attentions of Fw 190 and Bf 109 fighters taking off from Woensdrecht.

The leader's navigation was faultless as he approached Eindhoven. The plan was for the first two Bostons to attack the building at low level, dropping eleven-second delay-fused 250-lb bombs, as the remainder of the formation pulled up to 1,500 feet to drop their bombs in level flight before diving back to low level to escape to the north. Once the first element of surprise passed, the formation came under heavy attack from the anti-aircraft defences. The Bostons joined up in small groups, crossing the Dutch Coast north of Rotterdam before returning to their airfields in East Anglia two and a half hours after take-off.

The raid was a great success with the factory severely damaged and production dramatically reduced for six months. Sadly, the cost was high with fourteen aircraft lost, including one of the Ventura Squadron Commanders. The raid attracted great publicity in the press, and the Dutch Resistance acknowledged that it had given a great boost to the morale of the Dutch people.

During the following weeks, numerous operations were flown against ports, airfields and oil installations before the Bostons were temporarily withdrawn from operations in order to participate in large-scale Army exercises, which included experiments at laying smoke screens. By the

Bostons depart the Philips radio valve factory after the very successful raid on 6 December 1942. (*Air Historical Branch*)

summer, 'Circus' operations had recommenced. These daylight operations now attracted large fighter escorts, which often involved five Squadrons of Spitfires – a far cry from the days of unescorted raids by the Blenheims. More innovative tactics were introduced. On 26 July 1943 the Bostons attacked Wevelgem Aerodrome near Courtrai in Belgium, but, initially, they set course for the Dutch coast to confuse the enemy radar and DF stations. After twenty minutes the formation turned back for the English coast where they picked up their fighter escort as they headed for the target. Enemy fighters did not appear until after the Bostons had attacked the airfield.

On 2 August 1943 the crews of 88 Squadron were given the chance to put into practice their smoke-laying techniques. Flying a Boston IIIA (BZ 323), Deeks and his crew led the first of twelve pairs of Bostons to a position 8 miles off Boulogne, where Royal Navy minesweepers were operating. The Bostons positioned themselves between the ships and the clearly visible French coast before laying a smoke screen from four containers fired off at ten-second intervals. The screen was very effective, and the Bostons left the area with an escort of eight Spitfires just as the second pair of Bostons arrived to reinforce the screen. A similar operation was mounted a few weeks later to cover a large-scale amphibious exercise in the English Channel. Few of the crews appreciated that this was a prelude to their role during the great D-Day invasion the following year.

Two raids flown in late 1943 highlight how the tactical Squadrons varied their tactics. On 5 September twenty-four Bostons of 88 and 107 Squadrons attacked Woensdrecht airfield in Holland with containers of 40-lb HE bombs. Flying their Boston IIIA (BZ 323), Deeks and crew led a section of 88 Squadron. The whole formation met up with the fighter escort over Bradwell Bay before climbing to the bombing height of 12,000 feet with no fewer than nine Spitfire Squadrons forming the escort. From the time the bombers crossed the Dutch coast, they came under constant attack from light and heavy flak batteries with a particularly intense barrage over the target. With shells bursting all round the formation, Deeks commented laconically 'it made bombing no easy job'. Post-attack photographs confirmed the success of the attack.

The tactics were different on 3 October when twelve Bostons of 107 Squadron, led by Wing Commander R. England DFC, attacked the Chaingy power station near Orléans. Deeks's pilot, John Reeve, had been promoted to Squadron Leader and posted as a Flight Commander to 107 Squadron, taking his crew with him, and they were leading the second section. After coasting out near Beachy Head, the formation flew at very low level over the Channel increasing speed to 250 knots as they approached the French coast, firing their front guns to silence the inevitable light flak. Making full use of the low hills and valleys, the formation made regular changes to their route as they flew around Paris and headed for Orleans. The attack had been planned for a Sunday, and the formation was greeted by the waving French population as well as the less welcoming crews of the flak batteries. The cathedral at Orléans could be seen on the horizon, and the final run-up to the target commenced. The tactics were similar to the Eindhoven raid, with the first section remaining at low level to drop their eleven-second delay-bombs as Deeks's section climbed to 1,500 feet to drop 500-lb MC bombs. A large explosion was observed in the middle of the target, and post-attack analysis of the photographs taken by Deeks confirmed extensive damage. As the Bostons dived away from the target, John Reeve saw a long goods train that he raked with the forward-firing gun. The Spitfire escort appeared over northern France to escort the bombers home.

Freddie Deeks (left) and his crew stand by their 107 Squadron Boston. His pilot, John Reeve, is standing next to him. (*J. Pelly-Fry*)

This raid highlights how the planning of attacks had become more coordinated and sophisticated. The air staff at Headquarters 2 Group had planned the attack to coincide with similar attacks by 88 and 342 Squadrons on two other power stations in the Paris area with the aim of depriving much of the French rail network of electric power. The combined raid was so successful that the Paris–Tours railway had to revert to steam, and six transformers were put out of action for six months. The official report pointed out 'It shows the effect of simultaneous attacks if these are successful.'

By the end of October 1943 Freddie Deeks's long tour on Bostons was coming to an end, but not before he flew on a major raid that ended in tragedy. On 22 October thirty-six Bostons were tasked to attack the engineering and repair depot at Courcelles in northern France. Once again the formation was led by Wing Commander England with Deeks and his crew leading the second section. The formation flew at low level over the sea, but due to the poor visibility, the formation crossed the coast a few miles off track. In an endeavour to regain track, the leader turned, causing his formation to spread out. As they crossed the small port of Veere near the Scheldt Estuary, the formation encountered intense light flak and, within a few seconds, four of the leading six Bostons were shot down to crash in flames, including Wing Commander England. The remaining bombers in the leading Squadron poured fire into the flak positions, but two more Bostons were lost. Reeve took over the lead, but the combination of poor visibility and the very confusing landscape of slag heaps and railway yards meant that the formation passed 2 miles from the target, and the survivors had to bring back their bombs. This devastating loss had a cruel effect on the Boston crews, and Air Vice-Marshal Embry described the loss of the highly experienced Richard England as 'a severe blow to the whole Group, he was a great leader'. Ironically, the day after his death came the announcement that he had been awarded the Distinguished Service Order for 'his inspiring leadership, great courage and exceptional skill'.

After two more sorties, Freddie Deeks completed his second tour of operations when he was posted to serve as an instructor with 1482 (B) Flight where he flew in the Mosquito for the first time. It was at this time that the *London Gazette* announced that Flight Lieutenant F.J. Deeks had been awarded the Distinguished Flying Cross for his outstanding work as a low-level navigator during his time in Malta and in 2 Group.

After a six-month rest, he crewed up with the New Zealander Squadron Leader R. Young DFC, and they were posted to 487 (NZ) Squadron at Thorney Island to fly the Mosquito FB VI. Deeks and his pilot started operations in early August 1944 just as the Allied armies were ready to break out of the Normandy beachhead to commence their headlong dash across northern France into Belgium. Their first sortie on 9 August set the pattern for their tour of operations when they took off at night to patrol the area surrounding the River Seine north-west of Paris. Their task was to continue where the rocket-firing Typhoons had finished at the end of daylight, harass the enemy and, in particular, disrupt transport movements. The Mosquitoes would drop flares on suspected targets before carrying out a dive-bombing or strafing attack with cannons if a worthwhile target had been illuminated. They returned from their first operation having dropped their 500-lb bombs on trucks that had carelessly displayed lights.

Immediate support of the battle area and attacks against the transportation system in northern France became the nightly routine for the light bombers of the Second Tactical Air Force (2 TAF) who often mounted over 200 interdiction sorties each night. Deeks and his pilot went out almost every night to patrol specific areas with orders to attack any transport targets. These included motor transport, trains, barges and ferries. If a target were found, Deeks would fix the position using his GEE navigation equipment before broadcasting the position to call in other patrolling Mosquitoes.

A diversion from the night attacks occurred on 31 August. Deeks and his pilot, flying Mosquito VI (NT 123), took off in the morning as part of a six-aircraft formation to attack an SS barracks housed in a school at Vincey near Epinal on the River Moselle. The French Maquis had reported the presence of 2,000 SS troops in the area. Once across Allied lines, the six aircraft let down to low level to follow the valleys to the target, which was a very distinctive building. The Mosquitoes climbed prior to dropping their four 500-lb eleven-second delay-bombs that exploded in

A spectacular view of Freddie Deeks sitting next to his pilot Squadron Leader Young in their 487 (NZ) Squadron Mosquito FB VI over the North Sea in August 1944. (*Author's Collection*)

the buildings. Troops could be seen running for cover as each Mosquito carried out three cannon firing attacks inflicting further serious damage. This highly successful attack destroyed the building for the loss of one of the Mosquitoes, whose crew was able to join up with the Maquis before returning to England.

By the end of August the armies were making rapid easterly progress, and the 2 TAF bombers patrolled in the areas ahead of the advance. To reduce the transit flying time, 487 Squadron moved to Hartford Bridge to begin patrols in Belgium and Holland, sometimes flying as far east as the Ruhr in their relentless search to destroy the Germans' transport infrastructure. Deeks attacked the ferries in the Walcheren area where the Allied armies were meeting pockets of stiff German resistance. In late September the Münster–Hamm railway was attacked, and a few days later it was the turn of the Osnabrück railway to feel the effects of Deeks's and Young's bombs and cannons. On 5 October a train was attacked in northern Holland and brought to a standstill after a cannon attack with the engine wrecked. The patrol continued to the south where barges were attacked on the Dortmund–Ems canal. This series of attacks was typical of the very many mounted every night by the tactical bombers. The Mosquitoes roamed over western Germany as they interdicted the routes leading to Arnhem and Walcheren, and the railways supplying the retreating *Wehrmacht*. The light bomber force had made giant advances since the days of 1940 when the Blenheims suffered such crippling losses.

Deeks and his pilot had flown thirty-five night patrols when they took off on 20 November in a Mosquito VI (PZ 332) to patrol the railway north of the Ruhr. Due to poor weather they were unable to locate a suitable target so decided to drop their parachute flare. By chance, this illuminated the airfield of Metelen, which soon became the recipient of four 500-lb bombs. Landing after a four-hour sortie, Freddie Deeks had completed his third operational tour and his eightieth war operation.

After a further period as an instructor at the 2 Group Support Unit, he volunteered to fly Ansons with the 88 Group Communications Flight based at Fornebu in Norway. In mid-1946 Deeks left the RAF only to rejoin three years later when he was trained on Valetta transports before moving to the Far East to join 52 Squadron engaged in air supply in support of the ground forces during the Malayan emergency. This tour lasted three years during which he flew many operational sorties over the jungles of Malaya.

After a ground tour at Bomber Command, Deeks returned to flying and was trained as a night-fighter navigator on Meteor NF 11s. At the end of the conversion course Deeks was posted to Malta, the scene of his earlier dramatic wartime flying exploits, to start a three-year tour on 39 Squadron equipped with the Meteor NF 13. During this period the Suez crisis developed and regular detachments of the Meteors were sent to Cyprus, but they never went into action. After a further ground appointment Freddie Deeks retired from the RAF in 1961.

Finally, in 1994, the government of Malta announced that the President had approved 'The Malta George Cross Fiftieth Anniversary Medal'. It was awarded to those who had defended the island in the desperate days of the siege of Malta, which led to the award of the George Cross to the people of the island. Appearing on the list of recipients was Flight Lieutenant F.J. Deeks DFC. It was fitting that his gallant service in Malta was still recognised so many years later.

Chapter Nine

Escape From Italy – Roy Marlow

Living in south London and witnessing the Battle of Britain and the London Blitz, Roy Marlow was determined to join the Royal Air Force. In October 1940 he cycled from his home in Ewell to the RAF recruiting office in Croydon where he volunteered for aircrew duties: he was two months short of his sixteenth birthday. He was a strong boy, having already played three schoolboy international football matches for England, and he was able to persuade the authorities that he was three years older than his actual age. After successfully completing the various aptitude tests and medicals he was accepted for training as an air gunner.

With his basic training complete, Marlow reported in July 1941 to the recently formed 9 Air Gunners School at RAF Llandwrog near Caernarvon. The unit was equipped with some well-used Whitley bombers used for airborne gunnery training against drogues towed by Lysanders. An innovative training aid was the moving target range at nearby Hell's Mouth, where a large model aircraft travelled at speed on a trolley running on an oval track, and the trainee gunners practised firing at it from a portable gun turret. On completion of the nine-week course, Marlow was awarded his air gunner's brevet and promoted to Sergeant. The sixteen-year-old found himself sharing the Sergeants' Mess with long-serving senior NCOs, some having spent twenty years as corporals with others old enough to be his grandfather!

Marlow completed his operational training at 20 OTU at Lossiemouth in northern Scotland,

Roy Marlow with his new air gunner's brevet and Sergeant's chevrons. He was just seventeen at the time. (*Roy Marlow*)

where he converted to the Wellington, flying almost eighty hours during a Scottish winter. He and his crew were posted to the Middle East, and they were sent initially to Harwell where they collected a new Wellington aircraft. After a series of flights to complete fuel consumption checks, they flew to Portreath in Cornwall where they waited for suitable weather before setting off on the nine-hour flight to Gibraltar. Their stay on the Rock was brief and they took off at dusk the following day to complete the transit to Malta under the cover of darkness, arriving just before dawn. The aircraft was handed over to another crew who flew it to Egypt. For Marlow and his crew there was a three-week wait until they were allocated to another Wellington for delivery to Egypt. They eventually delivered the bomber to Heliopolis, and then made their way to join 70 Squadron.

The Squadron was equipped with the Wellington Ic and had moved to Landing Ground (LG) 104 near Daba in the Western Desert, where Marlow was allocated to Sergeant F. Leach and his crew. He flew his first operation on 24 May 1942 when nine Squadron aircraft attacked Maturba. Over the next few days he flew five more operations, and on the night of 5/6 June he took off in 'M' for Mother (Z 9096) for another bombing operation against Maturba. Over the target the aircraft was hit by anti-aircraft fire and the starboard engine caught fire, and eventually was extinguished. As they headed for base the port engine overheated, and a crash landing became inevitable. Leach ordered the crew to take up crash-landing positions, and with Marlow passing to the pilot his estimate

Ground crew work on the Wellington Ic aircraft of 70 Squadron at the Advanced Landing Ground at Al Daba. (*Air Historical Branch*)

Some Wellingtons returned from bombing raids at very low level! (*Roy Marlow*)

of the height of the aircraft, the aircraft was put down safely, allowing all the crew to escape with bruises as the aircraft burst into flames.

By daybreak the aircraft was a smouldering wreck with no chance of salvaging any survival aids. The six-man crew set off to walk to the north and very soon came across an entanglement of barbed wire with a sign 'MINEN'. Looking back, they could see that the Wellington had first hit the ground less than 200 yards from the minefield before slithering to a halt. After making a detour, a vehicle was heard and, within minutes, a German patrol arrived on the scene. The German officer treated them courteously, and gave them water before driving them to their camp where they were handed over to the Italians. After an uncomfortable night in a slit trench they were taken to a prisoner of war (POW) compound where they were split up, and Marlow saw his colleagues for the last time. Within days, the garrison at Tobruk fell and thousands of Allied prisoners arrived to swell the already overcrowded transit camp. Conditions rapidly deteriorated in the merciless sun, and Marlow resolved to escape. However, without water and miles from Allied lines, there was no chance for him to make an attempt.

After two weeks, the Italians began to move the POWs to permanent camps, and Marlow was in the first convoy to set off for Tripoli, some 800 miles to the west. The three-week journey was a nightmare in the open trucks under the desert sun with inadequate rations, and no accommodation for the overnight stops other than barbed-wire compounds. The convoy of thirty trucks finally arrived at the permanent camp where some shade was provided by trees, but the food of rice water and stale bread offered little improvement on previous rations. Water was the most important requirement, and each prisoner was rationed to one mug per day. It was delivered, daily, by a bowser, and this gave Marlow his first idea for an escape attempt.

It was virtually impossible to scale the barbed wire surrounding the compound – an Australian had been shot attempting to do so – and a tunnel in the sandy conditions was out of the question. Marlow decided that the bowser gave him his best chance of escaping from the compound. The following day he squeezed between the lorry's cab and the water tank, and succeeded in getting away, only to be spotted within a few miles. He was soon back in the camp and placed in a wire cage, without shade, and on bread and water for seven days. Within days he contracted a severe case of dysentery, which led his condition to deteriorate rapidly. Like all his prisoner colleagues, he was suffering from malnutrition even before his brief escape. He was persuaded to report to the first aid post, but it was all he could do to crawl the 100 yards from his compound. The seriousness of his condition was soon apparent to the doctors, and they arranged for him to be transferred to the hospital in Tripoli where he spent the next three months, which included his eighteenth birthday in November. Once he was well enough to travel in December, he was transferred to a hospital ship bound for Naples. On arrival in Italy he was taken to a hospital at Lukka near Pisa where he was cared for by nuns and Allied doctors who had been taken prisoner during the North African campaign.

By April 1943 he had recovered sufficiently to move to a permanent POW camp, and was taken by train to the large, purpose-built Campo 82 at Laterina near Arrezo, 50 miles south-east of Florence. Escape would be difficult from such a substantial and well-guarded establishment, so he soon made enquiries about joining an outside working party. Knowing that as a sergeant he was likely to be given a supervisory job, he removed his 'stripes' and was soon allocated to a party sent to work in the gardens of a count's residence some 50 miles away, where a small compound had been hastily prepared for the prisoners. On arrival Marlow noticed that a small section of the outer wire had not been completed, and he immediately started considering what opportunities this might offer for an escape. During the rest periods over the next few days he noted the habits of the guards, but was alarmed to see the arrival of new barbed wire and fresh stakes, clearly intended to make the compound more secure. Work on improving the camp's security started the next day and Marlow decided it was time to leave. He had alerted a soldier in the Durham Light Infantry to his plans, and they rose at 0300 and headed for the wire.

There were two guards patrolling the wire, and both displayed a lack of interest in their mundane job. Having observed their routine for few minutes, Marlow and his colleague were soon able to throw a blanket over the six-foot-high barbed-wire fence and scramble over. They quickly got clear of the area before resting to decide on their next move. News of the Allied landings on Sicily had recently arrived at the camp, so they decided to head south in the hope that they would meet up with the advancing armies. They travelled by night and sheltered in woods, but heavy overnight drizzle hampered their progress. During the daytime they had noticed a railway line heading south, and the next night they made their way to a small town with a railway siding where they tried to board a goods train. At that point they were seen, arrested and beaten before being dragged to the station. The following morning they were back at Laterina camp, but their four days of freedom cost Marlow twenty-eight days in solitary confinement on bread and rice water, with ten days in chains and his entitlement to Red Cross parcels was withdrawn for two months.

On completion of his 'sentence' Marlow was given a warm welcome by his fellow prisoners, who generously fed him from their parcels, and his strength soon returned. He was put in a group of other escapers whose movements and activities were closely monitored. However, this did not prevent them from exploring a manhole cover, and they were soon digging a tunnel, which kept them busy for the next month until it was discovered. Another thirty days in solitary confinement followed.

As the summer of 1943 wore on, the POWs were encouraged by increasing sightings of Allied aircraft when, on the morning of 8 September, they awoke to find that the Italian guards had disappeared – Italy had signed an armistice with the Allies. There was great rejoicing and many believed that freedom was a matter of days away. The senior British officer told the prisoners not to attempt to escape, but Marlow decided that it was more likely that the prisoners would be transported to Germany, and he prepared his kit in readiness for another bid for freedom. On 12 September he was in charge of a group of former escapers when there was an opportunity to slip away. At 1700 they cut the wire and walked out of the camp. A few hours later the Germans arrived, surrounded the camp, and the remaining prisoners were all transported to Germany. Marlow was free and determined that his third attempted escape would be successful.

He decided to travel alone, and headed for the east coast near Ancona, thinking that it was only a matter of time before the Allies attempted a landing in the area. He travelled at night, but was keen to obtain some civilian clothes to replace his conspicuous uniform. He found an isolated farmhouse, and after maintaining a watch for suspicious movements he approached the farm and was amazed to discover that the farmer's wife was English – she had been a nurse during the First World War and had nursed her future Italian husband when he had been wounded. Marlow was fed well, given a good set of clothing and advised not to head for the coast – which was a secure area requiring a special pass – but to travel south.

Initially he travelled at night, but once well clear of the area near the camp he travelled by day in order to make a greater distance. He was able to cover 6 or 7 miles each day through the mountainous terrain, and his tanned complexion, stubble beard and civilian clothes allowed him to pass without arousing suspicion. He approached isolated farmhouses and was overwhelmed by the generosity of the poor farmers who almost always fed him and provided a barn for sleeping. Throughout this period he was very conscious of the great risks being taken by his helpers, and he made sure that he always left before daybreak.

Three weeks after his escape he had walked some 60 miles and was near the small town of Umertide. The weather was poor so he decided to approach an isolated house to get some food. He was invited in, and once he had identified himself the owner fetched an English-speaking friend who had lived in America. A plan was devised for him to catch a train and be escorted to Rome where the Allies were expected in the near future. Because of a misunderstanding he missed the train rendezvous and lost contact with his helper, so he resumed his southerly journey on foot, avoiding all the towns. German activity increased, and he decided to keep to the mountains where the farms were more isolated and there was less chance of a surprise encounter. But with the onset of winter this route was often difficult, and he was frequently forced down into the valleys.

Marlow had decided to learn Italian from the earliest days of his capture, and the daily opportunities to converse with the farmers gave him increased confidence, in addition to making him more fluent. This was to prove a great bonus in the days ahead. One day he was forced to walk through a small town, and he soon became conscious of being followed. He tried to shake off his pursuer by heading back for the hills, but the person persisted. Once in the woods he confronted the young man who immediately asked if he was English. This shook Marlow considerably as he was convinced that his appearance would not attract any attention. Eventually the pair returned to the youth's house where Marlow was well fed and given a bed. He had become so conditioned to sleeping rough that the comfort of a bed prevented him from sleeping, so he abandoned it in favour of the floor! It transpired that the young man and a few of his friends were anxious to fight the Germans, and they had collected together some basic weapons including a few hand grenades. They invited Marlow to be their leader in a private war against the Germans.

The following morning they gathered their equipment and food and set off for the snow line in the mountains. They camped in small, rough, pre-prepared shelters for two days before arriving at a camp occupied by six friends. It was soon clear that they were very inexperienced in the art of guerrilla warfare, and Marlow decided to stay just long enough for one action. He selected a good vantage point above a road where they could ambush a vehicle. They identified their rendezvous points and escape routes, and then waited for a target. In due course a German lorry appeared and the band opened fire at 20 yards' range, shattering the driver's cab as Marlow tossed in a grenade. The lorry sheared off the road and careered down a ravine. The band headed back to the mountains where they were able to observe the arrival of German troops at the scene. They regained their camp and had settled for the night when a loud explosion woke them – it was shellfire. The Germans had traced their camp. Marlow split from the others and headed further up the mountains until he was well clear of the area, before resuming his journey south.

The weather had deteriorated to heavy drizzle, and Marlow had begun to feel unwell. He was tired, undernourished and very wet, and had also started to develop some very large and painful boils. He managed to get a meal and a change of clothing from a peasant farmer, but his progress south in the worsening weather was slowing. A fever developed and he realised that he was in trouble and must get some help. Lights from a small village in the valley below beckoned him, and he made his way to the first house he came across, where he knocked on the door. A middle-aged couple opened it, and, in Italian, he told them that he was an escaping British prisoner of war and needed a drink. He was given a cup of wine, which he immediately drank, before collapsing at their feet. Roy Marlow had arrived in the small village of Goriano Valli set in a valley high in the Apennine Mountains.

He woke to find himself between crisp white sheets with an old lady looking at him. After his collapse, he had been moved to the house of the

The village of Goriano Valli where Marlow spent many weeks being sheltered during the bitter winter of 1943. (*Roy Marlow*)

elderly parents of the leading woman of the village. He had been asleep for forty-eight hours. Over the next ten days he made a slow recovery and was visited by most of the villagers. His intention was to regain his health and strength, and wait for the winter to pass before resuming his journey south. He was still plagued with the painful boils, but he carried out a detailed reconnaissance of the area, made numerous shelters and stocked a number of caves so that he could make a hasty retreat to the mountains should the village be visited by Germans. He also became very familiar with the layout of the village, and this was to prove a vital element in his survival. The winter was one of the most severe the region had experienced, and it effectively halted the Allied advance south of Cassino, well to the south of Marlow's position. He was faced with remaining in the mountains for the winter.

A few weeks after his arrival at the village he was roused by a commotion and shouting of 'the Germans are coming'. He rushed from the house and headed for one of his refuges as the Germans broke down doors in their search for 'the Englishman'. News of his presence in the area had obviously leaked to the enemy. Over seventy troops made a thorough search of the village before they finally departed. Marlow returned to find great distress in the village, but his presence had been kept secret. He immediately decided that he must not put these wonderful and generous people at further risk, so he moved back to one of his shelters, although he came down to the village each day to collect food. It was at this time that he met Sabatino Tiberi and his family, who were to treat him like a son, giving him a great deal of help at the risk of death or deportation. They were to become life-long friends. He attended church on Christmas Day, but insisted on staying in his caves overnight.

The weeks slipped into months, but he was still plagued with the discomfort of the boils, which were regularly dressed by his friends on his visits to the village. As the weather began to improve, and his strength began to return, he made plans for his onward journey. At the end of March he visited his helpers for a meal and was persuaded to stay the night because the weather was so bad. In the early hours he was woken by the old lady to learn that the Germans had arrived and surrounded the village. They started to round up all the men between sixteen and sixty, and there was no escape for Marlow, who walked straight into a patrol. Fortunately, his command of the language was good and he was able to pass for an Italian, which gave him some time to think about his predicament.

The Germans set up a parade with all males having to produce their identity cards. This was the one aspect that Marlow had overlooked. Someone smuggled a Fascist Party member's card to him, but this failed to satisfy the German officer conducting the interrogations, and he was detained. He resolved not to admit his true identity as he was driven off to a nearby town for further interrogation. He managed to maintain his 'Italian' identity and was placed in the cells overnight before further interrogations the following morning. During an interval he persuaded his guards to let him sit in the courtyard outside where a wheelbarrow was leaning against the low wall. As lunch approached, his guards left to eat, leaving just one who appeared disinterested and casual. Seizing his chance, Marlow sprang forward using the wheelbarrow as a launch platform, and leapt over the wall and sprinted down the street. His intimate knowledge of the valley helped him to escape. Instead of heading for the hills, as the Germans might have expected, he made for the river. He was seen at a distance and shots rang out, but missed him as he dashed for a secluded spot to wade across before crossing a railway line. In this way, the German troops in their lorries would have had to make a very wide detour to find a bridge, giving him time to make his escape into the hills on the opposite side of the valley.

Roy Marlow's escape was characterised by his clear thinking, initiative and always being one step ahead of the enemy. Once in the hills he made a wide detour to the north, away from the obvious route, which would have been to the south. He also reasoned that the last place the Germans would look for him would be back in the village of Goriano. As darkness fell, he crept back to the Tiberi house where he was received with unbounded joy and given a meal, but he ignored their pleas for him to stay and rest in the house. He was constantly conscious of the dangers all the villagers ran, so he elected to return to his prepared hiding places in the hills where he remained for four weeks. The villagers kept him supplied with blankets and fed him, although he made the occasional visit to Goriano when he felt it was safe to assist the Tiberis in their fields, returning to the hills each night. By mid-May he could see from the northerly movement of the German forces, and increased Allied aerial activity, that it was now only a matter of time before the advancing armies arrived to liberate his valley.

Towards the end of May he saw the large bomber formations attacking Cassino, and within a few days came the moment he had longed for. From his hiding place he heard the noise of great rejoicing in the village square as the villagers came to fetch him to join in the celebrations. The Germans had withdrawn to the north, and peace had arrived in the valley on a perfect spring day. Eighteen-year-old Marlow picked up his blankets for the last time and returned to the village, and to the wonderful family that had cared for him with such courage and devotion. He had been on the run for eight months since his escape from the prison camp at Laterina.

Within a few days, Marlow had to make the final parting from the village and the valley that had been his home for so long. The Tiberi family tried to persuade him to remain, but they all knew that he must return. On about 20 June, he bade his final, emotional farewells, and the head of the family, Sabatino Tiberi, escorted him on the 20-mile walk to the town of Sulmona, which was in Allied hands. They parted on the outskirts of the town with a brief embrace and a wave, and Marlow headed into the town.

Three days later he was given a lift to Rome where he received medical attention before being flown to Naples. On 12 July 1944 he arrived back in England, just over two years after he had been shot down. After debriefing in London, where he was told that his promotion to Warrant Officer had been confirmed, he went on a well-earned leave.

In 1978, Roy Marlow returned to Goriano Valli to meet his 'second family', the Tiberis. He is pictured in the centre with Madam Tiberi, her son Valentino and his family. (*Roy Marlow*)

The Deputy Director of Military Intelligence (Prisoners of War) recommended Roy Marlow for the award of the Military Medal 'in recognition of the initiative and devotion to duty which he displayed during his escape'. However, the Air Ministry considered that it would be more appropriate for the award to be upgraded to the Distinguished Conduct Medal. Unfortunately, this request was not approved, and the *London Gazette* of 27 March 1945 announced the award of the Military Medal.

Roy Marlow never forgot his helpers in Goriano Valli. Through the RAF Escaping Society he regained contact with them and made an emotional visit to his second home thirty-five years after his first encounter. Little had changed in the valley, but Sabatino Tiberi had died, and his son Valentino was the head of this remarkable and courageous family who had saved the life of an equally courageous and determined teenage air gunner.

Chapter Ten

Stirling Engineer – Fred Fray

By the mid-1930s it was becoming increasingly apparent that the rise of the German Nazi Party posed a serious threat to the peace of Europe. The Royal Air Force had experienced a series of debilitating reductions since the end of the First World War, and was ill-prepared for a war against the rapidly expanding military might of Germany. Not before time, a series of measures to expand the size and capability of the RAF was introduced. Among these expansion schemes was a programme to significantly increase the number of boys entering apprentice training at the RAF School of Technical Training at Halton. Conceived by Trenchard after the First World War, the RAF apprenticeship scheme created a worldwide reputation for excellence, and for six decades it was to provide the backbone of the RAF's ground tradesmen. Many of these men would serve with distinction as aircrew in the forthcoming war.

Fred Fray (right) during his training as an aircraft apprentice at Halton. (*Author's Collection*)

Fifteen-year-old Fred Fray joined 32 Entry at Halton in August 1935, together with 915 other boys, a number that was almost double the previous intake. He was born in north-west India, but had been sent to England to start his schooling when he was five. He lived in Hull with his maiden aunt, and after attending Hymers School he joined the RAF. He passed out from Halton in 1938 in the new trade of Fitter 2. In the RAF Handbook of the day it was noted that, 'The men in this trade will be employed in the work of maintaining aero-engines, the most highly skilled work in the Royal Air Force.' He was posted to RAF Leconfield in East Yorkshire to join 97 Squadron operating the Heyford bomber.

By the time that the Phoney War came to an end in the spring of 1940 measures were well in hand to expand the bomber force, including an increase in the number of Operational Training Units. In April 1940, 10 OTU was created at Abingdon to train bomber crews to operate the Whitley, with the nucleus of air and ground crews being drawn from 97 Squadron. Promoted to Corporal, Fred Fray was one of the ground crew.

The expansion of the bomber force, together with the imminent arrival of the first of the four-engine bombers, the Stirling, had generated a review of crewing arrangements. The mainstays of the bomber force at the time were the twin-engine Wellingtons and Whitleys, both of which employed two pilots. The planned increase in the number of bombers would create a huge demand for pilots if this policy continued. In addition, the new bombers were far more complex to operate, and a specialist engineer was considered necessary. After a year of prevarication at the Air Ministry, the staff at Bomber Command became exasperated and called for a meeting to resolve the issue. This meeting proved to be a milestone, resulting in a plan to immediately recruit suitably qualified tradesmen to be employed in the new aircrew trade of flight engineer. Only men in certain highly skilled trades were eligible, and these included the trade of Fitter 2. At the time of this decision the four-engine Stirling had been in service for eight months, and had been using two pilots, so there was an urgent need to recruit the new flight engineers. During his service with 97 Squadron and 10 OTU Fray had taken any opportunity to fly, and this new aircrew category gave him the long sought-after opportunity to become aircrew. He was one of the first to volunteer.

Following approval for the establishment of flight engineers, an Air Ministry order was published to outline the duties and responsibilities they would be fulfilling. These were listed as follows:

1.   To operate certain controls at the engineer's station and watch appropriate gauges.
2.   To advise the captain of the aircraft as to the functioning of the engines, fuel, oil and cooling systems both before and during flight.
3.   To ensure effective liaison between the captain and the maintenance staff including debriefings after flight.
4.   To carry out practicable emergency repairs during flight.
5.   To act as standby gunner.

Training to fulfil these duties was met through a series of short courses based on the acknowledged expertise of the volunteer tradesmen:

1.   A three week course of air gunnery training at a Bombing and Gunnery School followed by:
2.   Short courses of training at manufacturers' works

On satisfactory completion of these courses, operational training was carried out at the conversion units, and at the end of this phase the Flight engineer was, where necessary, promoted to temporary sergeant. Once the scheme had become established, these basic training requirements were extensively developed and included a specific flight engineer's ten-week course at RAF St Athan. In addition, the responsibilities of the post increased and the Flight engineer managed all the aircraft systems including hydraulics and electrics.

Fred Fray was one of the first to be selected for flight engineer training, and in November 1941 he joined 26 Conversion Flight (later re-numbered 1651 Heavy Conversion Unit) at RAF Waterbeach near Cambridge where he was introduced to the Stirling. After a period of ground lectures and practical experience on the aircraft he left for RAF Newmarket to join 1483 Flight for his three-week air gunnery course.

Following a period of ground training, Fray got airborne on 12 April 1942 in Wellington N 2778 for his first air exercise, an air-to-sea firing detail off the North Norfolk coast. Over the next ten days he flew eleven exercises including air-to-air, air-to-ground and cine-gun exercises against Duxford Wing Spitfires and Whirlwinds from Coltishall. At the end of the course he was assessed as 'Good, a most promising air gunner' and

The Flight Engineer's position in a Stirling I with technology more akin to a ship's engine room. (*Author's Collection*)

awarded his air gunner brevet. (The flight engineer's 'E' brevet did not appear until September 1942, although a number of unofficial brevets with 'FE' had appeared in the meantime.)

Fred Fray reported back to Waterbeach in April 1942 to commence his air training on the Stirling. The engineer's panel was well laid out and neatly set on the starboard fuselage wall behind the co-pilot's seat with various mechanical controls placed along the front of the main spar within easy reach. The technology was more in keeping with a ship's engine room with oversize levers and large hand wheels, but the size and comfortable spacing of the controls reduced operator error and the effects of battle damage. Most of the Flight engineer's airborne training was conducted during sessions of circuits and bumps, with the first four sorties monitored by an instructor. With just ten hours' experience on Stirlings Fray joined 214 Squadron's Conversion Flight for a week of concentrated training before moving to Stradishall in Suffolk to join the Squadron. After a single long-range training sortie to learn the art of fuel log keeping, he was ready to embark on his first operation on 17 May 1942. He had a total of just forty-one hours' flying experience.

By May 1942 the Commander-in-Chief of Bomber Command, Air Marshal Arthur Harris, was beginning to make his presence felt. Among many innovative measures he dispensed with the co-pilot in his four-engine bombers and expanded the role of the Flight engineer. Initially this was not a popular move, but, once established, it became a very sound practice, and the rapport established by the captain and his 'mate', the Flight engineer, was a crucial partnership in the safe operation of the aircraft. In the coming months this was epitomised by the team work of Fray and his pilot.

Just after 2200 on the night of 17 May 1942, Fray took off on his first operational sortie in Stirling W 7527 with four 1,500-lb sea mines to drop off the Danish coast. Two nights later his was one of sixty-five 'freshman' crews sent to bomb the U-boat pens at St Nazaire. These two sorties were typical of the way a new crew was introduced to the bomber war, but things proved to be very different when they took off for their third sortie.

To counter the considerable criticism levelled at the efficiency of Bomber Command, and the constant attempts by the Royal Navy to divert the bomber force to attacking naval targets, the new Commander-in-Chief devised an operation to finally silence them – the Thousand Bomber Raid. By mustering all his reserves and the bombers in the training units he was able to produce 1,046 aircraft for his planned raid on 26 May against the port of Hamburg. The weather proved to be unsuitable so the raid was delayed until the night of the 30th when this great force took off for the secondary target of Cologne. Taking off just after 2300, Fred Fray and his crew joined the stream of bombers for an uneventful attack on Cologne. Three nights later they went out again with a similar force, this time to bomb Essen, but cloud cover prevented a good attack. These Thousand Bomber Raids certainly made their mark on history and the attack was a great turning-point in Bomber Command's war.

Aircrew and ground crew of 'O for Orange,' 214 Squadron at Stradishall in August 1942. Fred Fray is in the back row, third from the left, while his long-term skipper, Clarence Ince, is in the centre. (*Author's Collection*)

On their sixth sortie Fray and his crew were forced to turn back when their captain was taken ill, and after landing he was withdrawn from flying for a period. They were allocated a new pilot, Clarence Ince, who had just completed his training, and they remained together as a crew for the rest of their tour. This was the beginning of a unique partnership, as Ince and Fray would fly two operational tours together during which they established a superb working relationship that would see them counter many difficulties and dangers. For their first sortie with the new 'skipper', the crew were briefed to attack Emden. Over the target they lost the starboard inner engine, and Fray and Ince coaxed the aircraft home safely. Their partnership had started well under difficult circumstances, and they quickly earned each other's respect.

Throughout the summer months, the crew almost always flew Stirling I, R 9355 as they attacked targets in the Ruhr and the major German ports. The bomb load was mixed and often included the 2,000-lb bomb, but incendiaries were always carried. The introduction of the Gee navigation aid heralded the start of improvements in navigation and bombing accuracy and Fray recorded the use of the new aid on a raid to Duisburg on 23 July. A few nights later Clarence Ince had to use all his skill to shake off the searchlights as his aircraft was 'coned' over Hamburg. More excitement occurred three nights later when Fray's gunners shot down a Bf 109 fighter as they left the 'lightly defended' target at Saarbrücken.

On the night of 11 August Fray and his crew attacked Mainz, and they reported that the town was clearly seen in the light of the flares dropped by the leading aircraft allowing them to identify the target by reference to the islands in the river. Bomber Command assessed the raid as particularly effective with much damage to the centre of the city. During the summer of 1942 the Wellingtons and Stirlings of 3 Group had been experimenting with 'flare aircraft' and the use of 'raid leaders', and by mid-August the Target Finding Force had been established working initially through the headquarters of 3 Group. It was soon renamed to become one of the air war's most famous titles – the Pathfinder Force. A week after the successful attack against Mainz, the Pathfinders flew their first sortie when they attacked Flensburg, but success eluded them.

The first successful Pathfinder-led raid was to Kassel on the night of 27 August. Of the 306 bombers involved, only 5 were Stirlings – Fray's crew flew one of these. Before reaching the target, an oil leak in the port inner required the engine to be shut down, but the captain pressed on to the target with the aircraft load of incendiaries. On the way home Fray was kept busy transferring and balancing the fuel between tanks.

The difficulties faced by the new Pathfinder Force were graphically illustrated when an attack was mounted against Saarbrücken on 1 September. They illuminated and marked a town they believed to be the target, and the Main Force carried out an accurate attack, with Fray's crew dropping 1,530 incendiaries and reporting a 'terrific explosion'. Unfortunately, devastation had been brought to the small non-industrial town of Saarlouis some 13 miles away from the planned target.

At 2100 on the night of 8 September Fray settled in to his familiar seat just behind his captain Clarence Ince in their faithful Stirling R 9355 for a raid on Frankfurt. It was his twenty-seventh operation. Just after dropping their load of incendiaries, the aircraft was rocked by a direct hit by flak. The starboard outer engine caught fire, and other hits were registered in the port wing and the belly of the aircraft. Fray and Ince soon had the fire under control as they shut down the engine and turned on to a direct route home. The starboard inner engine soon started to give problems, and Fray discovered that the Stirling was losing fuel. It needed all Ince's piloting skills and Fray's engineering knowledge to keep the battered Stirling airborne. As they approached the English coast, it was obvious that they would have to make an emergency landing as soon as possible, so Ince headed for the crash strip at Manston. With damaged hydraulics he made an approach to the airfield, but on finals the fire-damaged starboard outer engine fell away from the wing, and the inner finally cut, but Ince managed to make a crash landing with just the port engines operating. The aircraft was a write-off and Ince was injured, but the rest of the crew escaped. The pilot's outstanding flying earned him the Distinguished Flying Cross, but he was strong in his praise of the cool and professional work of his flight engineer Fred Fray.

With their pilot injured, the rest of the crew were declared 'tourex' and Fray left to be an instructor at 1651 Heavy Conversion Unit at Waterbeach.

Ground crew at Oakington prepare MG-W, a 7 Squadron Stirling I, ready for another night's operations. (*Author's Collection*)

Shortly afterwards he was joined by his pilot Clarence Ince who had recovered from his injuries. For the next four months they spent many hours instructing and flying countless circuits and landings. Normally they would have expected their rest tour to last for twelve months, but they decided to team up again and volunteer for duties with the Pathfinder Force. On 2 January 1943 they joined 7 Squadron based at RAF Oakington commanded by the legendary Wing Commander Hamish Mahaddie. The four-engine Stirling still equipped the Squadron with the conversion to the Lancaster still some months away.

After a short settling-in period to become familiar with the Pathfinder techniques, Fray and his new crew attacked the French port of Lorient on two successive nights with incendiaries and flares. A few nights later, on 4 February, they embarked on the long haul to Turin with a load of four 1,000-lb bombs. The starboard inner engine was lost over the target, and the crew struggled for the next four hours to get their crippled bomber back to England. It was under such difficult circumstances that the Flight engineer became the key member of the crew as he managed the fuel and aircraft systems while nursing the three serviceable engines. By this stage, Fred Fray and his pilot had flown over twenty operations together. On their next sortie their superb working relationship would be put to its severest test.

Just after 1800 on 14 February, Fray held the throttles wide open as his pilot lifted their Stirling E-Easy (R 9278) off the runway at Oakington to set course for Cologne. The crew were about to cross the enemy coast over

Holland when a Messerschmitt Bf 110 night fighter attacked their aircraft. The port wing and tail were damaged, while the port fuel tanks were pierced and the fuel control-cock cables were severed. The electrical system was also damaged. After evading the fighter, and assessing the damage to the Stirling, Ince decided to press on to the target which was bombed successfully. Fray's superb knowledge of the Stirling's fuel and electrical systems allowed him to balance the fuel and keep all four engines running despite the severe damage sustained by the fuel and electrical systems. It was crucial that he 'managed' these systems accurately as his pilot struggled to control the badly damaged aircraft. Eventually, a successful emergency landing was made at Oakington. Three weeks later it was announced that Clarence Ince had been awarded a Bar to his Distinguished Flying Cross for 'his fine example of courage and devotion to duty'. He would have been the first to acknowledge the crucial role played by his flight engineer. Two weeks later Fray was awarded his permanent Pathfinder badge.

Fray and his colleagues were allocated Stirling J-Jig (R 9266) for the remainder of their tour. In this time they attacked some of the most heavily defended targets in Germany including Bremen, Wilhelmshaven,

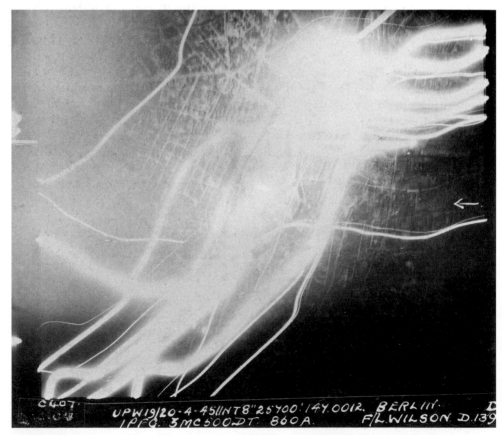

Pathfinder Force markers fall over the centre of Berlin. (*Author's Collection*)

Nuremberg, Stuttgart and Hamburg, and on 1 March they attacked the 'Big City' Berlin for the first time. The Pathfinders had difficulty producing concentrated marking resulting in the bombing being spread over a wide area. However, over 300 bombers attacked, and the weight of bombs was such that widespread and severe damage was inflicted. By the end of March, Fray and his crew had carried out two further attacks against Berlin, but returning on 29 March their aircraft was hit by predicted heavy flak. Inspecting the aircraft after landing, the ground crew counted fifty-two holes.

By April the Ince/Fray crew were becoming one of the most experienced on the Squadron, and were regularly operating in the marker role. The raid on Stettin on 20 April proved to be the most successful attack beyond the range of the marking aid Oboe, and reports claimed that the Pathfinder marking was 'carried out perfectly'. On the long haul home from the target the recently repaired J–Jig was hit by light flak over Denmark, and fuel was lost from number seven starboard tank. Once again, Fred Fray had to display all his knowledge to allow his pilot to nurse the aircraft home. By now he had flown over forty operations, all on Stirlings, and on 15 May it was announced that he had been awarded the Distinguished Flying Medal. The citation concludes with the words, 'His exemplary conduct and high standard of efficiency have set a praiseworthy example.' This does scant justice to his remarkable performance as a flight engineer. On seven occasions he had returned from the target on three engines. On two other occasions his aircraft had been severely damaged by fighters and by anti-aircraft fire resulting in the loss of an engine and fuel. On two further occasions his aircraft had suffered flak damage. There is no doubt that flight engineers earned their gallantry awards the hard way.

In May, Fray's crew flew in the role of back-up markers against targets in the Ruhr. The attack against Dortmund on 23 May was the heaviest during the Battle of the Ruhr, and the first time that over 100,000 tons of bombs had been dropped on a single target. The contribution from Fray and his crew was three 2,000-lb bombs in addition to their five target indicators. A few nights later they attacked Wuppertal when the attack was claimed to be the outstanding success of the Battle of the Ruhr – the compiler of the Squadron operations record book remarked that it was 'an absolutely wizard show!' On 11 June the Main Force attacked Dusseldorf with a diversionary raid of seventy-two aircraft attacking Munster. No 8 Group provided all the aircraft for this latter raid, and it was designed as a mass trial of the H2S bombing radar aid. The Station Commander, Group Captain Fresson, flew with Ince and his crew on this unique raid that was later assessed as a complete success.

On the night of 21 June Fray took off for Krefeld on his fifty-first operation and forty-fifth alongside his captain Clarence Ince. Just after midnight his aircraft (R 9266) was shot down over the target by anti-aircraft fire. 22-year-old Flight Lieutenant Clarence Ince DFC and Bar ordered his crew to bale out. They got out successfully, but he was still at the controls when

A portrait of Fred Fray drawn by fellow prisoner A. Cox whilst at Stalag Luft VI, Heydekrug, November 1944. (*Author's Collection*)

the Stirling crashed and exploded. He had given his life to save his crew. He has no known grave and is remembered on Panel 119 of the Runnymede Memorial.

The Squadron Operations Record Book notes that the raid on Krefeld was 'a disastrous night for the Squadron with four of the most experienced crews missing including the Flight Commander, Squadron Leader C.A. Hughes DSO, DFM, Flight Lieutenant J.S. Watt DSO, DFC and Flight Lieutenant C. Ince DFC & Bar'. Two nights later the Squadron veteran, 23-year-old Wing Commander R.G. Barrell DSO, DFC and Bar, was lost. The men of the Pathfinders paid a heavy price for their elite status.

Fred Fray was soon captured after his parachute descent and quickly found himself at the *Luftwaffe* reception centre at *Dulag Luft* near Frankfurt where he met up with some of his crew. Within a week or two he was transferred to *Stalag Luft VI* at Heydekrug in Lithuania as POW 137. This camp was the most remote of all the POW camps, with escape virtually impossible. Fray remained there for the next eighteen months. With the Russian Army advancing, the camp was closed in December 1944, and all the prisoners were forced to march to *Stalag Luft 357* near Fallingbostel, some 40 miles north of Hanover.

During his time as a POW, Fred Fray made friends with Warrant Officer 'Dixie' Deans who had been shot down in his Whitley in September 1940. Deans's story of his time as a POW is one of the most remarkable even among the legendary stories of wartime prison camps. In a succession of POW camps he embarked on a variety of activities ranging from maintaining morale among his fellow prisoners, through organising cooperatives of exchangeable goods, promoting escapes, and establishing an intelligence network of great value to MI 9 in London. The climax of his astonishing career was to lead 12,000 British prisoners of war to freedom through war-torn Germany. Fred Fray was one of those prisoners.

As the Allied armies swept eastwards, the British POWs were ordered to set off with minimum personal possessions on a march lightly guarded by their German captors. Deans was the acknowledged leader of the camp, and he insisted on the strictest discipline during the march while he negotiated with the German commandant. After ten days the food supplies ran out, and Deans made arrangements to collect Red Cross parcels from Lübeck as the prisoners halted at Gresse. After a harrowing journey he returned with enough food for the prisoners and coordinated the distribution to the near-starving men. The day was fine and the prisoners spread out to enjoy their first meal for days. Above circled nine Typhoon fighters, and as the prisoners watched, the fighters peeled off and dived, firing their rockets and dropping their anti-personnel bombs. Fray and his colleagues dived for cover in disbelief, but sixty of the prisoners were killed and hundreds wounded – many died later as a result of their wounds. A tragedy that is always a potential risk in the 'fog of war'.

The incident convinced Deans that he must warn the advancing British forces of the presence of such a large body of POWs, and prevent further accidents. He therefore demanded that the German Commandant, *Oberst* Ostmann, release him. The Commandant agreed, and Deans cycled through the lines to secure an interview with the local Corps Commander, General Barker. Deans returned to bring out the British prisoners to a safe area near Lübeck. Warrant Officer Deans then took the surrender of *Oberst* Ostmann. He was subsequently awarded the MBE.

After a few days of recuperation at Lübeck, Fred Fray was flown back to England on 7 May 1945 after almost two years in captivity. One of his first duties after a period of leave was to attend Buckingham Palace on 23 October to receive his Distinguished Flying Medal from His Majesty The King. He returned to the RAF, but his flying days were over, and he was commissioned as an engineering officer and continued to serve for a further three years before retiring to Gloucestershire.

The role of the Flight engineer is often overlooked. Yet, many stricken and badly damaged bomber, transport and maritime aircraft were nursed home thanks to the skill, ingenuity and courage of flight engineers. Their array of gallantry awards is testimony to their value as dedicated members of aircrew. No one better epitomises these stalwarts than the ex-Halton apprentice, Fred Fray.

Chapter Eleven

Over Madagascar and Italy – John Harris

During his schooldays at Eastbourne College, John Philip Gladstone Harris had been a member of the Army section of the school's Officer Training Corps (OTC). After leaving school he continued his interest in the Army by accepting a commission in the 6th (Territorial) Battalion of the Devon Regiment in September 1938. At the outbreak of war he was mobilised, remaining in England on home defence duties. In June 1940 he responded to a call for Army officers to transfer to the RAF for flying duties, and he was commissioned as a Pilot Officer on 1 July 1940. Six weeks later he reported to 9 Service Flying Training School at Hullavington in Wiltshire where he trained on the Tiger Moth initially and then the Hart and Audax aircraft before gaining his pilot's wings on 2 November.

Former Army officers were usually assigned to army cooperation or reconnaissance Squadrons, and Harris was sent to Old Sarum the home of 1 School of Army Co-operation for operational flying training and conversion to the Lysander. On completion of the course in January 1941, he was posted to 231 Squadron based at Newtownards in Northern Ireland and equipped with the Lysander III. The Squadron flew anti-invasion patrols each dawn, frequently combining them with regular patrols and reconnaissance flights along the border with neutral Eire. However, it spent the majority of its time flying in support of large-scale Army exercises, often operating from field sites. Although routine, and probably increasingly tedious for young pilots who wished to see action, the constant training provided valuable experience. In the spring of 1942 there was a call for volunteers to form a new Flight of Lysanders for overseas operations, and Harris was quick to offer his services.

No 1433 Army Co-op Flight was formed at the end of March, and Harris was among the first group of pilots to join. There followed frantic activity to get the new unit ready to move overseas. Six Lysanders were dismantled and crated before being transported to the Clyde. The flight sailed aboard HM Troopship *Capetown Castle* on 13 April for 'a destination unknown'. Three weeks later the ship docked in Durban and the personnel disembarked. Once the crated Lysanders arrived, the Flight embarked in the *Llandaff Castle* for Madagascar – the first indication of its destination.

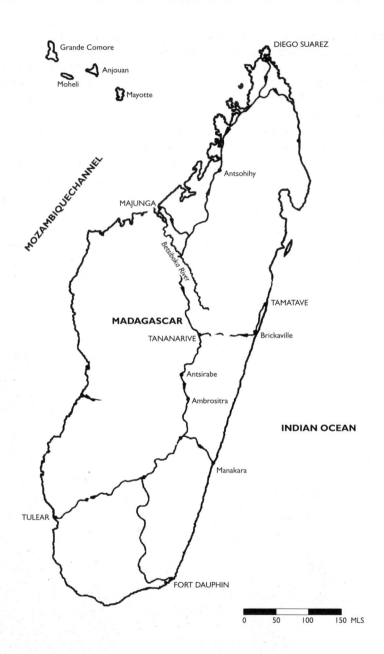

By April 1942, Japan had taken control of South-East Asia and was casting its eyes on Ceylon as a potential naval base for operations in the Indian Ocean. At the western end of this huge ocean was the large island of Madagascar, over 1,000 miles long and almost 400 miles wide. The French colony was under the control of the Vichy authorities – the same authorities who had allowed the Japanese to occupy French Indo-China. Understandably, there was great concern that they would also allow them access to the ports in Madagascar. A Japanese sub-marine presence so close to South Africa would have presented a severe threat to the crucial shipping routes around the Cape of Good Hope, and to the Middle East via the Red Sea. Plans for the occupation of the island were made, and Operation 'Ironclad', the capture of the port of Diego Suarez at the northern tip of the island, was mounted on 5 May. The landings were opposed strongly, but the port was in Allied hands within three days. Air support was provided by Swordfish, Albacores, Martlets and Fulmars from the aircraft carriers HMS *Illustrious* and *Indomitable*, and by units of the South African Air Force. Most of the Vichy Air Force was destroyed, and the nearby airfield of Arrachart was occupied, becoming the home for the 'Air Component' under South African command.

On 29 May the six Lysanders of 1433 Flight arrived at Diego Suarez in their crates and were transported to Arrachart where they were to be assembled. As the crates were being unloaded, an unidentified spotter aircraft flew over the port. It transpired later that it was a Japanese reconnaissance aircraft catapulted from the submarine *I-10* surfaced some

Lysander V 9499 of 1433 Flight at Camp Arrachart, Diego Suarez. (*A. Barnett*)

50 miles from the island. The following evening, two Japanese submarines, the *I-16* and the *I-20*, moved closer to the island and each launched a two-man midget submarine, which entered the anchorage at Diego Suarez. They both fired a torpedo with one striking the battleship HMS *Ramillies*, and the other sank an oil tanker. The battleship was badly damaged, but managed to reach Durban under her own steam where repairs were affected. The following morning the Lysanders took off to search for any sign of the attackers. A ground patrol cornered the crew of one of the midget submarines, and they were killed in a gun battle. Three weeks later, a Lysander spotted one of the midget submarines abandoned on a beach.

Other ports in Madagascar could provide facilities for Japanese naval forces, and the South African commander was anxious to occupy the whole island. The British wanted to avoid a fight and hoped that the Vichy authorities would surrender, but it soon became apparent that they had no intention of doing so. Plans were made to assault Majunga on the west coast and Tamatave on the east coast before mounting an advance on the capital Tananarive. During this period, Harris was promoted to Flight Lieutenant and appointed as the Flight Commander. The Lysanders were kept busy on communications work, but their main role was to assist in the reconnaissance of the two ports and the only road that connected Diego Suarez with the rest of the island. By mid-July, approval had been given to

The first casualty as Lysander V 9427 ends up in a ditch at Camp Arrachart. (*A. Barnett*)

Armourers hard at work loading 20lb HE bombs on the stub wings of a 1433 Flight Lysander at Ivato. Six bombs were carried on each stub wing. (*A. Barnett*)

assault Majunga, and 1433 Flight was placed under the control of 22 East African Brigade for tactical reconnaissance and close support.

At the end of August the Flight left a small maintenance staff at Diego Suarez and the remainder embarked once again on the *Llandaff Castle* and sailed south. On 10 September, the troops of 29 Brigade assaulted Majunga, and soon captured the town. The Lysanders, led by Harris, flew down and arrived at the small airfield almost before the arrival of the troops. No 22 East African Brigade landed almost immediately and their task, with 1433 Flight in direct support, was to travel as quickly as possible along the only road to the capital Tananarive. The advance went well until the troops reached the wide River Betsiboka where the large suspension bridge had been sabotaged. Fortunately, the job had 'been botched' and the whole span was resting complete four feet below the surface allowing traffic to pass at a slow pace. On 19 September, the Lysanders moved forward to a grass airfield where the ground crew set off on the difficult overland journey that involved crossing numerous rivers where the bridges had been destroyed, including crossing the broken Betsiboka bridge.

For the next few days, the Flight flew continuously in support of the advance to the capital, which eventually fell on 23 September. Within a few days 1433 Flight moved into the former French airbase at Ivato on the

John Harris at the rear pays his respects as Flight Sergeant F. Keeper is laid to rest at Tanarive cemetery after dying of wounds received when his aircraft was engaged by ground fire. (*A. Barnett*)

outskirts of the capital and, for the first time since arriving in Madagascar, enjoyed some modest permanent buildings and facilities. However, it was short lived as the Vichy authorities still refused to surrender and the Allied advance south recommenced with 1433 Flight moving to the highland town of Antisirabe, 50 miles south of the capital. On the advance the Lysanders provided close support for the advancing East Africans by strafing and bombing enemy formations. During these operations on 9 October, one aircraft piloted by Flight Lieutenant Carlyle, V 9440, was forced down by ground fire. The air gunner, Flight Sergeant F. Keeper, was seriously wounded, and he died a few hours later. He was buried in the Tanarive cemetery with full military honours. By 10 October only two Lysanders were left serviceable so the Flight was withdrawn to Ivato. It signalled the end of the Flight's operational flying in Madagascar. By 2 November the campaign was successfully concluded and the whole island was in the hands of the Allies. The Lysanders had flown twenty-nine operational flights in addition to many reconnaissance sorties. As the Flight Commander, Harris had been at the forefront of the operations flying almost daily on army support and reconnaissance sorties. The

Flight had endured some appalling conditions with torrential rain, tented accommodation and, sometimes, with as many as 25 per cent of personnel suffering from malaria or jaundice. No campaign medal was awarded for the actions in Madagascar!

Once hostilities ended, a number of replacement aircraft arrived, and others were repaired. With hostilities over, the Flight was heavily involved in photographic survey work using the F 24 camera with a five-inch lens. Small detachments were sent to Tulear in the south and to the other main towns of Diego, Majunga and Tamatave to conduct aerial surveys to supplement the modest mapping of the area. These tasks in remote areas created plenty of resupply and communications flying for the pilots. The Flight also embarked on a series of meteorological flights recording temperatures up to 17,000 feet. On one flight to 16,500 feet Harris recorded that there were 'many anvil-shaped cumulo-nimbus visible on all sides'.

At the beginning of January, Harris was promoted to command the Flight with the rank of Acting Squadron Leader. The routine of survey flying, meteorological climbs and communications flying continued to April when it was announced that the Flight would be withdrawn. Harris sailed for Durban on 14 April 1943 before travelling to Egypt for air staff duties, reverting to the rank of Flight Lieutenant. On 11 September he joined 70 OTU based at Shandur, alongside the Suez Canal, to start training on the Baltimore. Together with the Boston, the American-built twin-engine Baltimore was the mainstay of the Middle East light bomber force having replaced the Blenheim. It was also used extensively by the South African Air Force whose Squadrons provided a significant proportion of the bombing capability. On 10 December, Harris joined 223 Squadron based at one of the satellite airfields of Foggia in southern Italy.

No 223 Squadron was a veteran of the North Africa and Sicily campaigns having moved to the Italian mainland in September 1943. It was equipped with the Baltimore IV and formed part of 232 Wing of the Desert Air Force. Weather had restricted the Squadron's operations in the period leading up to Harris's arrival, and he was unable to fly his first operation until 30 December when he flew as part of a twelve-aircraft formation to bomb enemy gun positions at Tollo. For most sorties, the Baltimores carried the 500-lb MC (Medium Capacity) and 250-lb bombs or a mixture of both.

The main tactic for the light bomber Squadrons was to attack with twelve aircraft flying in two boxes of six. One hour before take-off the ground crew started the aircraft and warmed the engines. The crew arrived thirty minutes later and engines were started fifteen minutes before the aircraft taxied out in order. Three minutes before take-off the marshalling officer gave the signal to 'clear engines' (check magnetos, oil pressures and temperatures) to each individual aircraft. The leader was signalled to enter the runway where he closed the gills before receiving the take-off signal. As he commenced his take-off roll, the next aircraft entered the runway to prepare for take-off. Once the leader was safely airborne and clear of the airfield, the second aircraft took off with the procedure repeated until all

Boxes of Baltimores en-route to bomb the railway complex at Sulmona. (*Air Historical Branch*)

twelve aircraft were airborne. Spare aircraft stood by with engines running to fill any gaps created by unserviceable aircraft. All aircraft had to be airborne in ten minutes.

Once airborne, the leader flew straight ahead for five minutes climbing to about 1,500 feet before turning downwind on a reciprocal heading. The next five judged their turn after take-off to get in position with the leader. His box was complete by the time he came abeam the airfield when he turned away through 45°. In the meantime, the second box formed up in the same way, and as the leader started a wide turn to fly back up the length of the runway, the second box joined behind and the formation set off on the route to the target. Due to his inexperience of bomber operations, Harris flew as an ordinary member of the formation initially, but he was soon designated to lead the second box of six aircraft.

At the beginning of 1944 the British Eighth Army had advanced up the east coast of Italy to Ortona as the US Fifth Army was advancing on the western side towards Rome. Due to unusually bad winter weather, the advance had slowed towards the end of 1943 and the German forces had dug in on the 'Gustav Line', dominated by the mountain and monastery of Monte Cassino. In an attempt to break the deadlock, Allied troops landed at Anzio on 22 January, but the initial surprise was not exploited and the stalemate on the 'Gustav Line' continued. In response to the Anzio landings, and the attempts to break the 'Gustav line', Field Marshal Kesselring, the German Army Commander, started to move reinforcements to the areas, and these became the targets of the light bombers.

On 24 January Harris was flying FA 561 in a formation of twelve Baltimores tasked to attack the town of Penna with the objective of creating a roadblock. The formation took off at 0755 to form up as two boxes before making a rendezvous over Termoli at 8,500 feet with the fighter escort provided by 3 SAAF Wing. The formation headed for the target and climbed to the bombing height of 13,500 feet. Arriving over the target one hour after take-off, the bombers dropped their loads of 250 and 500-lb bombs achieving three hits on the main roads and starting large fires. Two hours after take-off the bombers landed. This type of sortie set the pattern for the next few weeks as the armies fought to break the 'Gustav Line'.

Operations in February were dogged by atrocious weather, but Harris attacked road and rail communications, ammunition dumps, tank repair shops and supply depots. By mid-March the weather had improved, and 223 Squadron moved to Biferno airfield and transferred to 3 SAAF Wing. This coincided with the beginning of a major air campaign by the Mediterranean Allied Air Forces (MAAF) to support the ground forces. Operation 'Strangle' was designed to interrupt, and destroy if possible, the enemy's lines of communication in preparation for the Allied offensive planned to start in May.

Two schools of thought had developed during the winter on how best to 'interdict' the rail system. Professor S. Zuckerman, scientific adviser to MAAF, concluded that attacks against large railway centres, which contained important repair facilities and large concentrations of locomotives and rolling stock, would be the most likely to achieve the aim. Invariably, these facilities were associated with marshalling yards and a number of key nodal points in the railway network were selected for attack. The other school of thought, supported by many Army commanders, maintained that such a scheme was one of attrition and could not achieve results quickly. They wanted a policy that would have an immediate effect on the battle. This could best be achieved by creating a geographical 'line of interdiction' and attacking bridges, viaducts, road junctions and railway lines, which would prevent any trains passing this line to support the battlefield. The Deputy C-in-C of MAAF, Air Marshal Sir John Slessor, reconciled the differences, and it was agreed that the heavy bomber forces would attack marshalling yards and repair shops in the north of Italy with the medium and light bombers and fighter-bombers of the Tactical Air Force responsible for cutting, and keep cut, all the lines supplying the German front. Stemming from this agreement came 'The Bombing Directive' of 19 March. (The same combination of attrition and

Above: Bombs arrive at the beginning of another intensive day of bombing sorties by Baltimores of 223 Squadron in Italy. (*Air Historical Branch*)

Opposite: The winter of 1943 will long be remembered for the atrocious weather with many airfields flooded. These 500-lb bombs provide the ground crew with a dry route. (*Air Historical Branch*)

interdiction formed the basis of the 'Transportation Plan' used to such great effect in the build-up to the landings in Normandy.)

On 18 March Harris took off in FA 410 as part of a twelve-aircraft formation to attack the San Lorenzo marshalling yards where the target was a petrol and motor transport dump. The Baltimores attacked from 7,200 feet in good visibility, and both boxes observed good results with many direct hits on the railway tracks, buildings and railway trucks. Harris was flying in the second box, whose bombs scored a direct hit on the centre of a bridge. Good photographs were obtained confirming the success of the attack. This raid was the prelude to an intensive period of bombing attacks by 223 Squadron and, within a few days, Harris had bombed the road/rail junction at Popoli, the marshalling yards at Sulmona, a road/rail bridge at Perugia and railway trucks at San Benedetto.

Throughout April and early May the light bombers continued their daily attacks against the lines of communication, but as the new ground offensive, Operation 'Diadem', approached, they also attacked supply and ammunition dumps. Overnight on 11/12 May Monte Cassino was attacked by the Second Polish Corps. British troops crossed the 'Gustav Line' as the US and French armies broke through to the Liri Valley. For the next four days Harris and his colleagues bombed German gun positions, and on 15 May as Kesselring started to withdraw, the Baltimores, operating in close support of the Fifth US Army, destroyed seventeen guns in a small area. The following day, Harris and his navigator, Flight Sergeant D. Freemantle, led a twelve-aircraft raid for the first time when they attacked a large tented camp with 250-lb bombs and 40-lb fragmentation bombs from 11,500 feet.

The Poles captured Monte Cassino on 18 May and the advance continued with the Baltimores still acting in direct support of the ground forces. The Fifth Canadian Division was held up, and Harris led an attack against forty artillery pieces, allowing the Canadians to move forward. The Canadian Army Headquarters sent a signal 'bravo – good bombing – excellent results'. Other raids were flown to create roadblocks allowing fighter-bombers to follow up to attack convoys caught up in the choke points. This phase of the Italian campaign demonstrated the effectiveness of a 'Tactical Air Force' operating in direct support of the armies.

On 30 May there was a brief interlude as 223 Squadron bombed targets in Yugoslavia in support of General Tito's partisan army. Harris led the first of two raids against a German garrison in the village of Prekaja. The formation took off at 1027 and headed for the island of Viz where they rendezvoused with an eight-Spitfire escort. Bombs exploded on a large building at 1155, and Harris landed to learn that he had been promoted to Acting Squadron Leader. Four days later he was appointed as 'A' Flight Commander, and celebrated by leading the Squadron on his 100th operational sortie.

By the beginning of June the light bomber force had reverted to the interdiction of lines of communication, in particular the railway network. Harris led a number of raids against rail bridges on the main line running along the Adriatic coast. On 14 June he led twelve aircraft against the viaduct at Macerata. Messerschmitt Bf 109 fighters had made a rare appearance over the past few days, so six Spitfires provided an escort. The formation bombed from 13,000 feet, scoring hits on the railway and several near misses. Heavy flak was encountered, but all the aircraft returned safely.

The direct effect of the interdiction programme was to force the enemy off the railways and on to the roads over most of the area between the Rimini–Pisa main line and the battlefront. This became apparent by the end of May when the Germans had virtually abandoned large sections of line, concentrating on repairs to certain sections only. The requirements of maintaining the extended lines of communications on a motorised basis demanded the progressive withdrawal of increasing numbers of motor transport from the forward battle area. The convoys and roads then became the targets for the fighter-bombers, forcing the enemy to run his convoys at night causing further delays to his re-supply system. This was an important secondary benefit of the attacks against the railway system.

With the fall of Rome on 4 June, the Allied armies advanced northwards allowing the light bomber force to strike at the main railway networks in the north of Italy. 223 Squadron moved to a landing ground at Pescara on the Adriatic coast, and this put the main railway line from the important junction at Rimini to the industrial north in range of the Baltimores. On 25 June Harris led an attack against the marshalling yards at Rimini, and two days later the rail network at Cesano received his attention.

July brought no respite for the crews of the light bombers and Harris led attacks against port facilities, in addition to further attacks against the railway system. After attacking gun positions threatening the Polish Corps advancing towards Ancona, he received a signal from the Polish Army Headquarters: 'Thanks for your efficacious bombing of the hostile batteries.' On 26 July he took off at 1252 in FA 563 to lead a formation to attack the marshalling yards at Russi. The Spitfire escort joined up, and the first box bombed on Harris's orders, achieving a straddle and direct hits on the railway. A large warehouse exploded as the second box ran in to bomb, scoring further hits. The bombers turned for home and landed at 1529. Harris had completed his 116th and final operation. He left the Squadron on 3 August when the diarist recorded the departure 'of one of our key members who, as well as being a remarkably efficient Flight Commander, was an integral part of the Squadron itself. He will be greatly missed.' A few days later, 223 Squadron amalgamated with 454 (RAAF) Squadron and became 30 (SAAF) Squadron.

At the end of August, it was announced that Harris had been awarded the Distinguished Flying Cross for his outstanding service. The recommendation drew attention to his operational flying on Lysanders with 1433 Flight and the lack of a rest before he embarked on a second operational tour. It concluded:

> When he was stood down from operations he had completed 75 light bomber sorties and had led the Squadron on 24 occasions. By his intense enthusiasm for operational flying he has been an inspiration to us all, and some measure of his success can be judged by the fact that on three occasions the Army sent back messages of congratulation on the raids he has led. I cannot speak too highly of his excellent work as a Flight Commander during the last six months of intensive operations, nor of his coolness and devotion to duty under fire. Most strongly recommended for the award of the DFC.

Harris was posted to command the Baltimore Flight of 75 OTU based at Shallufah near the town of Suez. He was entirely responsible for all pilot training, crew conversion and operational training. In addition to RAF and Dominion crews, he was also responsible for training Yugoslav, Greek and Free French aircrew. He spoke French well and was personally responsible for the conversion of all French pilots. He flew intensively until the end of July 1945 when he was finally rested. With the exception of just one short break, he had been flying continuously for five years in the extreme climates of Madagascar, the Middle East and an Italian winter. Shortly after moving to Gianaclis near Alexandria for administrative duties, it was announced that he had been awarded the Air Force Cross for his service with 75 OTU, the citation concluding: 'This officer has never spared himself in his efforts to bring Allied crews up to a high standard.'

John Harris resigned his commission in January 1946 to retire to live in Nairobi, retaining the rank of Squadron Leader. On 23 May 1947 it was announced that he had been awarded the Efficiency Medal (Territorial) 'having completed the qualifying period while serving with the RAF'. His awards reflected an efficient, courageous and distinguished career as a pilot and leader. Sadly, he died in Nairobi in June 1961 aged forty-five.

Chapter Twelve

Spitfires to Moonlighting – Bob Large

Londoner 'Bob' Large volunteered for service in the RAF at the beginning of July 1940, and started his pilot training seven weeks later at the height of the Battle of Britain at the Airwork Reserve Training School at Perth. He flew for the first time on 26 August in Tiger Moth N 6531, with his instructor Sergeant Winning. After ten hours he flew his first solo, and completed the elementary phase of his training in October when he was selected for training as a fighter pilot. He made the short journey from Perth to Montrose where he joined 8 Flying Training School for advanced training flying the Miles Master. The intensive advanced flying course lasted just three months during which he completed seventy-five hours flying before being awarded his wings and sergeant's chevrons on 8 January 1941 with an above average assessment. He was just nineteen, and had been in the RAF barely six months.

Large converted to the Spitfire at Hawarden with 57 OTU, and within a month he joined 66 Squadron based initially at Exeter before moving to Perranporth. The Squadron had been heavily engaged as part of 11 Group during the Battle of Britain, and had recently moved to the West Country for a rest period. It was in the process of exchanging its old Mk I Spitfires for the Mk IIa, and Large flew his first sortie in the new Mk in X 4926 on 21 April when he did a climb test to 30,000 feet. The Squadron was engaged mainly in sector patrols and convoy patrols, and this allowed Large a relatively quiet environment in which to build up his fighter experience.

The quiet routine was broken on 20 June when Large took off as the Number Two to Flight Lieutenant 'Dizzy' Allen, a Battle of Britain veteran with a number of confirmed victories, who was leading Black section. They were vectored on to a formation of Heinkel 111 bombers, escorted by five Messerschmitt Bf 109 fighters of *Jagdgeschwader 2* (*JG 2*), some 30 miles south of Plymouth. The two pilots engaged the fighters, and each was credited with destroying one.

Within a month of this success Large was posted to 616 (South Yorkshire) Squadron based at Westhampnett as part of the Bader Tangmere Wing. The Squadron had been very heavily involved in Circus operations over northern

France, and had suffered a number of casualties. Replacements were drawn from the fighter Squadrons operating in less busy areas, and Large flew his first operational sortie with his new Squadron on 14 July, which was also his first sortie in a Spitfire Mk V – P 8748. As one of the 'new boys', Large was detailed to fly a number of routine convoy patrols while the old hands, who included Billy Burton, Johnnie Johnson, 'Cocky' Dundas among many other future 'aces', flew on the almost daily bomber close escort and target support sorties.

The role of the close escort Wing was the direct protection of the bombers, and they had to resist the temptation to look for a fight. The target support Wing's role was to clear the target area and to cover the withdrawal of the bombers and their close escort Squadrons. Other Squadrons provided high cover, and there were usually freelance and diversion Squadrons whose job was to attack the fighter airfields before the main attack.

On Monday 9 August the Tangmere Wing was detailed for Circus 68 as target support for bombers attacking Gosnay. As was his normal practice, Douglas Bader was leading with 616 Squadron when the Wing took off at 1040. One of the Spitfire Squadrons failed to make the rendezvous, and the remaining two pressed on without top cover. Shortly after reaching the French coast, the Messerschmitt Bf 109s of Adolph Galland's *JG 26* pounced on the Spitfires. In the confusion, Douglas Bader was shot down, and a few moments later, Flight Lieutenant 'Buck' Casson, one of 616 Squadron's Flight Commanders, was also shot down. This loss of the Wing Leader and one of the Squadron's Battle of Britain veterans was a huge blow. A search was immediately launched in the hope that the missing pilots had reached the English Channel and were in their dinghies. Throughout the rest of the day the Squadron continued to search, and Large took off in W 3521 to search the area off Calais before landing at Hawkinge short of fuel. As darkness fell, the search was called off. Five days later it was announced that both pilots were safe as prisoners of war.

A 616 Squadron Spitfire IIA (P 8367) undergoes first-line maintenance at Westhampnett in the summer of 1941. (*J .E. Johnson*)

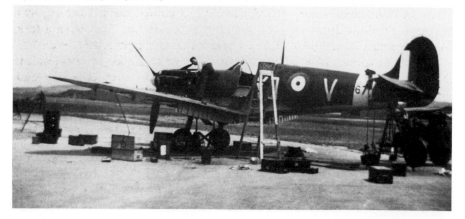

Despite the loss of its Wing Leader, the Squadron continued to fly offensive sweeps and bomber escort sorties without meeting any opposition. In the meantime, the International Red Cross had announced that Bader had lost one of his artificial legs during his bale out, so plans were made to drop a replacement pair. It was decided to do this during a routine bombing sortie on 19 August. Large was flying in W 3460 as one of the close escorts for 82 Squadron Blenheims. The bomber leader dropped the crate containing the legs near St Omer before the formation proceeded to its target. With the safe delivery of the legs, Bader was mobile again, and a few days later he made his first escape attempt!

Two days later the Tangmere Wing was escorting Blenheims to Lille when it ran into trouble. Large was again flying W 3460 when the Wing was attacked from above in weather conditions that favoured the Bf 109s. No 610 Squadron suffered the most, losing four pilots, including Denis Crowley-Milling who eventually got home after successfully evading capture and reaching Gibraltar. No 616 Squadron continued to fly bomber escorts and offensive sweeps for the rest of August, and Squadron pilots, most notably Johnnie Johnson who was starting to build up his score to eventually become the highest scoring RAF fighter pilot, achieved some successes. The end of August 1941 virtually signalled the end of the fighter offensive over the Pas-de-Calais. Large and his colleagues flew a few convoy patrols, but an escort to Blenheims bombing a convoy on 11 September marked the end of 616 Squadron's 'high summer', and the Squadron was finally withdrawn for a rest after a very hectic six months. Seventeen pilots had been lost, and it moved to Kirton-in-Lindsay to train the replacements. Shortly afterwards, Bob Large was commissioned as a Pilot Officer.

The remainder of 1941 passed quietly with routine patrols and convoy escort duties before a move in the New Year to the small airfield WB2 at Kings Cliffe, a satellite of Wittering. Equipped with the Spitfire Mk Vb, the overall daily routine remained the same with much emphasis on training the new pilots. The tedium was relieved for a few days when ten aircraft flew to Matslask on 12 February, and Large flew as part of a six-aircraft escort to Whirlwind fighter-bombers seeking the German battle cruisers *Scharnhorst* and *Gneisenau* during their epic Channel dash. Nothing was seen and the Squadron returned to the normal routine. An unusual task was undertaken in early April when Large escorted a captured Heinkel 111 and a Messerschmitt Bf 109 from Wittering to local airfields for recognition training. Although the German aircraft carried RAF roundels and serial numbers, it was considered prudent to give them a Spitfire escort.

April saw more activity and Large flew on five offensive sweeps and bomber escorts over northern France operating from West Malling as a Wing with 412 and 609 Squadrons. The Focke-Wulf 190 had appeared on the scene and it was soon apparent that the Spitfire Vbs were no match for the new German fighter; the Squadron lost two pilots in an early encounter. Towards the end of May, the Squadron started to re-equip with the Mk VI version of the Spitfire. This development of

Pilot Officer Large (left) receives congratulations on his appointment to a commission from his 616 Squadron colleague, 'Trapper' Bowen RCAF. His Flight Commander, Johnnie Johnson, looks on. (*J.E. Johnson*)

the Mk V was designed to combat the threat posed by the high-flying Junkers 86P bomber and reconnaissance aircraft. The Mk VI was fitted with a pressure cabin, extended wing tips and a four-bladed propeller – all designed for better performance at high level. Large had his first sortie on 23 May when he commented that the aircraft 'was too hot at low level'. Others were to find the same and this restricted the use of the aircraft to the high-level operation. In the event the threat failed to materialise. On one height climb, Large managed to reach 39,500 feet.

Fighter pilots were renowned for their high spirits and aggression. Colleagues claimed that Bob Large possessed enough of both to equip a whole Squadron, and he often found himself 'on the carpet' for some high-spirited misdemeanour. On 8 May he was conducting an air test over the east coast when he spotted a twin-engine, twin-finned aircraft that looked like a Dornier 17 bomber. He closed in and was about to open fire when he noticed the RAF roundels on the wing. He broke away and 'beat up' the aircraft, coming sufficiently close to remove its radio aerial. He returned to base and was soon ordered before the Station Commander, Group Captain Basil Embry, when he became the recipient of a huge 'rocket'. The damaged aircraft, a Flamingo, had landed at Wittering without radio and parked in front of the hangars. Out stepped Marshal of the RAF Lord Trenchard!

A few days later, Large had an altercation with a fighter control officer, and he found himself under close arrest pending a court martial. Basil Embry, himself one of the most aggressive pilots and commanders in the RAF, recognised talent and spirit and allowed Large to fly on offensive patrols 'on the understanding that you come back!'

July saw the Squadron flying an increasing number of offensive patrols from West Malling, and during a two-week period, Large flew ten operations over France. The last of these on 30 July proved to be a black day for 616 Squadron. The Squadron was launched on a Ramrod to St Omer and told to remain initially at 500 feet as it headed for France. Large was flying BS 108 with his usual wingman, Sergeant Mike Cooper from Kenya, flying alongside in loose formation. The order to climb was late, and as the Squadron climbed through 20,000 feet, fifty-plus Fw 190s of *JG 26* bounced the formation. The Spitfires were at a great disadvantage and Mike Cooper and Pilot Officer J. Mace were soon shot down. Large's aircraft was hit by *Hauptmann* Johannes Seifert, a Knight's Cross holder, but he managed to 'clobber' a Fw 190s before he inverted his stricken Spitfire and baled out. He came down in the sea close to Mike Cooper, and air sea rescue launches picked them up. Sergeant D. Lee was also hit and he nursed his Spitfire back to Biggin Hill, but his engine failed on finals and he was killed in the crash. Large was credited with a 'probable', and it was later confirmed that Mace was a prisoner of war.

When Canadian troops and British Commandos made their 'reconnaissance in force' against the French harbour town of Dieppe on 19 August 1942 they were supported by the largest array of RAF aircraft yet mounted for an operation. Sixty-eight Squadrons flew almost 3,000 sorties – all in just sixteen hours. 616 Squadron moved from Great Sampford to Hawkinge for the operation, and pilots came to readiness at dawn to provide top cover taking off at 0700 for their first patrol over Dieppe. The Squadron mounted four major operations throughout the day, and Bob Large flew on all four patrols. The second was to give support to 416 (RCAF) Squadron in the battle area as the troops endeavoured to withdraw. Fifty Fw 190s were seen, as well as a lone bomber, this latter was attacked and destroyed by the Flight Commander, Tony Gaze. No sooner had the Squadron landed it was called into action again when a number of inconclusive fights with Fw 190s took place. Large had 'several squirts' at the enemy fighters and claimed a 'damaged'. In the early evening the Squadron scrambled for the fourth time, this time to give cover to the last of the naval vessels as they withdrew. During the four patrols Large had accumulated over six hours' flying time. Two Squadron pilots were lost, although one was picked up from the Channel having baled out and taken to his dinghy.

For the next few months, the Squadron remained very active on sweeps and escorting USAAF B-17 Flying Fortress bombers over France. On 2 October twelve Squadron Spitfires took off to join Circus 221 to provide close escort to six B-17s attacking Longavesnes airfield near St Omer – Large flew as White 3 with his friend Flight

Sergeant Mike Cooper flying as White 4. As the formation was leaving the target, twelve Fw 190s appeared about 6,000 feet below, and Large set up a diving attack. He caught a straggler, and started firing from 500 yards holding a five-second burst with the result that the enemy fighter caught fire in a steep dive. Postwar analysis indicates that *Unteroffizier* Hans Stoller of *2/JG 26*, who managed to bale out despite being wounded, flew the German aircraft. Large had to break away from the engagement as other fighters threatened, and he exhausted his ammunition in a head-on attack on another Fw 190 before heading for the coast with Cooper flying line abreast with enemy fighters giving chase. Almost immediately a Fw 190 closed in on Cooper and attacked him from below hitting his aircraft in the radiator. A glycol leak started almost immediately, and Cooper had to bale out at 17,000 feet landing in the sea 2 miles off the French coast. As he watched his friend

An extract from Bob Large's logbook showing details of his part in the rescue of Sergeant Mike Cooper, an action that earned him the DFC. (*R. G. Large*)

clamber aboard his dinghy, more Fw 190s attacked Large but, with no ammunition, he had to fly hard to escape from them. He noted Cooper's position, broadcast a 'Mayday' call, and raced back to Hawkinge.

On landing, his aircraft was refuelled and he immediately took off, accompanied by Flight Lieutenant J. Fifield, to relocate Cooper – there had been insufficient time to rearm the Spitfire. He spotted Cooper, but was almost immediately attacked by four Fw 190s, which were eventually driven off by Fifield and other Spitfires of 402 (RCAF) and 416 (RCAF) Squadrons appearing on the scene as escort to a Walrus air-sea rescue aircraft piloted by Flight Sergeant Tom Fletcher DFM. Large continued to orbit the dinghy as the other Spitfires kept more enemy fighters at bay, and as the Walrus dropped a smoke float to keep Cooper in sight. In the meantime, it had become apparent that Cooper was floating in an enemy minefield. Royal Navy patrol boats and RAF High Speed Launches sent to rescue Cooper decided it was too risky to enter the area, so Fletcher landed in the minefield, despite coming under fire from shore batteries, and taxied between the mines that were just visible on the surface. A rope was thrown to Cooper, but the Walrus rear crew were unable to get him on board, so Fletcher had to make another perilous orbit among the mines for a second attempt. This was successful, and with Cooper safely on board, Fletcher took off with shells splashing around him, and with Large and the other Spitfires giving top cover. Fletcher was recommended for the Victoria Cross for this very gallant rescue, but this was reduced to a Bar for his DFM. The *London Gazette* issued on 3 November announced that Bob Large had been awarded an immediate DFC 'for his gallantry and forethought, which set a praiseworthy example'.

During November and December the Squadron was constantly engaged in offensive sweeps and escort sorties for B-17s. Large flew no less than thirty-three operations during this hectic period, but his long tour with 616 Squadron was coming to an end. In the New Year he was posted as an instructor to the Fighter Leaders School at Aston Down after flying continuously on operations for almost two years during which time he flew 188 operational sorties, and was credited with two destroyed, one probable and one damaged, the latter achieved at a time when top cover and close-escort sorties afforded fewer chances for the high-flying Spitfire VIs to engage the enemy.

Within a few weeks of arriving at Aston Down, Bob Large was grounded for six months after a road accident. He was posted to be the personal staff officer to Air Vice Marshal Hollinghurst, the AOC of 9 Group, an unlikely appointment for such a high-spirited officer – a fact that the AOC soon discovered! During his tour, Large flew a variety of interesting communications aircraft including many sorties in a Leopard Moth (R 9381) and a Vega Gull (X 9436). After six months the Air Vice-Marshal agreed that Large's fighting spirit was being wasted and allowed him to return to operations. He offered him 'any fighter Squadron you want'. However, Large had other ideas and, without consulting his boss, he visited a friend flying Lysanders from Tempsford, and was able to persuade the Squadron commander of his suitability. When the posting notice arrived on the AOC's desk without warning, there was a minor eruption when he exclaimed that he could think of no one less suitable than his errant staff officer – not least because he only had fourteen hours' night-flying experience! Nevertheless, he relented and agreed to release Large for these very special duties.

After making two parachute descents from a static balloon, Bob Large arrived at Tempsford on 25 February 1944 for duties with the Lysander Flight of 161 Squadron, often referred to as 'the Moonlight Squadron'. The task of 161 Squadron was to deliver and pick up agents from France, a role requiring highly skilled pilots with a very special ability and courage. They flew alone, at night, and into hostile territory, never knowing whom the reception committee would be.

The Lysander had entered service with the RAF in 1938 to join Army Co-operation Squadrons, but experience during the Battle of France in the spring of 1940 highlighted the aircraft's vulnerability. It had been designed for short landings and take-offs from rough ground. Powered by a single Mercury XX engine, it was a robust aircraft fitted with a fixed undercarriage, a 100-gallon fuel tank behind the pilot, and a gunner's position that could accommodate up to three people. The wings were equipped with automatic leading-edge slats and trailing-edge flaps giving the aircraft a remarkably slow landing speed. It was the ideal aircraft for the special duties role. A fixed ladder was fitted to the rear cockpit on the port side, and a large streamlined fuel tank holding 150 gallons was fitted between the undercarriage legs. This increased the radius of action significantly and operations up to eight hours were flown. Painted all black, the Lysander III (SD) became universally known as the 'Black Lysander'.

Training a pick-up pilot was built around short field landings and take-offs, cross-country flying and night flying. Although the Squadron was based at Tempsford, fields at Somersham and Caxton Gibbett were used to simulate landing grounds in France, and these were prepared in exactly the same fashion as those prepared by agents in the field. The 150-yard flarepath was laid out into wind in an inverted 'L' with three pocket torches. Torch 'A' was with the receptionist in charge of the landing ground at the downwind end where the passengers were waiting. Torch 'B' was 150 yards upwind with torch 'C' 50 yards to the right of torch 'B'. The flarepath had to be at least 100 yards from the downwind hedge, with no trees or obstructions on the approach, on a clear, firm level strip of land about 600 yards long. Rutted cart tracks had to be avoided but the most important feature was to avoid soft mud. Once the aircraft was heard close by, the chief receptionist at torch 'A' flashed the agreed code letter, and once this was acknowledged by the Lysander pilot, the other torches were switched on. The pilot completed a low approach, landed at 60 knots, and immediately taxied back to the take-off position and lined up ready for take-off. As soon as

The field at Somersham near Tempsford where pilots and 'receptionists' were trained for pick-up operations. (*Public Record Office. CN 5/33*)

the aircraft stopped, the receptionist moved to the foot of the fixed ladder to help the descending passengers and their luggage before the returning passengers climbed into the rear cockpit. The engine was kept running, coffee was exchanged for champagne, the chief receptionist switched on his torch, which was the signal for the other torches to be lit, and the pilot took off a few minutes after landing.

During the dark 'moonless' periods, the Squadron pilots instructed the agents and receptionists how to prepare these strips, and this included emergency withdrawals simulating enemy attacks. Until pilots were satisfied, agents were not cleared to prepare and act as a receptionist at a flarepath in France.

A particular skill that Lysander pilots had to perfect was mail pick-ups (MPU). Initial practice was carried out during daylight before perfecting the technique at night. The aircraft did not land but flew a few feet off the ground trailing a wooden hook attached to a weighted cable. On the ground there were two poles with a torch on top of each and a wire loop stretched between them with a mailbag attached to the loop. The Lysander pilot had to be very accurate since the wooden hook would break if it hit the ground or, of greater concern, would hit and damage the elevators. As the hook engaged the wire, the pilot climbed away and the winch operator in the rear cockpit winched the bag on board. Operationally, all this was carried out at night, with two torches as a reference, in an unarmed aircraft over enemy territory!

Accurate navigation was essential if a single torch was to be found in a field after a three- or four-hour flight. Pilots spent many hours preparing their maps. Bob Large used half-million scale topographical maps to draw the tracks between the turning points, mark the headings to fly, the distances, and the enemy gun defences using the latest intelligence. For the approach to the target field, a larger scale map was used. All the maps were stuck together and then cut into a long strip with the track in the middle, and folded so that it would fit into the top of a flying boot. Ideally, the operational sorties were flown in moonlight when water features were particularly clear, and these were ideal for route turning points and initial points into target fields.

After six weeks of intensive training Bob Large was ready to fly his first operation. During the moon period the Lysander Flight moved to Tangmere, where all operations were conducted from the Sussex airfield. Large's first pick-up was Operation 'Rubens' on the night of 9/10 April when he took Vicomte Elie de Dampierre (known as 'Berger') in Lysander 'L' to a large field near Angers. He was on the ground for a few minutes before taking off with Captain Jean Godet in the rear cockpit. Inbound aircraft made their first radio call as they crossed the English Channel when they called 'Postgirl' for a bearing. If the sortie had been successful they transmitted days of the week, whereas numbers were used to indicate that the operation had been unsuccessful. On this occasion he was told to divert to Dunsfold because of fog at Tangmere. Diversions were only

A Lysander III SD of 161 Squadron. Large flew this aircraft on numerous occasions. The long-range fuel tank and the passenger ladder on the port side were standard fits for the Special Duties Lysanders. (*Public Record Office. CN 5/33*)

Flight Lieutenant Bob Large DFC pictured in late 1944. (*R.G. Large*)

ordered if the weather was very bad, since taking the 'Joes' (agents) to strange airfields caused major security problems.

On 30 Apr/1 May Large flew a 'double' with Flying Officer J.P. Alcock flying the second aircraft on Operation 'Organist'. Each aircraft flew independently to an easily identified landmark – usually a river – where they rendezvoused. The first set off for the target field followed a few minutes later by the second. The first completed the pick-up and called 'clear' as soon as it was airborne when the second landed. In this way, the aircraft were on the ground for the minimum amount of time, thus reducing the risk to the ground parties. After dropping off his 'Joe' in a field near Châteauroux, Large picked up Violette Szabo, one of the great heroines of the SOE. He was fired on by light flak on the return flight, and the aircraft ground-looped on landing – his starboard tyre had been shot to pieces. He had been airborne for almost seven hours.

On 9 May Large flew on a 'treble' with Squadron Leader Len Ratcliffe and Lieutenant Per Hysing-Dahl on Operation 'Mineur'. They flew independently, and arrived within three minutes of each other to make a successful rendezvous near Bléré on the River Cher. Ratcliffe set off first for the field near Touraine, and landed his two 'Jocs'. Large followed ten minutes later with Hysing-Dahl landing as Large climbed away from the field. The three aircraft brought out eight agents on what was only the second successful 'treble'. Normally a Hudson would have been used, but there were no suitable fields in the area.

Poor weather curtailed operations during July, and Large did not fly his next operation until the end of the month. With Flight Sergeant Tommy Thomas in the rear cockpit, he took off for a mail pick-up operation,

'Toupet III', deep in France near Nevers. This was successfully completed, but they encountered a blanket of radiation fog covering the south of England, and they were diverted to Bolt Head, an airfield on the top of cliffs near Salcombe in Devon. With thick fog over the airfield, and the fuel tanks almost dry, mortar flares were fired through the cloud to assist the landing. In the meantime, Large was preparing to bale out when he made one last attempt by letting down over the sea and flying to 'nought' feet. In fact, he came out over the airfield and was able to complete a very tight circuit to land after a seven-hour flight.

On 6 August Large took off from Tangmere on his final operation with 161 Squadron – another long-range mail pick-up at night, Operation 'Butterwort'. He was unable to get a fix near his target due to low cloud, so he made for the River Loire where the conditions were much better. He got a visual fix of his position and successfully found his field where the reception committee lit their torches as they heard his Lysander approaching. After dropping a mailbag, he completed a dummy run over the pick-up point before snatching another bag on his next approach. After a six-hour flight, he landed his single-engine Lysander 'G' back at Tangmere as dawn broke.

With Allied armies moving rapidly through northern France, and the Maquis taking control of other large areas, operations for the Tempsford-based Lysanders reduced significantly after the August moon period, and most pilots were posted to other appointments. The unique 'moonlight' operations were virtually over. However, Large remained with the Squadron for a 'special operation' to be mounted into Germany. After a few weeks this was cancelled, and Bob Large found himself with little useful work so he decided to go to London to negotiate a new posting to an operational Squadron. He returned a day late and was immediately charged with being 'absent without leave'. Incredibly, he was court-martialled and, even more incredibly, found guilty and dismissed from the service. Higher authorities approved the findings until the decision reached the King, who, on the advice of the Secretary of State, promptly overturned the sentence.

Bob Large tried to return to his old Squadron, No 616, which was flying the Meteor jet fighter in Germany, but he was unsuccessful. However, he was posted to 504 Squadron, the second Squadron to be equipped with the Meteor, and he flew his first sortie in a Meteor I on 7 April 1945 after a few sorties to practise asymmetric flying in the Oxford. In September the Squadron was renumbered 245 Squadron, and he continued flying the Meteor until he left the Service in March 1947. He then became a commercial pilot, but spent his weekends flying Meteors with 601 (County of London) Squadron where he became an expert aerobatic pilot.

In 1990 Bob Large learnt that the French government had made him a Chevalier of the Légion d'Honneur for his services to France during his time as a special duties pilot carrying agents. In many respects, Bob Large was the archetypal fighter pilot. Something of a rebel, full of high spirits, somewhat ill disciplined, but above all tremendously courageous. One of his fellow 'moonlight' pilots put it succinctly, describing him as 'a fantastic chap'.

Chapter Thirteen

Supplying the Partisans – Jack Strain

With the war eighteen months old, nineteen-year-old Jack Strain enlisted into the Royal Air Force Volunteer Reserve for aircrew duties. After initial training at Wilmslow and Newquay, he sailed for Canada where he trained as an observer under the British Commonwealth Air Training Plan. Observers first learned the techniques of navigation at an Air Observer School before going to a Bombing and Gunnery School to learn the art of bomb aiming and air gunnery. Students were awarded their observer's brevet and promoted to sergeant before completing the return journey across the Atlantic Ocean.

On return to the United Kingdom, it was routine for Canadian-trained observers to complete a short navigation course at an Air Observer School to familiarise themselves with flying over a blacked-out country that suffered from indifferent weather. With this short course at 2 Air Observer School at Millom completed, Jack Strain was posted in January 1942 to 21 OTU at Moreton-in-Marsh to convert to the Wellington in the bomber role where he crewed up with Sergeant Tony Payne. By the time he had completed the bomber conversion course, the Wellington had been withdrawn from front-line service with Bomber Command, but it continued to provide the mainstay of the RAF's bomber force in the Middle East, and Jack Strain and his crew were posted to the region to join a bomber Squadron.

As Wellington aircraft became surplus to requirement in Bomber Command, many were flown out to replace the losses of Middle East Squadrons. Crews posted to the area were used to ferry the aircraft via Gibraltar, and Strain and his colleagues set off from Portreath in HF 887 on 6 June 1942 arriving in Gibraltar after a nine-hour flight across the Bay of Biscay. The traditional onward route to Egypt had involved a stop at Malta but, with the island under siege, an alternative route had to be found. The nearest land in British hands was in Egypt, well out of range of the Wellington. To increase the range of the aircraft, the front gun turret was removed and the aircraft was fitted with a long-range ferry tank. After two days in Gibraltar, Sergeant Payne lifted the heavily laden Wellington off the short runway and headed for Mersah Matruh, 200 miles east of

The Wellington ferried to Egypt by Jack Strain and his crew. The front turret was removed to reduce weight and was re-fitted before the aircraft was allocated to a squadron. (*Jack Strain*)

Tobruk, and some 1,800 miles from Gibraltar. By any standards this was a major undertaking for an inexperienced crew, but Strain's navigation was perfect, and the crew landed at their destination after a flight of over twelve hours. The following day, and just three days after leaving England, they continued their journey and delivered the aircraft to a Maintenance Unit in the Canal Zone. Unfortunately, the crew were split up to become individual replacements on various Wellington Squadrons.

Within a few days, Strain was posted to 70 Squadron, one of the longest established and most experienced of the desert bomber Squadrons of 205 Group. The Squadron was based at Abu Sueir near Ismailia having conducted a rapid retreat from Benghazi ahead of the German armoured breakthrough in the Libyan Desert. With a shortage of crews on the Squadron, Strain was soon in action. By coincidence the aircraft he had ferried to Egypt was allocated to 70 Squadron, and he flew his first operation on 3 July in this aircraft when he attacked enemy troops and transports near El Daba.

Jack Strain's first few weeks with 70 Squadron proved to be one of the most significant periods in the Desert war. Rommel's *Panzer* army reached the Egyptian border, and General Montgomery arrived to assume command of the Eighth Army. The British retreat stopped at El Alamein when the army dug in, having been told by its new commander that there was to be no further withdrawal. Rommel's supply lines were stretched, yet he continued to mass his forces for one final thrust into Egypt and on to the Suez Canal. This exposed his rear positions, and the Wellingtons of 205 Group turned their attention to his motor transport (MT) parks, forward aircraft landing grounds and supply dumps. The port of Tobruk was crucial for the resupply of the German *Panzers* and it became a regular target for the Egypt-based bomber Squadrons earning the nickname 'the milk run'. Anti-aircraft defences at the port were considerable, and on his first two visits, Strain's aircraft was hit by flak. On a third, both pilots had to exert all their strength to pull the Wellington out of a dive after being caught by searchlights. Worse was to follow on 5 August, the first night of the Tobruk 'Blitz'.

On joining 70 Squadron, Strain had crewed up with American-born pilot Sergeant 'Tex' Holland, a man of similar spirit and courage who had enlisted in the RCAF. He was at the controls of DV 624, when the crew headed for yet another attack against the shipping in Tobruk. Strain had moved to his bomb-aimer's position in the nose as the aircraft approached the target, and had just released the bombs when the aircraft was caught by intensive anti-aircraft fire. The aircraft was hit in the wings and fuselage, and a particularly heavy burst blew off the front hatch close to Strain's position. He would have fallen through had he not caught the legs of the second pilot who was able to pull him to safety. He had been wounded in the arm by shrapnel, which severed an artery, but quick work by the wireless operator stopped the profuse bleeding, and Tex Holland turned for Egypt, landing at Heliopolis where Strain was transferred to hospital. He made a quick recovery, and returned to operations four weeks later.

In the meantime, Rommel prepared to launch his major attack on 30 August against the Alam el Halfa Ridge, and the Wellingtons of 205 Group pounded his positions with excellent support from flare-dropping Albacores of the Fleet Air Arm, which had illuminated the target. These attacks with the Albacores in support continued over the next four nights, and those on 2 September proved decisive, being assessed as the most successful of all the battle-area night attacks. The next day Rommel's advance was halted, and this marked the end of his efforts to reach the Suez Canal. The German Field Marshal was later to state, 'The continuous and very heavy attacks of the Royal Air Force . . . absolutely pinned my troops to the ground and made impossible any safe deployment or any advance according to schedule.' This intensive period of operations resulted in the loss of four Wellingtons of 70 Squadron.

Jack Strain returned to operations on 5 September when he attacked Tobruk, which had once again become the primary target after the enemy offensive had been halted. On this sortie his bombs started a major fire at the base of the main jetty, and two nights later he started another fire on the waterfront. Over the next seven weeks the Squadron pounded Tobruk with 250 and 500-lb bombs and incendiaries – Strain attacked the port ten times in this period including a mining sortie in the harbour. The anti-aircraft fire was intense over Tobruk, and the Squadron lost numerous aircraft. One crew captained by Sergeant Carter crash-landed near Tobruk,

and the crew spent the next 29 days walking 430 miles back through the desert to Egypt. They even attempted to ambush two Italian army trucks, but had to escape into the desert night as sleeping soldiers were alerted and opened fire on the crew. They carried on walking east!

After releasing the bombs on a target, Tex Holland was in the habit of taking the Wellington to low level where the gunners shot out searchlights and attacked motor transports on the Tobruk–Bardia road.

On the night of 23/24 October the second and crucial Battle of El Alamein commenced and the Wellingtons of 205 Group flew at intensive rates attacking Rommel's guns, armour, advanced landing grounds and supply routes. Strain had been re-crewed with the Flight Commander, Squadron Leader D. Crossley DFC, and they attacked the retreating German troops and their transports almost every night. Once again, the Fleet Air Arm's Albacores were used to provide very effective illumination of the target areas. Strain attacked an enemy landing ground on 27 October, and was able to claim a direct hit on aircraft, starting seven fires. As the Eighth Army surged forward, the Wellington Squadrons moved to airfields and landing grounds in the desert arriving at El Daba in mid-November and El Adem by the end of the month. During late November there was some relief from the routine of bombing the retreating Axis armies when the Wellingtons attacked the German airfields in Crete. Strain and his crew bombed Heraklion before operations were resumed to hound the German concentrations as they continued their headlong retreat towards Tunisia. To keep within range, the Squadron was constantly on the move, arriving at Benina early in the New Year before continuing westwards to Magrun. By this stage, Jack Strain was coming towards the end of his tour and, after flying four operations against transport and supply lines, he took off on 19 January 1943 in HX 778 for his thirty-seventh and final operation when he bombed Tripoli harbour. During his tour with the Squadron he had dropped 113,750-lb of bombs.

On 5 February it was announced that Jack Strain had been awarded the Distinguished Flying Medal. The long citation drew attention to his aggressive spirit and the outstanding bombing results that he achieved. The citation concluded:

> This NCO's tour of operations as a Navigator/Bomb Aimer has been distinguished throughout by extreme gallantry despite experiences which might have affected the morale of anyone less resolute. His cheerfulness and undaunted determination to strike at the enemy has proved an inspiration to the Squadron.

Tex Holland was also awarded the DFM and Squadron Leader Crossley received a Bar to his DFC. Shortly afterwards, Strain was commissioned.

Opposite: Bombing up at a desert Advanced Landing Ground. (*Jack Strain*)

A Hudson VI of 267 Squadron, with a Hurricane escort, flies supplies to the troops of the 8th Army at a forward position in the North African desert. (*IWM. CM 5008*)

Pilot Officer Jack Strain was posted to 267 Squadron for a rest from operations. The Squadron was equipped with the Mk VI transport version of the Hudson aircraft, and Strain flew his first sortie on 24 February 1943 in EW 937. The Squadron was based at Cairo West (LG 224), and was tasked to fly supplies and personnel throughout North Africa. In the course of the next few months, Strain averaged over eighty hours' flying time each month. With final victory in North Africa, there was a continuous and demanding requirement for air transport over a huge area, which now included routes to Casablanca, Algiers and Gibraltar. In addition, routes were established to Karachi in the east and to Khartoum and Takoradi in the south and west. This massive requirement coincided with the arrival of the much more capable Dakota aircraft, and on 6 June, Strain flew his first Dakota sortie in FD 840 to Marble Arch with stops at Castel Benito and El Adem.

Operation 'Husky', the invasion of Sicily, commenced on 11 June 1943, and the Dakotas of 267 Squadron were quickly in action resupplying the troops once a bridgehead had been established. Three days later, Strain was flying on a resupply shuttle service with Spitfire escorts between the Maltese island of Gozo and Lucata airfield in Sicily, taking ground personnel and equipment of a USAAF Fighter Wing. Within a few weeks, a detachment was established at San Fransesco in Sicily to support the invasion of Italy, and escorted resupply sorties were flown to the recently captured airfields in southern Italy. The landings at Salerno took place on 9 September and, four days later, Strain and his crew had a particularly hectic trip as they flew supplies to an airfield near Salerno. Kittyhawks of 21st USAAF Fighter Group escorted them, but this did not prevent them from coming under heavy anti-aircraft fire from the Allied naval forces.

The transport Squadrons in the Middle East were in constant demand, and 267 Squadron regularly mounted detachments of aircraft at airfields throughout the region. In November and December, Strain and his crew were based at Rabat Sale in Morocco, operating on the air transport service down the West African coast as far as Lagos in Nigeria. Achieving over 100 flying hours each month was a common occurrence. Soon there were other tasks for the transport Squadrons.

The delivery of supplies to the partisans in the Balkan countries had begun in May 1942, and the task had grown to such an extent that a specialist Squadron (148 Squadron), equipped with Halifax and Liberator aircraft, was established in March 1943 for the task. Before the collapse of Italy and the armistice on 8 September 43, Italian forces had occupied most of the Dalmatian coast, and following the Italian capitulation, the Germans and Marshal Tito's Yugoslav partisans moved swiftly to try and gain control of the coastline. In January 1944 the whole of the coast and all the Dalmatian islands except Vis and Lagosta were in German hands, and the extra troops involved gave the Germans eighteen divisions in the Balkan region. The demands to supply the partisans could no longer be met by the one specialist Squadron, and the special duties transport force was rapidly expanded. This included the transfer of 267 Squadron to the Italian theatre by the end of November 1943 when the Squadron transferred to 334 Wing and moved to Bari airfield in the south of Italy on the Adriatic coast. It soon established regular schedules to Tunis, Foggia, Naples and Algiers, but by March 1944 the Squadron's effort was almost equally divided between these routine services and special duties supply flights.

By spring 1944 the Germans were facing increasing opposition within the territories that they occupied. In Yugoslavia, Greece, Albania and Northern Italy, partisans were consolidating their resistance. In Poland, plans were being laid for an uprising. And, in southern France, the Maquis were preparing to support the long-awaited Allied invasion. Supporting these irregular forces placed an even greater demand on the RAF and USAAF special duty transport Squadrons, and 267 Squadron was soon heavily involved, with the demand continuing until the end of the war. Strain flew his first resupply dropping sortie with Flight Lieutenant Mike O'Donovan on 18 March 1944 when they took FZ 561 to drop supplies at night to the partisans in Greece.

The main task at this stage of the war was to supply arms and personnel to Yugoslavia. The difference between operations to Yugoslavia and other European countries was that at all times, large tracts of the country were in the hands of the partisans. The situation, however, was never stabilised

Dakotas of 267 Squadron at Bari. (*IWM. CNA 3334*)

as frequent small German offensives resulted in the partisans having to evacuate one area in favour of another. This led to an unlimited demand for supplies, and constantly changing dropping zones – 322 had been used by the end of the war. The control of large areas of country did, however, have some major advantages including the ability to make, and use, landing strips suitable for fully loaded Dakotas.

Jack Strain carried out a number of sorties over Yugoslavia before three crews of 267 Squadron, including his own, were placed on standby to fly 'a very special operation', for which, unbeknown to him, planning had begun in February 1944. The intention was to land in enemy-occupied Polish territory in the middle of the night to deliver two important agents, and collect a Polish General of the Polish underground. The operation was called 'Wildhorn' and it had to be delayed a number of times before it was successfully completed on 15 April. Shortly afterwards a second 'Wildhorn' sortie was requested, and Jack Strain and his crew were selected. The operation was known as 'Motyl' and the full crew were Flight Lieutenant M. O'Donovan the pilot, Jack Strain the navigator and Pilot Officer D. Thomas as the wireless operator. Pilot Officer Btochi of 1586 Polish Flight was selected as the second pilot and interpreter. Four long-range cabin fuel tanks had been installed to give the aircraft an endurance of fourteen hours. After numerous postponements, the crew positioned their aircraft, Dakota KG 477, at Brindisi on 29 May 1944 for a final briefing, and to collect General Kosak and Lieutenant Colonel Bisze of the Polish Army and 964 lb of ammunition.

At 1735 the aircraft with its two Polish passengers took off from Brindisi, and soon met up with two Liberators of 1586 Polish Flight, which escorted the Dakota during the daylight period of the Flight. Shortly after crossing the Yugoslav coast the three aircraft were fired on by light flak, which they avoided. Further flak was encountered south of Budapest, and soon afterwards the two Liberators broke formation and returned to Italy. The Dakota flew on at 10,000 feet and, with good visibility, Strain obtained pinpoints on the Danube and when crossing the Tartar Mountains. Radio communication was established with the Polish underground reception committee, and the appropriate identification signals were exchanged before the crude flarepath was lit. O'Donovan positioned the aircraft for landing, and after touchdown he just stopped before the end of the lights with ground mist beginning to creep on to the airstrip. He commented that it was 'a very bare 1,100 yards as briefed'. It later transpired that the stronger tail winds, and Jack Strain's perfect navigation, resulted in the aircraft arriving early, and the reception party had to hurriedly position the flarepath. In their haste, they placed the red markers at the beginning of the landing run some 200 yards into the field making the usable distance barely adequate for a Dakota. As soon as the Dakota rolled to a stop, Pilot Officer Btochi jumped from the aircraft to fill his pockets with Polish soil to take back to Brindisi. The two Polish officers and the ammunition were quickly unloaded, and two senior Polish Air Force officers and a diplomat climbed on board before the aircraft took off after spending less than ten minutes on the ground with the engines running. The four-hour return flight at night was uneventful and the aircraft landed at Brindisi almost nine hours after its departure.

Following the aircraft's arrival at Brindisi from this highly dangerous, but very successful, operation, the Polish Flight requested that the same crew take the Polish passengers to England, and this was agreed. The crew completed the journey via Gibraltar and, while in England, it was announced that the Polish Government-in-Exile had awarded Flight Lieutenant O'Donovan the Virtuti Militare (the Polish Victoria Cross) and the other three members of the crew were awarded the Polish Cross of Valour. A few weeks later, the third and final 'Wildhorn' sortie was flown when vital components of the V-2 rocket, captured by the Polish Underground, were recovered to Italy for onward transport to the intelligence agencies in England. This proved to be one of the most audacious and significant intelligence coups of the war, and there can never be too much praise for the gallantry of the men and women of the Polish resistance who carried out this remarkable action.

The official report for these incredible flights described them as 'probably the most difficult operations of their type attempted during the European War'. The aircraft had to penetrate over 800 miles into enemy territory,

Greek partisans unload Dakotas of 267 Squadron, the 'Flying Horse Squadron', in a Greek field. (*P.H.T. Green Collection*)

with virtually no support, to find a small field lit by a handful of torches marking an airstrip of marginal length for a Dakota.

Shortly after returning from England, Strain and his crew flew their first night sortie to land on a Yugoslav landing strip taking in supplies and personnel and bringing out Italian soldiers and wounded partisans. In all, thirty-six landing strips were prepared and used in Yugoslavia before the end of the war. Some became quite sophisticated with electric landing lights, others had Eureka radar homing aids. The partisans controlled the area for a few miles around these airstrips and patrolled the area whenever a supply sortie was expected, and few of these strips were overrun by the Germans. The strips were chosen and operated by RAF teams consisting of one officer and six men, and they were known as British Air Terminal Sections (BATS). Nine of these parties were formed, and their specialised knowledge, together with the way in which they organised the local partisans to load and unload Dakotas, contributed greatly to the effectiveness of supply operations. Moreover, apart from the obvious advantage of flying out wounded partisans, the use of these strips operated by the BATS parties reduced the quantity of parachutes and containers needed for delivering loads, and also enabled the recovery of materials used in the air drops. The BATS parties often remained in Yugoslavia for up to six months operating in harsh conditions, surrounded by the enemy, and their outstanding and gallant service has received scant attention.

By the end of June, the Squadron was sending out eight aircraft on supply sorties to the partisans almost every night. Throughout early July, Strain flew a number of sorties into landing strips, but occasionally the wrong identification signals were received and the Dakotas had to return to base. On one occasion the sortie had to be abandoned at a very late stage when German forces captured a landing strip. Although operations to Yugoslavia were intensive, the Squadron continued to send sorties to Greece, and airborne supply to the Italian resistance movement in northern Italy became more common. During an intensive period in August, Jack Strain flew into two Yugoslav landing strips, dropped supplies on two more night sorties over Yugoslavia, and made three attempts to drop supplies to the Italian partisans; two being baulked by bad weather. Early September followed a similar pattern with two air drops over northern Yugoslavia

Jack Strain pictured at the end of the war wearing his DFM, 1939–45 Star and Polish Cross of Valour ribbons. (*Jack Strain*)

near the Austrian border, and three landings in Yugoslavia to deliver stores and medical supplies, bringing out the wounded on the return flight. On one sortie he and his crew had just landed at a Yugoslav airstrip and were unloading their supplies when the local partisan leader summoned them to a banquet. As a gun battle raged in the surrounding hills, they fed on roast suckling pig and wild strawberries before returning to the more civilised surroundings of their Italian airfield!

By August 1944, Allied successes in the west, and the Russian advance into Romania, made it appear likely that German forces would soon begin withdrawing from Greece and the scattered islands in the Aegean Sea. With the various Greek resistance movements in open disagree-ment, there was a real risk of chaos once the Germans withdrew, and plans were drawn up for the immediate occupation of Athens as soon as this happened. Before these could be implemented, it was necessary to destroy the coast defence lines and the radar station at the southern end of the island of Kithera. A force of Royal Marine Commandos, members of the Long Range Desert Group, and the Raiding Support Regiment formed the attacking force, known as 'Foxforce'. However, before the force could start operations, a reconnaissance of the island was necessary. On 10 September Strain and his crew took off in KG 511 with the reconnaissance party of eight men and dropped them on the southern end of Kithera. During the transit to the drop zone, the raiding party sat in the back of the Dakota smoking, drinking whisky and playing poker. Such sang-froid is difficult for ordinary mortals to comprehend. The drop was carried out exactly as planned, and the subsequent operations by Foxforce were completely successful. They cleared the island before advancing to Athens to meet the main occupying force.

Five days after this operation, Jack Strain took off on his last operational sortie with 267 Squadron. With his regular pilot, Mike O'Donovan, he headed for the Yugoslav–Romanian border to drop supplies and personnel. After a five-hour sortie he landed back at Bari and finished his tour. Since joining the Squadron eighteen months earlier he had flown almost 1,500 hours and thirty-one resupply sorties, including six into landing strips in Poland and Yugoslavia. All these sorties required the most precise navigation, often to find a series of torches in a small field. Not surprisingly, he was assessed as 'above average'.

After leaving 267 Squadron he joined the staff of 205 Group and managed to fly on three more resupply sorties to Yugoslavia navigating a Wellington on each occasion. He returned to England in January 1945 to be a navigation instructor before completing the staff navigator's course at the Empire Air Navigation School. After a further six months as a navigation instructor at RAF Jurby he left the RAF to return to civilian life. During his service in North Africa he had applied to the London Hospital Medical School to train as a doctor. He completed his training and practised as a doctor in his home town Egremont for over fifty years.

Chapter Fourteen

Light Night Striking Force – Deryck Grainger

With war looming, nineteen-year-old Deryck Grainger volunteered for the RAFVR in June 1939 to be a pilot, starting his initial flying training almost immediately. He had just completed his annual three-week training period when he was mobilised in his home town of Newcastle. After completing the standard Initial Training Wing course, and with promotion to sergeant, he continued with his flying training. Selected for multi-engine training, he reported to 3 Flying Training School based at RAF South Cerney near Cirencester in June 1940. Despite the fierce fighting over southern England during the summer of 1940, including bombing attacks against South Cerney itself, the very hectic flying training schedules continued. Over seventy Oxford aircraft were based at the Gloucestershire airfield and its satellite at Bibury, where much of the night flying training was carried out. Grainger completed his pilot training on 29 September 1940, and was awarded his pilot's wings before departing for Cottesmore in Rutland, where he joined 14 OTU for training on the Hampden twin-engine bomber.

The Hampden was designed to meet the Air Ministry's specification B.9/32 for a medium bomber to replace the antiquated biplane bombers then in service. The aircraft was powered by Bristol Pegasus XVIII engines, giving it a top speed of 254 mph, and a large bomb bay allowed up to 4,000 lb of bombs to be carried. The aircraft entered Squadron service in August 1938 with bomber Squadrons in the newly formed 5 Group. Together with the Wellington and the Whitley, it formed the mainstay of Bomber Command's long-range bomber force at the outbreak of war, but early heavy losses during daylight raids forced all three aircraft types to be assigned to night bombing operations. The Hampden was the fastest of the three bombers, but it was lightly armed.

Grainger spent three months learning to fly the Hampden at Cottesmore, where he also flew the Napier Dagger-engined Hereford, an aircraft that never entered operational service. In 1940 it was the practice that all medium bombers carried a first and second pilot. The unorthodox fuselage and strange internal layout of the Hampden made movement within the aircraft almost impossible, so the second pilot acted as the navigator and bomb aimer. During the course at the OTU the junior pilots regularly flew on navigation exercises in the Anson, when they also practised bomb aiming. Pilot training consisted of dual instruction in the Anson followed by committing the Hampden's cockpit drills to memory. Once these had been mastered, an aircraft was jacked up in the hangar where the landing attitude could be demonstrated and the various drills could be practised. This was necessary since there was no dual-control version of the aircraft and the 'first solo' was exactly that. After a demonstration flight with an instructor, the pilot flew the aircraft for the first time with a gunner to keep him company. By the end of January 1941 Grainger had completed his basic pilot and navigator training at 14 OTU, and he was posted to 83 Squadron based at Scampton.

Grainger flew his first operation on 15 February when he attacked the oil installations at Homberg. He was flying as navigator and bomb aimer with Pilot Officer Royle and his crew in X 3096. Owing to searchlight activity, and the failure of one flare to ignite, the target could not be located, so two 250-lb bombs were dropped on the searchlight positions. The results of this first sortie were typical for this period of the bomber offensive when navigation was restricted almost entirely to dead reckoning, and bombsights were of a basic design. Throughout March, Grainger flew four more operations, each with a different pilot, and then he returned to the OTU to complete an intensive four-week captain's course before being allocated his own crew. He had served his apprenticeship and was ready to start flying operations as a captain in his own aircraft AD 907.

A Hampden of 83 Squadron prepares to take off from Scampton. (*P.H.T. Green Collection*)

The first operation for a new captain was usually a minelaying sortie and, on the night of 2 May, Grainger and his crew flew their first war mission together when they headed for the German convoy routes near the Frisian Islands. Commencing in April 1940, minelaying became a major role for the RAF's medium bomber force, but until the arrival of the heavy bombers only the Hampden, with its large bomb bay, was capable of carrying the 1,500-lb A Mk I-IV sea mine. The mines contained 750 lb of high explosive with magnetic or acoustic fusing, or a combination of both. The mine could be made to detonate on first sensing an impulse or it could be fitted with a time-delay fuse, some remaining inactive for months. 'Gardening' was the code name for aircraft sea mining operations when 'vegetables' were 'planted' in sea areas identified by the Admiralty who were responsible for all sea mining, whether carried out by aircraft, ships or submarines. The purposes of sea mining were several, and were seen by the Admiralty as a major operation to dislocate enemy sea-borne traffic and, in particular, to assist in the Battle of the Atlantic by hindering the passage of U-boats and blockade runners. There was the added advantage that mining operations forced the enemy to maintain large minesweeping fleets along the very extended occupied coastline of Europe.

At this time, the Hampdens were used for the long-range mining operations, usually to the Baltic, but the arrival of the German battle cruisers *Scharnhorst* and *Gneisenau* at Brest in May 1941 placed greater emphasis on operations against the French ports. Grainger's second sortie as a captain was to the French port of Quiberon where he laid his mine successfully before returning on the long route to avoid the defences on the Brest Peninsula, landing back at Scampton after a flight of over eight hours.

With the U-boat threat in the North Atlantic reaching serious proportions in the spring of 1941, most Bomber Command operations mounted during this period were directed against ports and industrial centres in Germany supporting the building of naval vessels and components. After his mining operations, Grainger next attacked the port and shipyards of Hamburg in what was later described as one of the most destructive operations so far in the war. On 12 May he was briefed to attack Mannheim, but, with poor visibility over the target, he and twenty-six other aircraft attacked the secondary target of Cologne. He and his crew reported a large explosion and fire, which was also observed by other crews. The records maintained by the Cologne authorities confirm that a number of important industrial targets were hit, and a barracks was destroyed, with heavy loss of life.

After this brief interlude over Germany, the Hampdens embarked on a series of sorties 'planting' sea mines, and on three consecutive nights, just over 100 mines were laid in the approaches to Brest and St Nazaire. The value of sea mining has often been ignored. Unlike bomber or ground-attack operations, the mining sorties did not generate immediate results, and provided little news for the propaganda machinery, but a great deal of enemy shipping was lost following these operations, and postwar analysis

A mixture of 250-lb and 500-lb GP bombs with nose fuses about to be loaded on to Hampden P 1333. (*IWM. CH 255*)

has highlighted their effectiveness and value. The effort Germany was forced to allocate to the defensive operation of minesweeping was very considerable, and significantly reduced its capability to mount offensive naval operations.

The bombing effort against 'maritime' targets continued throughout June, and Grainger flew two attacks against the German battle cruisers in Brest, three against the shipbuilding yards in Bremen, and one against the U-boat building yards at Vegesack. The difficulties of target finding and identification during this phase of the bomber offensive are well illustrated by the latter attack with all crews reporting failure to find the target, and others dropping their bombs on ETA or estimated positions. Similar problems occurred over Cologne on 10 July when cloud obscured the target, but Grainger's navigator was able to obtain a pinpoint on the river to the south of the city. He calculated a timed run from the pinpoint and the target was attacked despite the attention of the German flak batteries.

From the beginning of July it was back to German industrial targets for the main bomber force, but bad weather continued to thwart good bombing results. Grainger's next visit to Cologne on 20 July once again ran into bad weather over the target, but further trouble awaited him and his crew as they left the Belgian coast. Three German fighters, with one closing to 400 yards before opening fire, attacked them. Grainger's rear gunner, Sergeant Neil, returned the fire with his twin 0.303-in machine-guns with Grainger manoeuvring the Hampden violently as he headed for the protection of some thick cloud, which he reached before the fighter could inflict any serious damage.

Grainger completed his tour on 83 Squadron during the first week of August. He flew two mining operations, first to the Baltic and a second to the approaches to Kiel harbour before his final operation to Mannheim on 5 August when serious damage was caused to several areas of the city. After almost eight hours at the controls of his reliable Hampden, AD 907, he landed at Scampton at 0600 after completing his thirtieth operation.

Soon after Grainger had completed his tour on Hampdens, it became clear that the accuracy of Bomber Command crews did not match expectations or the optimistic beliefs of crews and staffs. The twin-engine bombers that bore the brunt of the early bomber campaigns lacked accurate bombing and navigation aids. They had been introduced into RAF service at a time when it was firmly believed that 'the bomber will always get through', and daylight operations would allow crews to visually navigate accurately to their targets, which would be easy to recognise and hit. In the event, daylight operations soon became untenable, and the bombers had to operate by night when the difficulties were greatly magnified. However, some operations caused considerable damage, and others diverted large numbers of combat-capable Germans to be employed

Sea mines being prepared in the mine dump ready for a night operation. (*IWM. C 4012*)

on defensive duties in order to combat the nightly bombing raids. The staffs and crews of Bomber Command gained considerable experience, and many very valuable lessons were learnt that helped pave the way for the massive bomber offensive that took the war to the enemy from 1942, and which played an enormous part in the eventual demise of the Third Reich. Above all, the gallantry of the crews that took these out-dated bombers to attack the enemy stands out as a wonderful chapter in the history of the Royal Air Force.

Following the completion of his tour of bomber operations, Deryck Grainger spent the next eighteen months as an instructor pilot at 12 Beam Approach Training (BAT) School – soon to be called 1512 BAT School – based at Dishforth but flying from Linton-on-Ouse with Anson aircraft. On 24 October 1941, Grainger was commissioned as a Pilot Officer, and four weeks later it was announced in the *London Gazette* that he had been awarded the Distinguished Flying Medal. The citation drew attention to his 200 hours of operational flying and commented:

> This airman pilot has shown great determination to find and bomb his targets. All his work is characterised by a dogged persistence. On one occasion he was detailed to attack Cologne but on arrival he found the target was obscured. He flew on to Aachen, his alternative target, but as conditions were similar he returned to Cologne where he eventually succeeded in identifying the main target, despite the short hours of darkness. On another occasion while attacking battle cruisers at Brest he remained in the target area for 25 minutes at a height of about 9,000 feet in order to make an accurate attack. Sergeant Grainger has been one of the most successful captains in his Squadron due to his exceptional ability, keenness and determination to press home his attacks, often in the face of enemy opposition.

The Air Officer Commanding 5 Group, Air Vice-Marshal J. Slessor, 'very strongly recommended' the award. On 24 March 1942, Grainger attended Buckingham Palace where His Majesty King George VI presented his DFM.

After his eighteen-month 'rest' tour with 1512 BAT Flight, during which time he accumulated over 600 hours flying time and was promoted to Flight Lieutenant, Grainger returned for a second tour of operations with Bomber Command. After attending a refresher course at 14 OTU at Market Harborough, he moved to Marham to convert to the Mosquito with 1655 Mosquito Training Unit. On 14 January 1944 he travelled to Graveley near Huntingdon with his Canadian navigator, Flight Lieutenant Jack Barron, to become a founder member of 692 Squadron of the Light Night Striking Force (LNSF) of 8 (Pathfinder) Group.

Three Mosquito Squadrons (105, 109, 139) had operated with 8 Group during 1943 flying 'nuisance' attacks and perfecting marking techniques with the new navigation aids Gee and Oboe. The Squadrons flew the Mosquito B IV, and the steady flow of the improved Mk XVI version allowed 627 and 692 Squadrons to be formed.

A Mosquito B XVI of 692 Squadron pictured at Graveley in October 1944. (*IWM. CH 17858*)

Grainger flew his first operation on 23 January when he took DZ 490 to Düsseldorf to drop four 500-lb bombs on the red Target Indicators (TIs) dropped by 105 Squadron. He was airborne for just two and a half hours – a far cry from the six and seven hours taken for a similar sortie during his Hampden days. Four days later he made his first attack against Berlin when six Squadron aircraft bombed from 28,000 feet – again, a significant capability compared to the early days of the bombing offensive. On the way to the target, the high-flying Mosquitoes dropped spoof route markers and flares in support of the 515 heavy bombers also heading for Berlin.

By early 1944 the German air defence system, under the skilful direction and leadership of *Luftwaffe* General Joseph Kammhuber, had become a formidable obstacle to the Allied strategic bomber effort. To combat this increasing threat, the planning of the main bomber offensive became more flexible and innovative. The high-flying, fast Mosquitoes of the LNSF were employed in various roles including spoof and 'feint' attacks with Window to confuse the air defences and divert their attention away from the main force. The arrival of the first Mk IV (DZ 647) modified to carry the 4,000lb bomb provided the planning staff with yet more flexibility for the employment of the Mosquitoes. This included tasking individual aircraft to follow behind the main force to drop their blast bombs at regular intervals to disrupt fire-fighting efforts. The availability of the 'cookie' heralded a new era for the 'anti-morale' Mosquito Squadrons of the Pathfinder Force who were to range over German cities nightly, ensuring disturbed sleep for the inhabitants, in particular the industrial workers.

On 23 February Squadron Leader S. Watts dropped the first 'cookie' from a Mosquito when he attacked Düsseldorf. Grainger dropped the bomb for the first time when he took DZ 647 to Düsseldorf six nights later, bombing blind from 26,000 feet. His aircraft suffered minor shrapnel damage. During the first week of March, he dropped another on Münchengladbach, when conditions were much better, allowing the 105 Squadron Mosquitoes to mark the target accurately, and he also flew a similar raid to Dortmund, observing that the searchlights and flak were becoming more accurate at the Mosquito operating height. The capability of the LNSF was, however, about to take another significant step forward with the arrival of the first Mosquito B Mk XVI.

From the outset, it was intended that the B XVI would carry the 4,000-lb bomb. The aircraft had the improved Merlin 72 engines and a pressurised cockpit, giving the aircraft a ceiling of 36,000 feet. No 692 Squadron flew its first operation with the aircraft on 5 March. More of the new aircraft arrived in the next few days, and the Squadron was able to send out four to attack Frankfurt on 13 March accompanied by three Mk IVs. Grainger took one of the new aircraft (ML 940) for his first operation on the type. H2S-equipped Mosquitoes of 139 Squadron, whose timing was perfect, marked the target and the Mk XVIs bombed from 30,000 feet. The aircraft met considerable heavy flak in barrage form, and it was estimated that over 100 searchlights were in action, some operating in cones. This raid was the heaviest mounted by the Squadron so far.

The rapid build-up of the Mk XVIs during the busy month of March allowed the Squadron to dispatch an increasing number of the more capable aircraft every night. By the end of the month, twelve were available, and they attacked Cologne on 4 April and Hamburg two nights later. Grainger was flying ML 695 on the latter when weather conditions in the target area were perfect. The lack of cloud, excellent visibility and a full moon allowed the aircraft to bomb visually from 28,000 feet. The

No 692 Squadron aircrew at Graveley in June 1944. Deryck Grainger is second left in the rear row. (*Joe Reed*)

opposition consisted of very many searchlights operating in cones with heavy flak, which was intense in the cones. On the return journey the weather deteriorated with fog and low cloud forming over Graveley as the Mosquitoes arrived overhead. Graveley was one of the airfields equipped with the Fog Investigation and Dispersal Operation (known as FIDO), and Group Headquarters ordered it to be lit. First to land was Grainger, to be followed at five-minute intervals by the rest of the Squadron. It was the first time any had experienced a FIDO landing, and the Squadron diarist commented laconically 'the general opinion was that there was nothing much to it'.

By the middle of April the main force of Bomber Command was diverted to bombing support operations in the lead-up to the invasion of Europe. The rapid build-up of the Mosquito XVI force was timely, allowing 'nuisance' raids to be continued over Germany on an almost nightly basis. During April, Grainger attacked Dortmund, Cologne, Essen, Mannheim, Hanover and Osnabrück. On 18 April he attacked Berlin with a 4,000-lb bomb for the first time. The Squadron sent out ten aircraft to attack 'the Big City', all carrying two 50-gallon overload fuel tanks for the four-hour sortie. By the end of April, 692 Squadron had flown 200 sorties, dropped almost the same number of 4,000-lb bombs and lost no aircraft. It had been a very busy and effective month.

On 1 May, Grainger attacked the *IG Farbenindustrie* complex at Ludwigshaven with ten other 692 Squadron aircraft on what was described as 'an unsatisfactory attack due to scattered markers'. The following night he took ML 966 to Leverkusen, a raid that elicited the comment 'everyone agreed that this raid on the chemical works at Leverkusen was as satisfactory as the previous night's work at Ludwigshaven was unsatisfactory'. The TIs dropped by an Oboe Mosquito were accurate, and nine 'cookies' were dropped in the space of two minutes. Crews reported that bomb bursts were seen well concentrated round the TIs, and a large fire started as the aircraft left the area. Ludwigshaven was the target again two nights later when the cloud tops were at 24,000 feet obscuring the markers, so the nine heavy bombs were dropped on dead reckoning. Damage may have been slight, but the nuisance value of the raid was undoubtedly worthwhile, and it was conducted under weather conditions that would have completely thwarted the heavy bomber force operating at their much lower bombing heights.

Ten Mosquitoes of 692 Squadron attacked Osnabrück on 8 May – it was Grainger's fifth operation since the beginning of the month. The route to the target was over north Holland with the navigators using Gee to the turning-point south-east of Emden where a route marker flare had been fired by the marker force. Using the blind-marking technique with red TIs, the H2S-equipped Mosquitoes of 139 Squadron marked the aiming point (the railway marshalling yards). The Master Bomber visually identified it and marked it with green TIs before broadcasting instructions over the VHF radio about the exact aiming point in relation to the greens. The ten bombers then dropped on the Master Bomber's instruction within

a ninety-second period. This raid provides an interesting example of the rapid development of navigation, bombing techniques, capabilities and accuracies achieved since Grainger's Hampden days, less than three years earlier.

The next operation flown by Deryck Grainger and his navigator demonstrated the great versatility of the Mosquito. After a day practising low-flying techniques, thirteen Mosquitoes of 692 Squadron, led by Wing Commander S. Watts DFC, took off in the early hours of 13 May and flew in loose formation at 10,000 feet heading for the Kiel Canal. Each aircraft was carrying a sea mine. Ahead of them were other Mosquitoes of 100 Group attacking flak positions in the target area, and looking out for German fighters. The route first took the attacking force north of Heligoland before they turned south-east towards the canal, which connected the Baltic with the North Sea. Navigators used the north-west Gee chain for navigation, and were assisted by 139 Squadron Mosquitoes marking the route with green Very flares. The marking force then headed for the final run-in point, which they marked with red spot marker flares. The following attack force split into two formations before descending to 8,000 feet. Once they reached the red spots, they dived down to 300 feet using the bright moonlight to confirm their position.

The section of the canal chosen for the attack was lightly defended, and the first five aircraft identified the canal before turning along it to drop their mines from below 250 feet at 0349. The second wave had some difficulty finding the target, but six more mines were eventually dropped successfully. Much of the success of the operation was due to the accurate reconnaissance of the canal in the days before the attack. One aircraft failed to return from the mining operation.

The raid was a spectacular success. The canal was closed for seven days before re-opening for restricted traffic for three days, when it had to be closed again for a further three days. Twelve days after the attack, over seventy ships were still waiting to enter the canal. Crucial iron-ore supplies to German industry and troop reinforcements to Norway were among the 1,500,000 tons of cargo held up. Twelve gallantry awards were announced for aircrew of 692 Squadron including the DSO for Wing Commander Watts and the DFC for Grainger and his navigator, Jack Barron. The citation for Grainger's award included the statement:

> . . . a brilliant attack was executed with the utmost determination. This officer showed outstanding courage and devotion to duty and is recommended for the immediate award of the Distinguished Flying Cross.

Air Vice-Marshal Donald Bennett, the Air Officer Commanding 8 Group, added:

Opposite: A 4,000-lb high-capacity bomb, or 'cookie', being loaded into the modified bomb-bay of a black-painted Mosquito B IV of 692 Squadron. (*Joe Reed*)

Squadron Leader Deryck Grainger DFC, DFM pictured as a Flight Commander of 16 OTU at Upper Heyford, January 1945. (*Joe Reed*)

Flight Lieutenant Grainger displayed outstanding qualities of determination and skill in pressing home his attack. For his part in this operation, which required extremely accurate and precise flying in spite of the intense opposition, he is strongly recommended for the immediate award of the DFC.

Air Chief Marshal Sir Arthur Harris confirmed the award on 25 May 1944.

During the summer months, the main bomber force could not attack Berlin due to the short period of darkness, but this did not present a problem for the fast-flying Mosquitoes, which could complete the round trip in four hours. Over a four-day period towards the end of May, Grainger attacked the city with 4,000-lb bombs on three occasions. He then flew on five consecutive nights to targets including Hanover, Leverkusen and Cologne. In six days, the Squadron mounted sixty-three successful attacks, which is not only a testimony to the skill and stamina of the aircrew, but also the outstanding work of the hard-working ground crew.

Following the brilliant success of the Kiel Canal attack, 692 Squadron were tasked with a second mining operation on the night of 1 June. Five Mk IV aircraft took off just before midnight with Grainger flying DZ 633 armed with a 1,500-lb Mk III sea mine. The aircraft flew over Denmark before descending below the 5,000-foot cloud base over the Kattegat east of Aarhus. With excellent visibility below the cloud, they identified the landmark selected as an initial point before flying a precise heading and time to drop the mines from 700 feet.

With the Normandy invasion imminent, 692 Squadron launched twelve aircraft each night to attack targets in Germany, and this effort was continued until the third week of June. The procedures had become routine with 139 Squadron marking the routes with flares before dropping TIs over the target. On the night of D-Day, Grainger attacked Osnabruck, and two nights later he attacked Cologne when the Squadron diarist recorded that persistent condensation trails formed at 20,000 feet making it possible to see that the Mosquitoes ahead had been bunched together well on the correct track, 'which ran down a lattice line on the Gee chart'. This raid was followed by another attack against Berlin, and Grainger made his seventh and final trip to 'the Big City' on 17 June.

After visits to oil installations at Gelsenkirchen, Homberg and Saarbrücken, Deryck Grainger and his navigator Jack Barron took off on 30 June in a Mk XVI/ML 144 to attack the oil plant at Homberg. The target was bombed in very clear conditions by eleven aircraft after very accurate positioning of the TIs by the Mosquito marker force. Good bombing was observed, and there was a violent explosion and the returning bombers could still see fires as they left the Dutch coast. At exactly 0200, Grainger landed at Graveley on the completion of his fiftieth and final Mosquito operation. It was his eightieth bombing operation of the war, and, by an amazing coincidence, he had bombed the same target on his very first operation on Hampdens. Within a few days, he was posted to 1655 Mosquito Training Unit at Marham.

During the autumn of 1944, Grainger attended a flying instructor's course at the Central Flying School achieving an A 2 instructor category on multi-engine aircraft. He was promoted to Squadron Leader, and returned to 1655 MTU on 1 January 1945 when the unit was redesignated 16 OTU based at Upper Heyford. He remained with 16 OTU for the next twelve months, and was finally retired from the RAF in January 1946. He had had an outstanding career as a gallant and determined bomber pilot. Shortly after he left the RAF, it was announced that he had been awarded the Air Efficiency Award.

Charles Patterson
Distinguished Service Order, Distinguished Flying Cross, 1939–45 Star, Aircrew Europe Star (with France and Germany Clasp), Defence Medal, War Medal.

John Neale
Distinguished Service Cross, Distinguished Flying Cross, 1939–45 Star, Aircrew Europe Star (with Atlantic Clasp), Africa Star, War Medal (with Mention in Despatches), Malta GC Fiftieth Anniversary Medal.

Bernard Evans
Distinguished Flying Medal, 1939–45 Star, Aircrew Europe Star, Africa Star, Defence Medal, War Medal (with Mention in Despatches), Air Efficiency Award.

Guy Lawrence
Distinguished Service Order, Officer of the Order of the British Empire, Distinguished Flying Cross, 1939–45 Star, Aircrew Europe Star, Defence Medal, War Medal (with Mention in Despatches).

Del Wright
Distinguished Flying Cross, 1939–45 Star, Atlantic Star (with Aircrew Europe Clasp), Defence Medal, War Medal, General Service Medal (with Malaya Clasp). Note: the Near East Clasp is missing.

Doug Nicholl
Distinguished Flying Cross, 1939–45 Star (with Battle of Britain Clasp), Aircrew Europe Star, Pacific Star (with Burma Clasp), War Medal, Air Efficiency Award.

Freddie Deeks
Distinguished Flying Cross, 1939–45 Star, Aircrew Europe Star, Africa Star, War Medal, General Service Medal (with Malaya and Cyprus Clasps), Malta George Cross Fiftieth Anniversary Medal.

Roy Marlow
Military Medal, 1939–45 Star, Africa Star, Italy Star, War Medal.

Fred Fray
Distinguished Flying Medal, 1939–45 Star, Aircrew Europe Star, Defence Medal, War
Medal.

John Harris
Distinguished Flying Cross, Air Force Cross, 1939–45 Star, Italy Star, Defence Medal,
War Medal, Efficiency Medal (Territorial).

Bob Large
Distinguished Flying Cross, 1939–45 Star, Aircrew Europe Star (with France and
Germany Clasp), Defence Medal, War Medal, Légion d'Honneur.

Jack Strain
Distinguished Flying Medal, 1939–45 Star, Africa Star (with North Africa 1942–43 Clasp), Italy Star, Defence Medal, War Medal, Polish Cross of Valour. Medals below are: Polish Freedom and Victory Medal, Warsaw Uprising Cross.

Deryck Grainger
Distinguished Flying Cross, Distinguished Flying Medal, 1939–45 Star, Aircrew Europe Star, Defence Medal, War Medal, Air Efficiency Award.

Harold Yates
Distinguished Flying Medal, 1939–45 Star, Africa Star, Italy Star, War Medal.

Arthur Hall
Distinguished Flying Cross and Bar, 1939–45 Star, Aircrew Europe Star (with France and Germany Clasp), Africa Star (with North Africa 1943–45 Clasp), Italy Star, War Medal.

Arthur Brett
Distinguished Service Medal, 1939–45 Star, Atlantic Star, Pacific Star, Defence Medal, War Medal (with Mention in Despatches), General Service Medal (with Palestine 1945–48 Clasp), RAF Long Service and Good Conduct Medal.

Frank Baylis
Air Force Medal, 1939–45 Star, Aircrew Europe Star (with France and Germany Clasp), Italy Star, War Medal, Croix de Guerre (Belgium).

Aubrey Young
Distinguished Flying Cross, 1939–45 Star, Italy Star, France and Germany Star, Defence Medal, War Medal.

Ken Brain
Distinguished Flying Cross, 1939–45 Star, France and Germany Star, War Medal.

Sandy Webb
Distinguished Flying Cross and Bar, 1939–45 Star, Aircrew Europe Star (with France and Germany Clasp), Defence Medal, War Medal, Air Efficiency Award, Bronze Lion (Netherlands).

Chapter Fifteen

Aegean Sea Strike Pilot – 'Binder' Yates

Just three months after his seventeenth birthday, Lancashire-born Harold Yates enlisted in to the Royal Air Force for training as a pilot in January 1941. Seven months later he had completed his initial training at 10 Initial Training Wing at Scarborough and was aboard a troopship on his way to Canada to commence his flying training.

Soon after the outbreak of war the demand for pilots and aircrew rose well beyond the capabilities of the RAF's flying training organisation in the United Kingdom, and this led to the implementation of the British Commonwealth Air Training Plan (BCATP), a scheme described by Sir Maurice Dean as 'one of the most brilliant pieces of organization ever conceived'. The introduction of the BCATP provided the facility needed to produce the annual requirement of 50,000 trained aircrew. The flying schools were established throughout the Commonwealth with the majority based in Canada. In early 1941 studies indicated that yet more flying training schools would be required, and the British government agreed a further scheme with the United States under the auspices of the Lend-Lease Act. Three separate schemes were devised, and one became known as the 'Towers Scheme' – the brainchild of Vice-Admiral John Towers, an early pioneer of naval aviation. By the end of the war, over 14,000 aircrew had been trained in the United States.

On arrival at the Reception Centre in Toronto, Yates and his colleagues assumed that they would be proceeding to a Canadian flying school. Instead, they were issued with civilian suits, and found themselves on a train bound for the US Naval Air Station at Grosse Ile in Michigan to join one of the first 'Towers Scheme' courses in October 1941.

After completing ground school, the RAF cadets commenced initial flying training on the Stearman, and the harsh regime required each trainee pilot to fly solo within ten hours. On completion of initial flying training, the cadets transferred to the large US Navy station at Pensacola on the Gulf of Mexico for advanced training on the Vought Kingfisher and the SNJ-3, better known as the Harvard. With 200 hours flying experience, Yates was awarded his wings and sergeant's chevrons on 31 July 1942. A month later he sailed back across the Atlantic to return to the United Kingdom.

Pilots trained overseas had enjoyed good flying weather and easily identifiable navigation landmarks such as well-lit towns and cities, a stark contrast to the fickle European weather and the total blackout. To adjust to this much more demanding flying environment, pilots completed a course at an Advanced Flying Unit before commencing operational training. Yates spent five months at 6 (Pilot) AFU at Little Rissington flying the Oxford; this training would have included a week spent at a Beam Approach Training Flight consolidating on instrument flying and standard beam approaches under simulated bad weather conditions.

In view of the naval flavour of their flying training, the majority of former 'Towers Scheme' trained pilots were posted to Coastal Command. On completion of his course at Little Rissington, Yates travelled to East Fortune near Edinburgh to join 132 (Coastal) OTU. The role of 132 OTU was to provide long-range fighter and strike training for the maritime role, and the unit was equipped with the Blenheim and the Beaufighter. Having converted to the Beaufighter, Yates and his navigator, Sergeant J. Walley, completed a wide-ranging course that included formation flying, air-to-air and air-to-ground gunnery, practice with air-to-surface radar, dummy shipping strikes and maritime tactics. On completion of the three month OTU course, specialist torpedo-dropping training was conducted at 2 Torpedo Training Unit based at Castle Kennedy near Stranraer. Here the crew were trained in the art of torpedo dropping utilising the excellent weapons range facilities in Luce Bay. With over 400 hours in his logbook, Yates was almost ready to join his first operational Squadron. He and his navigator were posted to the Middle East.

Crews posted to the area were used to deliver replacement Beaufighters to the theatre. Since this was a daunting task for an inexperienced crew, a short course was established to train such crews and to test the aircraft. They travelled to the Bristol Aeroplane Company factory at Filton to collect a new Beaufighter, which they flew on 3 September 1943 to Port Ellen on the island of Islay, the home of 304 Ferry Training Unit. The role of the unit was to prepare crews to navigate and fly their aircraft on long ferry trips overseas. The course was only two weeks, but the crews made extended training flights over the North Atlantic to measure the exact fuel consumption of the new aircraft. On completion, Yates and Walley flew to Portreath in Cornwall to wait for suitable weather for the long transit flight to Gibraltar. Two days later, on 22 September, they took off with maximum fuel, and without the aircraft's guns, which had been removed to reduce the weight and thus extend the Beaufighter's range.

The route was designed to fly well to the west of the Bay of Biscay to avoid the *Luftwaffe*'s long-range Junkers 88 fighters based on the French Atlantic coast, before turning towards the north-west tip of Spain to obtain a visual fix. Remaining 5 miles out to sea the crew followed the coast arriving at Gibraltar after a five-and-half-hour flight. Following an overnight stay, they set off for Egypt and, using the recently acquired airfields in North Africa, arrived just three days after leaving Portreath.

Two weeks later Yates and his navigator joined 603 (City of Edinburgh) Squadron just as the unit was leaving Sicily for Egypt to bolster the expanding anti-shipping force for operations in the Aegean Sea.

Following the unconditional surrender of Italy on 8 September 1943, Allied plans were made to establish a 'second front' in southern Europe by setting up bases in the Dodecanese Islands in the eastern Aegean to be used as a series of stepping stones to the Greek mainland. After the failure to capture the key island of Rhodes, and attempts to establish a foothold on the island of Kos had been foiled by the Germans, British troops had withdrawn from Kos to Leros and Samos. Beaufighters based in Libya and Cyprus provided support before commencing a concentrated campaign against the German resupply shipping in the area. By mid-October 603 Squadron, recently re-equipped with Beaufighter TFX aircraft, was established at Gambut III and El Adem airfields in the North African Desert.

The reversals suffered by the British forces in the Aegean campaign reduced the time available for 603 to settle at Gambut, and for the air and ground crews to familiarise themselves with their new aircraft. The Squadron was soon in action escorting USAAF B-25 Mitchell bombers and torpedo-equipped Beaufighters of the recently arrived 47 Squadron as they attacked supply ships and armed caiques around Kos. Yates and

Beaufighters preparing to take off from a desert airfield. (*IWM. CM5575*)

Walley flew their first operational sortie on 9 November when they took off in LZ 275 with three other Beaufighters to escort two torpedo-carrying Beaufighters of 47 Squadron on an anti-shipping sweep in the eastern Aegean. A convoy was sighted off Amorgos, but escorting Junkers 88 fighters intercepted the Beaufighters before they could attack the ships and, after a twenty-seven minute pursuit, the Beaufighters had to abandon their attack. After a four-and-a half-hour sortie the aircraft landed at Gambut.

By 10 November the Germans had assembled an invasion fleet at Kos and the nearby islands ready to land assault troops on Leros where the British forces were established. The following day Yates was flying as part of a nine-aircraft formation escorting 47 Squadron torpedo Beaufighters attacking barges near Leros, but Messerschmitt Bf 109s broke up the attack shooting down one of the attacking aircraft. The loss of the island of Kos had provided the *Luftwaffe* with forward airfields, and the German fighters posed a continuous threat to the Beaufighters throughout the period.

Despite the efforts of Royal Navy destroyers, bombers of 201 Group, and the Beaufighter anti-shipping Squadrons, the Germans landed on Leros on 12 November, and soon made significant progress. The availability of fighter cover gave the Germans a huge advantage and losses soon mounted among the RAF attacking formations. As the situation worsened, the Beaufighters increased their attacks acting as escorts to the torpedo Beaufighters and the cannon-armed B-25 Mitchells. Yates flew offensive patrols daily. On 12 November he was part of an escort formation attacking ships in the western Aegean when a merchant ship and two escorts were damaged by cannon fire, and two escorting Arado 196 fighters were damaged. Four days later, as the Germans made further progress in occupying Leros, Yates took part in the attack against a convoy including a Siebel ferry and flak boats. The convoy, heavily escorted by fighters, was located about 3 miles west of Calino when the eight Beaufighters attacked with cannons before the enemy fighters could intervene. The ferry was blown up, leaving only burning wreckage and large columns of black smoke, but in the ensuing fight four Beaufighters were lost. As the situation worsened on Leros Yates and his fellow aircrew flew daily in search of shipping, and strikes were achieved against supply ships. However, by 20 November the ill-fated Dodecanese campaign was lost.

In the first ten days of his operational career, Yates had completed nine anti-shipping sorties, which averaged almost five hours each, and had flown against heavy opposition with the loss of a number of his colleagues. One of the key lessons of combined operations had once again been highlighted – the need to control the air. With bases close to the operational area, the *Luftwaffe* achieved local air superiority against the Allies who were operating at maximum range giving them very limited time in the target area.

With the end of the Dodecanese operation, 603 Squadron was released from operational commitments to allow the aircraft to be modified to carry the three-inch rocket projectiles (RP) instead of bombs. The United Kingdom-based Squadrons had demonstrated how effective the rocket was in the anti-shipping role, and 603 was the first of the Middle East Squadrons to be converted. Four rockets were carried under each wing and could be armed with 25-lb armour piercing or 60-lb high explosive warheads. A programme of lectures and flying training for the aircrew was commenced and all crews were converted to the role before the Squadron recommenced operations in mid-December.

A Beaufighter attack on German 'F' Boats off Leros in late 1943. (*Author's Collection*)

Following the occupation of the Dodecanese islands by German forces, RAF and USAAF bombers attacked German shipping in Greek ports, and Royal Navy submarines took a further toll. This led to a shortage of shipping, and the Germans made increasing use of local caiques and schooners as supply ships, and as flak ships to supplement the small supply ships and the dangerous escort flak ships. Almost daily these became the targets for the Beaufighters. The ever-present Messerschmitt Bf 109 and Arado 196 fighters made the task of the aircrew even more hazardous.

On 15 December four RP Beaufighters, with four gun-armed Beaufighters acting as escort, mounted the first operation with rockets by a Middle East Squadron. Yates was flying one of the RP aircraft (LZ 340) as the formation took off in the early morning on an offensive sweep in the western Aegean. Nothing was sighted, and the aircraft landed after a five-hour sortie. After this quiet start, success soon followed for Yates and Walley who were in action on 23 December when their formation of four aircraft attacked a two-masted 60-ton caique with rockets and cannons before proceeding to Naxos in the central Aegean where landing barges were attacked and damaged in the face of intense flak.

Ground crew at Gambut work on the Hercules engine of a 603 Squadron Beaufighter as aircrew inspect a damaged part. (*J. Edgar*)

After Christmas, 603 Squadron was out in force on the 26th when nine aircraft, in two formations, took off for offensive sweeps in the central Aegean. Yates flew in the second formation of three aircraft, which was diverted by a wireless message to proceed to Stampalia where the first formation had met with an earlier success. On arrival, the three aircraft attacked a three-masted caique of 100 tons moored alongside a jetty, and two 60-lb rockets fired from the first Beaufighter blew the vessel up. Yates switched his attention to the jetty and fired all eight rockets 'obliterating it in spray and debris'. The three aircraft came under intense anti-aircraft fire, but escaped undamaged.

Poor weather limited operations during the first weeks of the New Year, but offensive sweeps were launched when possible with limited success being achieved. Yates and Walley had their next success on 25 January 1944 when they scored rocket and cannon hits on a 100-ton caique near Samos, but they came under intense and accurate light anti-aircraft fire from shore batteries before they had to evade enemy fighters, which had appeared on the scene. They landed after a five-and-a half-hour sortie.

With the reduction in the number of large enemy vessels, torpedo attacks by 47 Squadron became increasingly rare. However, 603 Squadron provided six aircraft as anti-flak escorts and fighter cover on 30 January for two 47 Squadron torpedo-armed Beaufighters. Yates was flying LZ 272 armed with rockets and cannons for the shipping strike off Melos. Two hours after a dusk take-off, a convoy made up of a 2,500-ton merchant ship, an 800-ton sloop and two 500-ton flak ships was sighted. The formation leader attacked the flak ships, scoring cannon hits as the 47 Squadron Beaufighters dropped their torpedoes. Three Arado 196 aircraft attacked the formation, but Yates continued his attack against an escort vessel despite intense light flak. He scored cannon strikes before achieving three rocket hits on the bow of the 800-ton vessel, which was left with a column of black smoke rising. As the formation left, there was a large explosion amidships on the merchant vessel. In the final attack Yates's aircraft was hit by flak but, despite his aircraft being extensively damaged, he attacked and damaged one of the enemy fighters. Both he and his navigator were wounded, but Walley was able to bind up the damaged and leaking hydraulic pipes as Yates struggled to reach El Adem, where he made a successful night crash landing. Both men were admitted to hospital and did not return to operations for almost two months.

During the period Yates and his navigator were recovering from their wounds, the Beaufighter anti-shipping Squadrons continued to search for and destroy enemy shipping in the Aegean, but losses to flak continued to mount. On 16 February the anti-shipping Squadrons lost one of their most gallant and charismatic pilots when Wing Commander J.K. Buchanan DSO, DFC and Bar, the Commanding Officer of 227 Squadron, had to ditch his stricken Beaufighter when returning from a shipping strike. Tragically, he died in his dinghy before rescue forces arrived to rescue him.

The SS *Drache*, a German troopship, comes under rocket fire at Leros. The ship was attacked by twelve aircraft and was left sinking. (*Author's Collection*)

Torpedoes were used successfully for the last time on 22 February when a large force of Beaufighters, including 603 Squadron, provided an anti-flak and escort force for torpedo-carrying aircraft of 47 Squadron who sank the 5,343 ton merchant ship *Lisa* with their torpedoes. The lack of worthwhile large targets led to the withdrawal of 47 Squadron, and they left for the Far East in March. One of 603 Squadron's most experienced pilots, Flight Lieutenant A. Pringle, achieved a spectacular success on the night of 6 March when he found two warships off Crete, and fired all eight of his 60-lb high explosive rockets at the leading ship. A fire started immediately and very shortly afterwards the German TA 15 destroyer blew up and sank. Pringle was later awarded the Distinguished Flying Cross for this and other successes while serving with the Squadron.

Yates returned to flying at the end of March when he was soon involved in further action. On 2 April he was one of a formation of four aircraft that found caiques moored alongside a harbour wall on Mikonos, one of the many islands in the central Aegean. Against light opposition, the formation made numerous rocket and cannon attacks, causing extensive damage, before flying to Naxos where they repeated the action against another caique moored alongside a jetty. A few days later, Yates led a formation on an offensive sweep in the same area when more caiques were attacked and badly damaged. The marauding Beaufighter Squadrons had taken such a heavy toll of enemy shipping that the German troops on the Aegean islands were running short of supplies, so all types of ships were pressed into service. The caiques would endeavour to hide during daylight hours and sail at night, but the Beaufighters ferreted them out with daily sweeps around the islands and night intruder sorties over the sea-lanes. Due to the earlier successes, many of these long-range sorties resulted in no sightings.

With fewer ships to attack, 603 Squadron turned its attention to the main radar site in southern Crete when a large-scale attack, Operation 'Blackeye', was mounted on 5 and 6 April against the Wasserman and Wurzburg early

A German merchant ship transferring supplies to a caique at Preveza comes under cannon attack. (*Author's Collection*)

Flying Officer 'Binder' Yates DFM, Cairo 1946. (*J. Edgar*)

warning radars at Palaiokhora and Leonda. Two sections of four aircraft, escorted by Spitfires of 94 Squadron, carried out the attacks. Yates was flying in the first section, and strikes by four rockets were seen to hit the base of the 130ft-high Wasserman tower at Palaiokhora as others fell near the Wurzburg radar and gun positions. The attack at Leonda by the second section was more difficult as the target lay close to a ridge of higher ground, but rocket strikes were seen among a group of buildings. The attacks were repeated the following day, but the defences were alerted and a number of Beaufighters were damaged, but not before forty rockets had been fired to inflict further damage. Photographs and radio signals interceptions confirmed the success of the attacks.

Yates and his navigator, Walley, who had only recently recovered from his wounds and returned to flying, flew a number of offensive sweeps throughout the rest of May, but targets were proving more difficult to find. On 3 June they flew their final operation together. As one of the most experienced crews on the Squadron they remained for a few weeks passing on their knowledge and skills to the newly arrived crews.

After Yates's departure from the Squadron, 603 continued to harass the remaining German shipping in the Aegean. As the Germans suffered further defeats in Russia, Italy and the Balkans, they attempted to withdraw their troops during September from the garrisons on the Aegean islands. Together with the only other remaining Beaufighter Squadron, 252 Squadron, the crews of 603 successfully attacked a number of troopships heading for Greek ports from Rhodes and Leros. With the loss of so many troopships, and the final German defeat in Greece in October, many enemy troops were left stranded on the islands in rapidly deteriorating circumstances until the end of the war. In November 603 Squadron left the Middle East to return to the United Kingdom, where it was re-equipped with Spitfire XVI aircraft used in the ground-attack role during the final Allied offensives in Holland and Germany.

On 29 July 1944 it was announced that Flight Sergeant Harold Yates had been awarded an immediate Distinguished Flying Medal. The Squadron Commander's strong recommendation made specific reference to Yates's attack when he damaged a German destroyer off Melos and his subsequent masterly crash-landing at night despite his wounds. He also commended Yates for: pressing home his attack on enemy RDF Stations on Crete in the face of intense and accurate flak.' He concluded 'This NCO pilot has completed an extremely aggressive tour of operations in the Aegean. He has throughout his tour shown a consistent devotion to duty and courage of a high order. Air Chief Marshal Sir Keith Park, the Commander-in-Chief, approved the award on 5 July 1944. Shortly afterwards, Yates was commissioned as a Pilot Officer.

Yates had developed into a highly skilled and experienced anti-shipping strike pilot and he was posted as an instructor to 79 OTU based at Nicosia. The role of the unit was to train new strike crews, and when rocket-firing practice was introduced into the flying syllabus in July 1944, Yates was a natural candidate for an instructor post. He remained at

Nicosia until the unit was disbanded twelve months later, when he joined the Middle East Communications Flight at Heliopolis in Egypt. He finally retired from the RAF in May 1946 when he was able to resume his career as a chemist.

Chapter Sixteen

Night Fighter Radar Ace – Arthur Hall

The thought of sailing on a rough sea or flogging through the mud as an infantry soldier did not appeal to Arthur Hall, so he decided to pre-empt his expected compulsory call-up by volunteering for aircrew duties with the Royal Air Force. He was just twenty years old when he presented himself at the local recruiting office in Leeds, but it was not until the end of 1940 that he finally reported to Padgate for aptitude and medical tests. The doctors discovered that he had a slight defect in his left eye and he was offered training as a navigator, which he accepted.

He reported to the reception centre at Babbacombe in May 1941where he was issued with a uniform and inoculated against an unending variety of maladies. Each recruit was invited to state a preference for one of the numerous Initial Training Wing locations and, living near Leeds, he requested Scarborough. He immediately discovered the whimsical humour of the RAF when he was marched the few miles to 3 ITW located in the Regina Hotel in Torquay! Within a few weeks, he experienced another taste of humour when he was sent for his navigator training to Millom, near Barrow-in-Furness, having already been prepared, briefed and kitted out to go to Canada.

Hall arrived at 2 Air Observer School at Millom in June 1941 where the airborne exercises were flown in Ansons. Towards the end of the course, a sudden increased requirement for night-fighter navigators occurred and Hall accepted a request for volunteers. Within a matter of days, twelve trainee navigators were sent to 3 Radio School at Prestwick to learn all about Air Interception (AI) radars – still a very rudimentary piece of equipment. The current AI radar was the Mk IV, which suffered considerably from 'ground clutter'. The equipment consisted of two basic cathode-ray tubes, one to measure range and direction, and the other height. The students soon discovered that there was a very definite 'knack' in using the equipment, and many otherwise excellent navigators found it too difficult, and were transferred to other roles. The course lasted four weeks, with all the airborne training carried out in very tired and old Blenheim bombers converted to carry four or five students and an instructor, in addition to the pilot. On completion of the course, the students were awarded their 'O' brevet. (Early in the war, some men, usually air gunners or ground tradesmen, were trained specifically as radar operators and they were known as 'observer (radio)' and wore the 'RO' brevet. Both categories qualifying after 1942 wore the 'N' brevet.)

Hall was posted to 54 OTU at Church Fenton in Yorkshire. During the first few days, pilots and navigator/radios formed crews, a very *ad hoc* and informal arrangement. Hall and a pilot called Michael Benn seemed to get on very well with each other, and they agreed to fly together. It was a few days later that Hall discovered that his pilot was the Honourable Michael Benn, the eldest son of Viscount Stansgate, a former First World War pilot, and elder brother of Tony Benn who followed him into the RAF before becoming a Labour politician. Flying training was carried out in Blenheims, and the course was geared more to the development of evasion tactics, interception techniques and an introduction to flying under the direction of the controllers at a Ground Control Interception (GCI) unit. Surprisingly, there was not a great deal of night flying. At the end of the three-month course, both Hall and his pilot were commissioned as Pilot Officers, and posted to join 141 Squadron based at Ayr. The Squadron was equipped with the Beaufighter Mk IF powered by Hercules engines, and armed with four 20mm Hispano Mk I cannons in the nose and six Browning machine-guns in the wings.

By the latter part of 1941, the *Luftwaffe*'s bombing raids had become very sporadic, creating little activity for the night-fighter crews based at Ayr. However, this did provide a good opportunity for Hall and his pilot to develop their skills and establish the teamwork that was the essential need for a successful crew. A move to Acklington in Northumberland in early 1942 provided more activity, although during March it was a type of activity that aircrew find unwelcome. A few days after an undercarriage failure on landing, which resulted in a very high-speed dash down the runway on the aircraft's belly trailing a shower of sparks, Hall and his pilot were sent to the satellite airfield at Drem near Edinburgh, where the Squadron maintained a small detachment in order to provide a quick-reaction capability should the important dockyards at Rosyth and in the Forth come under attack.

On 25 March 1942, Hall and Benn took off in X 7576 to patrol east of the Firth of Forth. The GCI controllers vectored them towards a possible target at 10,000 feet, but before Hall could gain a positive contact on his AI Mk IV set, the local air defence guns opened fire. They were not renowned for their accuracy, but on this occasion they managed to register a hit – unfortunately, the shrapnel hit the Beaufighter. The hydraulics of the aircraft were damaged, causing a small amount of flap to drop on the port side, and this made it very difficult for Benn to control the aircraft in roll. The problems became more acute at slow speed, and trying to land the aircraft in this configuration was out of the question. The ground controllers directed the aircraft over the moorland area of Northumberland before Hall and his pilot baled out at 6,000 feet.

The parachute descent in the pitch-black night seemed unreal before Hall saw trees rushing towards him, and he arrived on the ground in a heap. He gathered his parachute and set off downhill until the silhouette of a very large mansion confronted him. He knocked at the door to discover that he was at the baronial hall of the Marquis of Tweeddale who was entertaining the local Home Guard. Once he had established his identity, Hall was introduced to his lordship and invited to join the party where he passed a memorable evening. Michael Benn landed unhurt and found his way to a crofter's cottage where he enjoyed equally warm hospitality, but on a rather more modest scale. The irony was not lost on Hall, the twenty-year-old lad from Pudsey.

In due course, 141 Squadron moved to Tangmere for a short period before settling at nearby Ford airfield. Towards the end of 1942 the Allies landed near Algiers in North Africa to drive eastwards, and volunteers were called for to form a night-fighter Squadron in Algeria. Michael Benn volunteered, but Hall chose to remain with the Squadron and another navigator replaced him. Hall crewed up with a new pilot, Flying Officer Leslie Stephenson, and so one of the RAF's most successful night-fighter partnerships was formed, together with a lifetime friendship.

The Beaufighters of 141 Squadron were re-equipped with a new AI radar, the Mk VIII, at the end of 1942. This radar, operating with a 10 cm wavelength, was a great improvement on the Mark IV set; in particular, it had eliminated the 'ground clutter' problem. The di-pole aerials had disappeared and a rotating radar scanner had been introduced into the nose of the Beaufighter. The radar operator's display was a single cathode-ray tube and the range had been improved to 12 miles. Unfortunately, trade remained very slack with many of the *Luftwaffe* units having been withdrawn from northern France to the Eastern Front in Russia, and Hall had very few opportunities to note the benefits of the new radar.

In early 1943 the 1st Army in North Africa were involved in heavy fighting as the advance to Tunisia gathered momentum. The important resupply ports of Oran, Algiers and Bone were attracting increasing attention from the *Luftwaffe* bomber units, and this prompted the need to build up the strength of the night-fighter Squadrons in the region. Hall and his new pilot soon found themselves caught up in this activity and were posted to join 153 Squadron based near Algiers. They first went to the Bristol Aircraft Company at Filton to collect a new Beaufighter Mk VIF, EL 169, before taking it to Lyncham to prepare for a delivery flight to Algeria. Once ready, they flew to Portreath in Cornwall, the departure airfield to Gibraltar. On arrival, one engine had developed an oil leak, and on the subsequent air test following rectification, the aircraft hit a flock of seagulls on take-off, and the aircraft was badly damaged. It was another three weeks before the aircraft was serviceable, and Hall and Stephenson eventually set off southwards on 12 March. Stripped of armament to save weight, the Beaufighter flew at low level across the Bay of Biscay to avoid

A Beaufighter VIF taxis at a North African airfield. The aerials for the Mk IV air intercept radar are prominent on the nose and wings. (*IWM. CH 15213*)

the Junkers 88 fighters based in Brittany and near Bordeaux. After almost six hours' flying time, Hall and Stephenson arrived at the busy Gibraltar airfield, remaining for one night before heading for Setif in Algeria, then on to 153 Squadron's headquarters at Maison Blanche, a few miles to the east of Algiers and the former airport for the French colonial city.

As the 1st Army advanced eastwards through Algeria towards Tunisia, more ports became available for unloading supplies, but this created one disadvantage – the ports were in range of the *Luftwaffe* bomber units based in Sicily and Sardinia. As a result, enemy bomber activity increased, and the Beaufighters, which had recently been fitted with the AI Mk VII (similar to the Mk VIII radar), found more trade. Small landing strips were established along the coast east of Algiers at Djedjelli, Bone and Taher. They had very few facilities, but the rugged Beaufighter was happy to operate from these very basic and rough airfields, and 153 Squadron positioned two aircraft at each during the day ready for night operations. However, since the strips were not equipped with night landing aids, the fighters recovered to Maison Blanche once they had completed their patrol. A good GCI organisation, using mobile units, had been established and positioned near the important ports and, with the Beaufighter's AI Mk VII having a much better performance at low level than the old Mk IV sets, the Squadron's successes soon began to mount.

Hall's and Stephenson's first success came on 17 April when they took off at 1730 in EL 174 from Maison Blanche on a dusk sweep. They were soon vectored by 'Mumsie' control on to ten 'bandits' approaching Algiers from the east. Hall had just obtained a radar contact when the controller announced that they were friendly, and the attack was to be broken off. As the Beaufighter turned on to a westerly heading, Hall spotted ten aircraft in loose formation. Stephenson closed to formate on them in the dusk light when, suddenly, they saw the swastikas on the aircraft – they were Junkers 88s. As the enemy bombers scattered, control was informed as Stephenson attacked the lead aircraft, which dived away taking violent evasive action. Hall maintained radar contact until the aircraft was eventually re-sighted at sea level when Stephenson fired a few short bursts, setting the starboard engine on fire. He closed and continued firing as the port engine caught fire, and the enemy bomber dived into the sea. It was probably an aircraft of *III/KG 77*.

On 1 May two aircraft were tasked to maintain standby overnight with one crew to take off late at night and the other to do an early-morning patrol. Stephenson and Hall elected to fly the 0400 sortie since experience had shown that most activity occurred then. However, the night sortie was cancelled due to poor weather, so they 'pulled rank' on the junior crew, 'offered' them the early-morning sortie, and retired to the officers' mess. The next morning they asked the other crew if they had flown, and were astounded when Flight Sergeant A. Downing and his radar observer Sergeant J. Lyons reported that they had been scrambled, and had managed to shoot down no less than five Junkers 52 transport aircraft, which were trying to use the darkness to evacuate German troops from Tunisia. Downing had a reputation as a joker, so Hall and his pilot took some convincing until the telephone rang, and the Air Officer Commanding asked to speak to the crew 'who have just shot down the five German transports'. Both the NCOs were subsequently awarded the Distinguished Flying Medal for this unique engagement.

As the army advanced eastwards, greater use was made of the forward airstrips, and Stephenson and Hall moved forward on 11 May to Djdjelli, a strip to the east of the port of Bone. Once again they were flying EL 174 when they were scrambled at 1945 under 'Funless' control and told to vector on 060° to investigate multiple contacts. As the Beaufighter passed through 2,000 feet, twelve Junkers 88s were seen head on and Stephenson manoeuvred behind the formation allowing Hall to make contact on his radar. He directed his pilot on to one of the bombers until visual contact was made when Stephenson opened fire with a short burst from the cannons at a range of 300 yards. The enemy's starboard wing and engine caught fire, with bits breaking off and striking the windscreen of the Beaufighter. The Junkers dived into the sea enveloped in flames. As Stephenson pulled away from the scene, a second Junkers 88 was seen briefly before Hall gained radar contact. Stephenson closed to 700 yards when the enemy saw the Beaufighter and started violent evasive action as it fired at the night fighter. Both aircraft dived to very low level

Aircrew of 153 Squadron at Algiers. Hall is kneeling third from the right. (*Arthur Hall*)

over the sea and a chase using the radar developed before visual contact was regained. A two-second burst of cannon sent the bomber of *III/KG 76* crashing into the sea, where the crew were later rescued to become prisoners of war. After almost four hours, the Beaufighter recovered to Maison Blanche where Hall and Stephenson received a great reception from the ground crew and their fellow aircrew. It was the first time a 153 Squadron crew had destroyed two aircraft during one sortie.

On 13 May the last of the Axis forces surrendered in Tunisia, and the campaign in Africa came to an end. The Allies were now in a position to threaten 'the soft underbelly' of Europe, and the planning for the invasion of Sicily was already well advanced. Tunisia provided a springboard for such an operation, and the massive build-up of troops and stores presented attractive targets to the enemy bomber forces. The night-fighter force remained on high alert.

Stephenson and Hall flew V 8816 to the forward airfield at Taher on 24 May. Just after midnight they were scrambled by 'Funless' control to investigate two unidentified contacts approaching from the north-east. It was a very dark night and the Beaufighter – callsign Chevron 50 – was vectored towards the target until Hall gained a radar contact at 3,000 yards at 10,000 feet. He brought his pilot astern and slightly below the target, and Stephenson gained a visual contact at 500 yards when he called Hall forward so that both could positively identify the aircraft before it was engaged – it was a Junkers 88. A two-second burst of cannon fire sent the bomber diving to the sea, and it crashed just off the coast. Almost immediately, the GCI controller vectored the aircraft to another contact flying at low level. Hall gained radar contact and brought the 'bandit' into visual range when another Junkers 88 was identified. A two-second burst set the port engine on fire, and the aircraft crashed into the sea.

The night's work for the crew of Chevron 50 was still not complete. The aircraft climbed to continue the patrol at 3,000 feet when it was soon vectored to another contact. Hall gained a radar contact on an aircraft that was climbing steadily, and the Beaufighter crew followed at a distance of 3,500 yards. The enemy aircraft levelled at 10,000 feet allowing the Beaufighter to close to 500 yards where Stephenson gained a visual contact on another Junkers 88. Hall confirmed the identification just as the German started a bombing attack, and Stephenson fired immediately registering a number of hits. The enemy turned sharply, but there was no escape, and another two-second burst set the aircraft ablaze before it crashed into the sea 10 miles off the coast. Chevron 50 then set course for Maison Blanche and landed after being airborne for almost five hours.

News of the triple success was passed to the airfield and, despite the very early hours, there was great jubilation when Stephenson and Hall landed. The ground crew were particularly thrilled, being able to boast that 'we have now got six kills', and rightly so. Without their dedicated support and hard work, the aircrew would have achieved nothing.

With Tunisia clear of enemy ground forces, 153 Squadron were able to mount detachments from La Sebala airfield just north of Tunis. On 9 June, Stephenson and Hall were tasked to overfly the fortress island of Pantellaria to see if they attracted any gunfire in order to determine if the island was still occupied. They flew one sortie at 400 feet, and reported no activity. Control then tasked them to fly at 200 feet, and again they reported no activity. The following day, the army made an unopposed landing to occupy the island.

Ten days later, Stephenson and Hall were summoned to see the Squadron commander, who handed them a telegram from the Air Officer Commanding congratulating both on the immediate award of the Distinguished Flying Cross. These were the first awards to the Squadron for action in North Africa. The recommendation signed by Air Vice-Marshal H.P. Lloyd read:

Flying Officer Hall is the Radio Navigator flying with Flying Officer Stephenson who has destroyed six enemy aircraft at night. On the night of 23 May the skill displayed by this officer was outstanding and it was largely due to his efforts that the pilot was successful in destroying three enemy aircraft.

Flying Officer Hall, during his service with 153 Squadron, has distinguished himself by skilful and persistent work, not only in the air but on the ground also. His example has been a great encouragement to the whole Squadron. I strongly recommend this officer for the immediate award of the Distinguished Flying Cross.

After a night of celebration, the following day was almost their last. They flew EL 174 to Taher on detachment and were scrambled at dusk. They had just reached flying speed on the take-off run when the starboard engine exploded. Unable to climb the heavy Beaufighter away on one engine, Stephenson slammed the aircraft back on the runway. Ahead was a small wood, and the aircraft crashed through the trees at high speed shedding wings, the tail plane and most of the fuselage just a few feet behind Hall's cockpit. Both scrambled out and raced away from the burning trees and exploding ammunition, suffering only a few cuts and bruises. Seeing the wreckage later, they realised that they owed their lives to the Beaufighter being 'built like a tank' with the fuel contained in the wings rather than the fuselage.

The Allies landed in Sicily on 10 July 1943, and Hall and his colleagues of 153 Squadron provided cover for the convoys. A few weeks later, Stephenson and Hall completed their tour of duty in North Africa and returned for a 'rest' tour as instructors at an OTU. Hall was posted to 50 OTU at Winfield near Berwick-on-Tweed, a bleak satellite airfield of Charter Hall. He spent six months as senior navigation officer flying with pilots converting to the night-fighter role and to the Beaufighter. Like many seasoned operational aircrew, he found his 'rest' tour more dangerous and demanding than facing the enemy. After six months as an instructor, he was glad to learn that he was posted to Woodvale near Liverpool to join 219 Squadron equipped with the Mosquito NF XVII. The Squadron had recently returned from North Africa and was working-up with its new Mosquito aircraft, which were equipped with the improved AI Mk X. Hall's pleasure at returning to operations increased when he learned that he had been promoted to Flight Lieutenant and would be teaming up again with Leslie Stephenson.

As the pilots became acquainted with their new aircraft, the navigators spent a few hours airborne in a flying classroom Wellington X fitted with the new AI radar. By the end of March, the Squadron was declared operational and moved to Colerne near Bath where the expected increase in enemy activity failed to materialise. In readiness for the Normandy invasion, 219 Squadron moved in May to Bradwell Bay in Essex amid growing excitement at the prospect of returning to north-west Europe.

During the afternoon of 5 June, all the crews were called to the operations room where the CO informed them that D-Day had arrived, and the Squadron was tasked to operate behind the invasion coast to intercept any attempted attacks by the enemy against the invasion fleet and landing beaches. Hall and his pilot took off at 0200 on the morning of the landings and carried out an uneventful patrol 15 miles inland from the Normandy coast. More patrols were flown over the invasion area between Le Havre and Cherbourg throughout June and July before a new threat appeared in the form of the

A Mosquito NF XXX of 219 Squadron. (*via Andy Thomas*)

pilotless flying bomb – the V-1. Defence against this high-speed threat directed against London was based on a layered approach with zones allocated to fighter aircraft with others reserved exclusively for the anti-aircraft artillery. The Squadron accounted for sixteen 'doodlebugs', as they were known, with Stephenson and Hall claiming one. At the end of July, the Squadron started re-equipping with the bulbous-nosed Mosquito NF Mk XXX.

Numerous interceptions were made during early August, but they all proved to be friendly. However, the Hall crew's luck changed on the night of 15 August. Flying MM 688 from Hunsdon, they were patrolling south of Caen under 'Radox' control when they were told that there was 'trade' to the east. They were vectored to the contact at 8,000 feet, and Hall soon gained contact on his radar at 4 miles' range. Visual contact was gained at 700 yards, and Hall and Stephenson were able to positively identify a Junkers 188 as they closed to 250 yards. Dropping back, Stephenson fired his cannons from dead astern, which set the starboard engine on fire. A second burst, with one-ring deflection, set the whole aircraft on fire, and it dived steeply into the ground and exploded. The Junkers 188, which had only recently entered service, was a much-improved version of the Junkers 88.

Once the Allied armies began to advance from the Normandy bridgehead, the Squadron started to fly deeper into enemy territory, and it also attempted to intercept the *Luftwaffe* night fighters attacking RAF bombers returning from raids over Germany. It was in this latter role that Stephenson and Hall achieved their next success on the night of 12/13 September when Bomber Command launched two large raids against Frankfurt and Stuttgart.

The Air Intercept Radar Mk VIIIB with the vizor fitted, installed in front of the navigator's position in a Mosquito. (*IWM. CH 16607*)

They took off from Hunsdon at 2205 to patrol south of Brussels. Just before midnight, 'Milkway' control informed them of a 'bogey' 8 miles away and gave a heading to intercept. Hall gained radar contact at 5 miles on a target well above. Distance closed slowly as the contact was manoeuvring, suggesting that it was a night fighter seeking out the British bomber stream. At 300 yards, visual contact was made and Stephenson edged in to 50 yards almost directly below the target where the crew identified the aircraft as a Junkers 88. As normal, Hall used the Ross night vision glasses to confirm the sighting. The Mosquito dropped back dead astern before Stephenson opened fire from 200 yards, setting the starboard engine on fire. Two further bursts sent the enemy aircraft of *Stab II/NJG4* into a vertical dive, and it exploded as it hit the ground 10 miles from Erkelenz. The four-man crew baled out, but *Oberleutnant* Siegfried Kath died when his parachute failed to open.

The Squadron moved to the Continent in October 1944 to take up residence on the former *Luftwaffe* airfield at Amiens/Glissy. The settling-in period was marred by the loss of three aircraft soon after take off resulting in the deaths of six aircrew, including the Squadron Commander. The circumstances were a mystery until one night when Stephenson and Hall suffered a 'runaway' starboard engine just after taking off. The aircraft swung violently to port, and only the exceptional skill and experience of the pilot prevented a crash. The starboard engine was shut down and a single-engine landing was made. The engineers examined the failed engine and discovered that faulty fuel booster pumps had been fitted. The Squadron was grounded for a few days while the pumps on other aircraft were changed, after which there were no further problems.

The Allied armies advanced into Holland during September, and the Mosquitoes set up patrol lines deeper into Holland and western Germany. By early December, they were flying over Germany seeking out any hit-and-run aircraft attacking the forward troops. During the evening of 4 December, Stephenson and Hall were patrolling in MM 790 near Nijmegen at 8,000 feet when they picked up a target at 4 miles. 'Voicebox' control had no information and told the crew to follow and investigate. They closed to 700 yards suspecting a friendly aircraft, so they approached very low and at 300 yards obtained a visual contact. They identified a Messerschmitt Bf 110 carrying a long-range fuel tank, flying straight and level on an easterly heading. Closing to 100 yards, they gave it a one-second burst when the enemy aircraft burst into a huge sheet of flame and dived steeply into the ground where it exploded and burnt over a large area 10 miles north-west of the German town of Krefeld. No return fire was experienced – Stephenson had fired just forty-one rounds.

Arthur Hall and his pilot 'Steve' Stephenson, an outstanding night-fighter team. (*Arthur Hall*)

The Germans launched their Ardennes offensive on 16 December. Despite the poor weather conditions, the Squadron mounted an increasing number of patrols, and successes mounted. Stephenson and Hall were on standby on Christmas Eve when they were ordered to take off just after midnight to patrol south of Hasselt. After two hours, 'Rejoice' control directed them to investigate a contact thought to be friendly. They gained radar contact and closed up to visual range where they identified a Messerschmitt Bf 110. Following their standard tactics, they dropped behind and below, and shot the aircraft down as the rear gunner started to fire. Just fifty-two rounds had been fired from the Mosquito's four cannons. The crew landed at 0400 on Christmas morning having achieved their tenth and final victory.

During a spell of leave in England in preparation for an Investiture at Buckingham Palace, where they were each to receive their Distinguished Flying Cross, both Hall and his pilot received telegrams informing them that they had been awarded a Bar to their earlier gallantry medal. A few days later, with their families in attendance, each received their two awards from His Majesty The King. As so often in war, sadness was never far away, and a few days later, Arthur Hall learnt with great regret that his former pilot, Michael Benn DFC, whom he had flown with for fifteen months, had been killed in a flying accident.

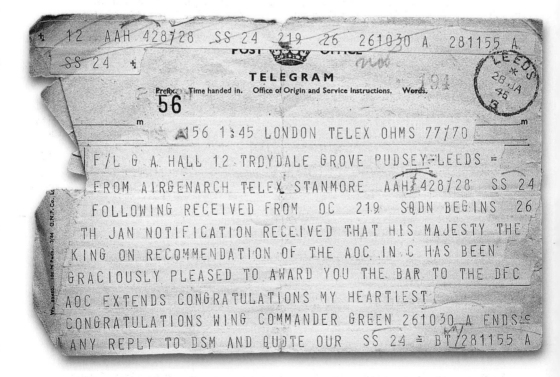

The telegram informing Arthur Hall that he has been awarded a Bar to his DFC. (*Arthur Hall*)

<u>SECRET</u>.   FORM 'F' PILOTS' PERSONAL COMBAT REPORT.   SERIAL NO. 219/7

From: No. 219 Squadron (149 Wing), AMIENS/GLISY.

To: H.Q. 2nd TAF.(2). H.Q. No. 85 Group (2); H.Q. 25 Sector, H.Q. 24 Sector.

<u>STATISTICAL</u>.
Date.   (A) 24/25th December, 1944.
Unit.   (B) 219 Squadron.
Type and Mark of A/C.   (C) Mosquito XXX A.I. Mark X.
Time attack was delivered.   (D) 02.45 hrs.
Place of attack.   (E) F.0567 (near Hasselsweiler)
Weather.   (F) $\frac{3}{4}$ moon, no cloud, good vis.
Our casualties a/c.   (G) Nil.
    "   "   personnel.   (H) Nil.
Enemy casualties in air combat.   (I) Me.110 destroyed.
    "   "   ground or sea combat (J) Nil.

<u>F/LT. L. STEPHENSON, D.F.C. (PILOT)</u>.   <u>F/LT. G. A. HALL, D.F.C. (NAVIGATOR)</u>
Dickens 17

        They were airborne at 00.50 hrs. from Amiens/Glisy and were taken
under Rejoice control where they patrolled north and south 30 miles east of
Hasselt. F/Lt. Stephenson continues:-

        "About 02.30 hrs. we were informed by control that there was an
aircraft, probably friendly, 20 miles south east of us at 6,000 feet. We were
given vector in that direction and lost height from 10,000 feet to 4,000 feet
and increased speed. At about 6 miles range we were informed that the bogey
had been proved friendly and so we prepared to turn back. A minute later the
controller decided that we should investigate after all. We turned back on a
vector of 100° and after a few minutes of well controlled interception we
obtained contact 4 miles range, slightly above, moving port to starboard.
Our height was then 3,500 feet. Target did a few gentle turns but no real
evasive action. Range was rapidly closed to 2000 ft. when a visual was obtained
on a twin-engined aircraft well above flying straight and level at about 235 m.p.h.
Our speed during the interception was 280 m.p.h. Closed right in below and in the
moonlight it was easily identified as an Me.110 with long range tanks. Dropped
back to 750 ft. and gave a two second burst from dead astern, height 4,000 ft.
It immediately caught fire and dived steeply down hitting the ground with a
large explosion. Just as it was in its steep dive the rear gun began firing
vertically white tracer into the air.   Time of combat 02.45 hrs., position
as given by control F.0567.
        I claim this Me.110 as destroyed."
        They resumed patrol and landed back at base at 04.00 hrs.

Cine-camera automatically exposed.
Ammunition expended - P.O.12; P.I.13; S.I.14; S.O. 13   Total 52 rds.

PILOT...F/Lt.   NAVIGATOR ....F/Lt.
        SQUADRON INTELLIGENCE OFFICER.................F/O.

Stephenson and Hall's combat report for a successful engagement on the night of 24/25
December 1944. (*Arthur Hall*)

The recommendation for the Bar to the Distinguished Flying Cross for Arthur Hall read:

> Since the award of the D.F.C., this officer has been responsible for the destruction of 3 enemy aircraft at night, and has completed 160 hours operational night flying over the Normandy beachhead, and later over the Dutch and German battle areas.
>
> F/L Hall has been responsible for a total of 9 enemy aircraft, including 3 in one night. He is a very competent Navigator(R) and the close teamwork he and his pilot have shown, has resulted in success.

The Squadron moved from Amiens to Gilze-Rijen airfield in Holland in early February. On the same night, Stephenson and Hall were patrolling in MM 702 near the front line west of the River Rhine when they gained radar contact at 10-mile range on a very slow-flying aircraft, and they soon started to overtake. Stephenson reduced the speed to such an extent that he had to lower the flaps, and eventually the undercarriage, in order not to overshoot the target. Once visual, they saw a twin-engine, twin-boom aircraft similar to the American P-38 Lightning. They looked from all angles but could not positively identify the aircraft, so decided not to engage. On landing, they discussed the encounter with the Intelligence Officer in detail. An inspection of the aircraft recognition documents identified the aircraft as a Focke-Wulf 189, a reconnaissance aircraft that had just appeared in the combat area for the first time. It had been a very fortunate night for an unsuspecting *Luftwaffe* crew.

By March, there was less and less trade for the night fighters, and they were regularly tasked to fly intruder sorties against the *Luftwaffe* airfields in Germany. The Squadron's last wartime victory was claimed on the night of 9/10 April when Flying Officers Ron Young and Guy Fazan shot down a Heinkel 177. Tragically, an Allied fighter shot down this crew nine days later and the pilot was killed. Guy Fazan walked back to the Squadron a few days later.

The European war ended with the Squadron based at Twente on the Dutch/German border where it continued to operate until the end of the war in the Far East. Stephenson and Hall remained with the Squadron after it returned to the United Kingdom, and Arthur Hall flew his last sortie in a Mosquito on 21 May 1946 from Acklington. He hardly ever flew again!

Few RAF crews achieved ten victories at night, and even fewer scored three in one night. Unlike *Luftwaffe* night-fighter crews who attacked bomber streams made up of many hundreds of aircraft almost every night, RAF crews faced very few targets by comparison. Together with his pilot Leslie 'Steve' Stephenson, Arthur Hall formed one of the RAF's outstanding night-fighter crews of the Second World War.

Chapter Seventeen

Halton 'Brat' at Sea – Arthur Brett

In the immediate aftermath of the First World War, when the RAF was fighting for its very existence, the then Chief of the Air Staff, Air Marshal Sir Hugh Trenchard, established the training organisations that would serve as the bedrock of the RAF for decades. Among these was 1 School of Technical Training (Boys) formed on 23 December 1919 on the former estate of the late Baron Rothschild at Halton Park. The first Aircraft Apprentices arrived in January 1922 to start their three-year engineering course. Enlisting as a Boy in No 9 Entry on 24 January 1924 was fifteen-year-old, Ramsgate-born Arthur Brett. He qualified as a Fitter Aero Engines in January 1927 when he passed out in the rank of Aircraftman Second Class (AC2).

Brett was almost certainly pleased when he joined II (Army Co-operation) Squadron based at Manston on 16 January, just a few miles from his home. However, this was short lived since the Squadron received orders on 8 April to 'proceed to China', about as far away from Ramsgate as was possible. Trouble had been simmering for a number of years in China when, in 1927, the situation around the International Settlement of Shanghai became very dangerous, and the city was threatened with invasion and occupation by Cantonese Chinese revolutionaries. The British government decided that a show of force was required, and a tri-Service 'Shanghai Defence Force' left for China in January. The air element was to be reinforced by 2 Squadron, which was given two weeks to prepare before embarking on HMT *Neuralia* at Southampton.

The Squadron was equipped with the Bristol F.2B Fighter powered by a Rolls-Royce Falcon III engine. Five aircraft had to be dismantled and crated ready for shipment to China. With such short notice, Brett and his colleagues would undoubtedly have been very busy trying to make the very short deadline to be ready to sail on 27 April. Having left the ordered routine of Halton only three months earlier, it was a stark reminder to the eighteen-year-old Brett that he was now part of a man's Air Force. After a long voyage, the Squadron finally disembarked and set up a base on the Shanghai Racecourse on 30 May. The aircraft were reassembled, test flown and were ready for operations by the middle of June when a number of photographic sorties were flown over the Squadron's area of operations. The Squadron continued operations until it was relieved on 6 September by a detachment of Fairey IIIDs from HMS *Hermes*. The II Squadron aircraft and personnel returned to England on HMS *Argus* and were re-established back at Manston by the end of October.

Life on an Army Co-operation Squadron followed a routine pattern with regular deployments to support exercises on Salisbury Plain, including the annual autumn manoeuvres when the Squadron operated from Advanced Landing Grounds. There was also an annual Armament Practice Camp (APC) at North Coates or Full Sutton when the crews participated in a concentrated training period of bombing and air gunnery on the Lincolnshire coastal weapons ranges. The ground crew would certainly have been kept very busy with so many detachments away from the parent station.

The Armstrong Whitworth Atlas started to re-equip the Squadron in 1929. Powered by the Armstrong Siddeley Jaguar engine, this would have presented a new challenge to Brett. A year later he was promoted to Aircraftman First Class (AC 1), almost four years after passing out from Halton – rather slow progress for an ex-Boy. In April 1931, he finally left II Squadron to join 40 Squadron that was re-forming at Upper Heyford, and was the first Squadron to be equipped with the Fairey Gordon.

As soon as he arrived on his new Squadron, Brett volunteered for 'aerial gunner' duties. In 1931, almost all aerial gunners were part time and continued to practise their basic trade. Brett took off for his first flight on

During his time on 40 Squadron, Brett flew many hours in this Fairy Gordon, K 1740, before it was transferred to MAEE at Felixstowe for float trials. (*P.H.T. Green Collection*)

1 May when he flew with Flying Officer Dawson in K 1742. His first attempt at aerial gunnery took place a month later, but most of his early flights were map-reading exercises and rear camera gun firing. His part-time flying duties attracted an additional one-shilling per day 'crew pay'. Although he flew one sortie on most days, he still had to combine this activity with his primary duties as an engine fitter. During his first year of flying Brett flew a wide variety of sorties including bombing, air gunnery, photography, map-reading and others. In effect, he was acting as the observer, an aircrew category that had ceased to exist at that particular time. During the first year he amassed a total of 160 flying hours, a considerable effort for a 'part-time' aircrew.

On 14 June Brett attended a formal air gunner's course at the Armament and Gunnery School at Eastchurch. On successful completion, he was re-mustered as a Fitter (AE)/Air Gunner, entitled to draw air gunner's pay, and to wear the distinctive air gunner's badge, a gilded winged bullet worn on the upper right sleeve of his uniform. His return from the course also coincided with the Squadron's departure to 1 Armament Practice Camp at Catfoss on the East Yorkshire coast.

The annual Armament Camp gave the pilots and their gunners a concentrated period of training devoted exclusively to gunnery and bombing. The Gordon was equipped with a foreward-firing Vickers 0.303 ins, air-cooled Mk II gun mounted on the port side of the cockpit. A Mk III Lewis gun was mounted in the rear cockpit. The aircraft could carry a mix of bombs on universal carriers mounted under the lower wings. The standard loads were two 250-lb bombs or four 112-lb bombs or sixteen 20-lb bombs. The release of the bombs could be controlled from either cockpit with the rear seat occupant lying in a prone position using a Mk VI bombsight. During the detachment, crews flew two or three times each day using the local Skipsea weapons ranges.

The Squadron returned to the newly constructed airfield at Abingdon where the facilities were some of the most modern in the RAF. Routine training continued with an emphasis on cross-country flying, long-distance reconnaissance flights, photography and camera gun exercises. Brett and his air gunner colleagues also used the wireless for air-to-ground communications and were, in effect, fulfilling the normal role of an observer. This was all in addition to continuing with their respective ground trades. They were probably the busiest members of the Squadron, yet many still held the lowly rank of AC 1. They certainly earned their modest flying pay.

In July 1934, Brett came to the end of his three-year period of flying as an air gunner, and reverted to his ground trade of Fitter (Aero-engines). His final sorties were part of a major exercise organised by Headquarters Air Defence of Great Britain (later known as Fighter Command) to test the country's air defence system. On 25 July he flew with Pilot Officer Mills in K 1748 for his final sortie when they 'attacked' the West India Docks from 12,000 feet.

With the introduction of the RAF's Expansion Scheme F, new Squadrons were formed by detaching Flights from existing units. After completing a course on the Kestrel engine, Brett moved with 'C' Flight to form 104 Squadron, which was equipped with the Hind, and he resumed his 'part-time' air gunner duties flying in K 4646 with the Squadron Commander, Squadron Leader Hewitt, on 16 June 1936. Within six weeks, he was posted to 209 Squadron equipped with Singapore flying boats and based at Felixstowe. During his time with 40 and 104 Squadrons, he had amassed almost 500 hours' flying time.

With the added complexity of the new generation of bombers, non-pilot aircrew training was reorganised and the full-time 'observer' was reinstated. The use of ground tradesmen as air gunners was steadily phased out, and the advances in wireless made it necessary for new air gunners to be proficient in its use, and tradesmen from the wireless specialisation provided the majority of recruits to the new, full-time wireless operators (aircrew). It was the advent of the wireless operator/air gunner, or WPO/AG as they became universally known. The special needs and peculiarities of flying-boat operations meant that fitters and riggers would continue

Brett was a member of the crew of this Short Singapore III of 209 Squadron during a detachment to the Mediterranean in October 1937. The aircraft is being lifted on to the slipway at Arzew in Algeria. (*P.H.T. Green Collection*)

to be employed on flying duties, and they doubled up as air gunners. Brett fitted into this latter category and, with his experience of the Kestrel engine, he was a natural choice to transfer to 209 Squadron equipped with the Kestrel-powered Short Singapore III.

The Singapore III, powered by four engines in a twin-tandem configuration, was the mainstay of the RAF's flying boat Squadrons leading up to the Second World War, and was the last in a long line of Short biplane flying boats. Brett was assigned to K 6914 as a fitter, and he spent most of his time with this particular aircraft, afloat, ashore and in the air.

During April 1937, his logbook contains eight entries 'Co-op with Bawdsey'. These three-hour flights were flown at various heights between 1,000 and 12,000 feet. Clearly, they were part of the trials conducted by the Bawdsey Research Station, which had been established the previous year to conduct trials for the new invention, Radio Detection and Direction Finding (RDF), later known as Radar. Further flights followed later in the year.

As the Spanish Civil War progressed, the British and French governments became increasingly concerned about the possibility of submarine attack during the attempted blockade of Spanish Mediterranean ports by Fascist forces supported by Italy. No 209 Squadron deployed five flying boats to the area to support an Anglo-French naval force. Brett was assigned to Squadron Leader P. Slocombe's aircraft, K 8567, and they departed for Malta on 17 September. On arrival, two anti-submarine patrols were flown before the aircraft flew to Arzew in Algeria to continue operations. During October, Brett flew on eight more seven-hour patrols before the aircraft moved on to Gibraltar to exercise with the Royal Navy. The detachment returned in December.

On 24 May 1938, Brett flew with a newly arrived pilot, Pilot Officer D. Spotswood (later Marshal of the RAF Sir Denis Spotswood and Chief of the Air Staff). They were to fly together on numerous occasions in the future, including the delivery of a Sunderland to Singapore. In June the first of the new Sunderlands were delivered to the RAF at Pembroke Dock. The first Squadron to be equipped with the new flying boat was 230 Squadron based at Seletar in Singapore, and a number of crews from 209 Squadron were allocated for the delivery task, including Brett. After a month converting to the aircraft, a final engine air test and a wireless test were carried out on L 2164. At 0435 on 5 August Flying Officer Gates and Pilot Officer Spotswood lifted the Sunderland off the water on the first leg to Singapore. The route took them via Malta, Alexandria, Habbaniya, Bahrain, Karachi, Calcutta, Rangoon, arriving at Seletar on 16 August after fifty-nine hours' flying time. In addition to monitoring the engines and being available for any aircraft in-flight rectification, Brett was part of the travelling ground crew responsible for mooring and servicing at the various staging posts en route.

After a ten-day rest at Seletar, the crew were given the task of delivering a Singapore III (K 6912) to Basra. They took off on 29 August, but it was to take them four weeks to get the flying boat to its destination. The aircraft suffered numerous engine problems and Brett was kept very busy servicing the engines and rectifying the many unserviceabilites suffered. The crew were stuck in Calcutta for fourteen days waiting for propeller spares, and a broken con-rod in the starboard rear engine delayed them in Karachi for another week. No doubt they were pleased to finally arrive at Basra on 29 October, and deliver the aircraft to the permanent staff at the Iraqi flying boat station.

By the time Brett and his colleagues had arrived back in England, the Squadron had moved to Calshot, and conversion to the Stranraer started early in 1939. Shortly after the war started in September 1939, the Squadron took delivery of the twin-engine Lerwick. By then, Brett had completed over three years on 'part-time' flying duties, and had accumulated almost 700 hours flying time during his tour of duty. He was promoted to Corporal and reverted to ground duties. He finally left the Squadron in November 1940, and was posted to Bermuda to join the Atlantic Ferry organisation, and was promoted to Sergeant.

During his twelve months on ferrying duties, Brett was assigned to the Catalina, and he flew on numerous air tests and crew familiarisation sorties. He completed his first Atlantic ferry flight on 4/5 March 1941, when he delivered AH 531 to Mountbatten, the Flight taking 24 hours 50 minutes. The following day the delivery to Greenock was completed. He flew on further delivery flights, making his last one on 10 June when he flew direct to Greenock in just over twenty-one hours. It was his final

The officers and ratings of 1771 Squadron at Machrahanish in September 1944. The CO gave Brett, the only member of the RAF on the Squadron, the honour of sitting in the centre of the front row. (*D. Manley*)

flight in the RAF as a member of the aircrew. In November he returned to England and to Lyneham to service the Liberators used to return ferry crews to Canada and Bermuda. Three months later he was promoted to Flight Sergeant. It had taken him thirteen years to advance to Leading Aircraftman, but just a further three to Flight Scrgeant. The exigencies of war no doubt!

Brett was seconded to the Fleet Air Arm in June 1943, remaining with the Senior Service until the end of the war in the Pacific. After a spell with 757 Squadron, the Naval Air Fighting Development Unit, equipped with the Hellcat, Corsair and Firefly, he moved to Yeovilton to join the newly formed 1771 Squadron as the senior engineering rate. So began a long association with the Squadron and the Firefly. Brett was the only member of the RAF serving with the naval Squadron, and he was responsible for the first-line engineering of the Squadron's fifteen Firefly FR 1 aircraft. In March 1944, the Squadron moved to RNAS Burscough (HMS *Ringtail*) near Ormskirk in Lancashire for intensive work-up training before embarking on the new aircraft carrier, HMS *Implacable*. This period included deck-landing practice on HMS *Trumpeter* operating in the Irish Sea. By late September the Squadron was ready to embark on its parent carrier.

HMS *Implacable* had been launched on 10 December 1942, but was not ready to embark its Squadrons for a working-up period in the Clyde until September 1944. Two torpedo-bomber-reconnaissance Barracuda Squadrons (828 and 841) embarked, with 1771 Squadron joining on 22 Scptcmber to provide a fighter reconnaissance and ground attack capability. The carrier completed her work-up at Scapa Flow and sailed on 16 October for its first operation – to find the German battleship *Tirpitz*. A pair of Fireflies, led by the Commanding Officer, Lieutenant Commander Ellis, located the battleship at anchor off Haakoy Island near Tromso. They remained outside the range of the ship's anti-aircraft guns, took photographs and reported its position. Other Squadron aircraft attacked a convoy, and, in a further strike later in the day, strafed aircraft on the airfield at Bardufoss. Later in the month, six offensive operations were launched against Rørvick, Bod and Lodinge, when the Fireflies were

Sergeant Arthur Brett of 1771 Naval Squadron. (*D. Manley*)

busy attacking flak ships and gun positions, with their four 20mm Hispano cannons, in support of the Barracuda Squadrons. It was during this period that the Squadron suffered its first losses when two aircraft failed to return.

In early November *Implacable* sailed again for Norwegian waters to provide cover to a surface striking force and escort carriers undertaking mining operations off the Norwegian coast. On 27 November, the carrier launched its own offensive sorties, and the Fireflies were regularly tasked with 'armed reconnaissance' sorties. In company with ten Barracudas, eleven aircraft attacked a convoy off Alster Island, sinking two ships and damaging four others. The Fireflies used cannons to suppress the light flak as the Barracudas torpedoed and bombed the major units. A full gale developed the following day, and Brett and his colleagues were busy securing aircraft on the deck in foul conditions, while maintenance on the unserviceable aircraft was carried out in the hangars below. Such conditions provided the hard-working maintenance ratings with some of their most difficult, and dangerous, times. The gale was so severe that *Implacable* suffered extensive damage to the hull and the undersides of the Flight deck extensions. She returned to Scapa for some emergency repairs before sailing again on 7 December to escort carrier minelaying operations. The following day, Fireflies attacked shipping in the Haugesund area, their last operation in European waters.

HMS *Implacable* off Japan in August 1945. (*D. Manley*)

HMS *Implacable* returned to Scapa for more extensive repairs, and 1771 Squadron disembarked to Hatston in the Orkneys. The carrier was out of commission for almost three months, and 1771 Squadron spent most of the time at airfields near the Clyde conducting a concentrated period of training with rockets on the weapons ranges near Ayr. On 7 March 1945 the training was interrupted when the CO, Lieutenant Commander Ellis, hit the stern of HMS *Pretoria Castle* during deck landing practice, and his aircraft crashed into the sea. Squadron aircraft searched for him for twenty-four hours, but to no avail.

With no fewer than eighty-one aircraft on board, *Implacable* sailed from Scapa for the Far East on 16 March. Short periods of flying took place off North Africa and Aden before the carrier arrived at Ceylon, where a more concentrated period of work-up training was possible. It was at this time that aircraft servicing arrangements were changed to a centralised system, and the Squadrons effectively lost their own maintenance ratings. Brett still had the distinction of being the only member of the RAF on board, and he became a key member of the deck engineering team supervising preparations for the launch and recovery of aircraft. A fundamental piece of equipment on the deck of wartime carriers was the safety barrier. With a straight deck, any aircraft missing one of the arrestor wires was brought to a halt by the barrier before it could plough into the deck park in the bow where other aircraft were parked. Some of the common reasons leading to a barrier engagement were aircraft returning damaged by enemy fire, the carrier's deck pitching, aircraft hook bouncing on contact with the deck, undercarriage failures and pilot misjudgement. The barrier was in frequent use, and aircraft were often damaged as a result, and on numerous occasions, the 'wreck' had to be rapidly 'committed to the deep' in order to clear the deck quickly for those aircraft that had still to land on. During the next few months, Brett and his colleagues who controlled the aircraft movements on deck were very busy.

The carrier spent two weeks working-up in Ceylon waters in April, and arrived at Sydney in mid-May. The other carriers in the British Pacific Fleet (Task Force 37) were operating in support of the Okinawa campaign, but *Implacable* proceeded to Manus in the Admiralty Islands north of Papua North Guinea to complete a final work-up. As the carrier headed for action off Japan, the Fireflies of 1771 Squadron and Avengers of 828 Squadron carried out attacks against the remnants of the Japanese Army holding out on the island of Truk in the Western Carolinas. By the end of the month, the carriers *Victorious* and *Formidable* had joined the Task Force, which rendezvoused with the US Task Force 38 on 16 July off the east coast of Honshu, Japan. This brought to sixteen the number of US and British aircraft carriers in the Force, and their task was to destroy the Japanese Air Force in a series of coordinated attacks prior to any invasion.

The following day Brett and his flight deck parties had a very early start when they ranged the aircraft on deck at 0200 in preparation for the first

A Firefly FR I of 1771 Squadron comes to grief landing on HMS *Implacable*. (*D. Manley*)

British attacks on mainland Japan. Eight Fireflies, armed with eight 60-lb rockets each, took off at 0345 to attack radar sites and airfields at Sendai and Matsushima, returning after a flight of three hours. The morning of 18 July followed a similar pattern with the Fireflies of 1771 Squadron attacking Koniocki airfield on Honshu. Lieutenants Catterall and Manley were flying DV 131 when its hook broke as they landed on the carrier's deck. The aircraft crashed into the barrier and was badly damaged. It could not be cleared quickly, and with other aircraft running low on fuel and waiting to land on, the aircraft had to be pushed over the side. It was bad weather that next interfered with flying, and the ship was unable to launch any aircraft over the next few days.

Flying resumed by the end of the month when shipping, airfields and railway installations were attacked by the Fireflies and Avengers, escorted by Seafires of 801 and 880 Squadrons. Whenever the weather allowed, the Squadrons flew at maximum intensity with just under 1,000 sorties flown on the eight days when flying was possible. By early August the Japanese had still not agreed to terms of surrender drawn up at the recent Potsdam conference, and it was decided to drop the first atom bomb. Weather delayed the attack, but on 6 August the first bomb was dropped on Hiroshima. This did not provoke a Japanese response, so the carriers continued to mount attacks against shipping and railways. On 9 August *Implacable* launched her attack Squadrons against targets on the Japanese mainland with 1771 Squadron strafing Matsushima airfield. Later that day, the second atomic bomb was dropped and the city of Nagasaki was destroyed.

Seafires of 801 Squadron provide an escort for two Fireflies of 1771 Squadron operating off Japan.
(*D. Manley*)

Early on the morning of 10 August Brett and his team of maintenance ratings prepared the aircraft for another strike sortie, and Fireflies took off at 0820 to carry out a sweep of the airfields and railway system in central Honshu. Four hours later, they landed back on board at the end of their final war sortie. That evening, Emperor Hirohito decreed that the Potsdam Proclamation should be accepted, but it was another five days before the war with Japan was officially ended. In the meantime, *Implacable* had sailed for Sydney where all the aircraft were disembarked in order to prepare the carrier for the recovery and repatriation of Allied prisoners of war and internees.

Although aircraft engineering servicing had been centralised on *Implacable*, Brett remained very much part of 1771 Squadron, so disembarked with them to Nowra near Sydney, remaining as the senior engineering rating until the Squadron disbanded on 16 October 1945. On return to England, Brett was able to secure a posting near his home in Ramsgate when he was appointed to 567 Squadron, an anti-aircraft cooperation Squadron equipped with Spitfire XVIs and Vengeance IV aircraft. In the meantime, it had been announced that Flight Sergeant Arthur Brett had been awarded a Mention in Despatches for his service on 1771 Squadron, almost certainly for his work during the Squadron's operations off Norway.

On the disbandment of 567 Squadron in June 1946, Brett was posted to Palestine for aircraft engineering duties. On 11 June 1946, he learnt that he had been awarded the Distinguished Service Medal, 'for distinguished service during the war in the Far East'. This prestigious naval decoration was rarely awarded to Royal Air Force personnel (twenty-three in the Second World War), and it indicates the very high regard that the Royal Navy had for him and his two years' service. No doubt, he was very disappointed when the medal arrived in the post! His Royal Navy Commanding Officer remembers that 'it was an unusual distinction for an RAF Flight Sergeant to be the Senior Rate on a Squadron, but his seniority and experience gave him a special "kudos" on board. He was an excellent fellow.'

Brett retired from the RAF in January 1949 after twenty-five years' service. Despite having over 1,200 hours flying as aircrew, when he acted as air gunner, bomb aimer, wireless operator, flight engineer and occasional observer, he was never entitled to wear an aircrew brevet since he ceased to be employed on flying duties just before the introduction of the single-wing 'AG' badge.

Chapter Eighteen

Photographic Reconnaissance Navigator – Frank Baylis

Lancashire-born Frank Baylis started his wartime service at the age of sixteen years when he joined his father's Home Guard Battalion in Blackpool. As soon as he was eighteen he volunteered for aircrew service in the RAF and was accepted for navigator training, but he had to wait until March 1942 until he was called up. During his Home Guard service he had been a member of the Signals Platoon, and during the navigator aptitude test he passed the Morse exam with ease so was earmarked to be a navigator/wireless operator. After attending the Initial Training Wing at Babbacombe, he completed his wireless course at RAF Cranwell, flying in Dominie and Proctor aircraft, and qualified as a wireless operator. Navigation training followed at 31 Air Navigation School at Port Albert, Ontario, and Baylis was awarded his navigator's brevet and sergeant's chevrons on 9 June 1943. This was followed by a General Reconnaissance course at Charlottetown. On the flying training exercises, the Anson aircraft was loaded with a sea mine in case a submarine was located during one of the training sorties.

On return to England, Frank Baylis was sent to 3 General Reconnaissance School at Squires Gate where the Canadian-trained navigators were introduced to flying under wartime conditions, and where they also received instruction on the new Marconi 1154/55 radio sets. The course was geared to the two-seat maritime role but, on completion of the course, Frank Baylis was posted to RAF Dyce near Aberdeen to convert to the photographic reconnaissance (PR) role at 8 (OTU).

At the outset of the war in 1939, the embryonic PR organisation was very much a law unto itself under its unconventional, but brilliant, chief, Sidney Cotton. However, by mid-1940 it was placed under the command of Wing Commander Geoffrey Tuttle, and came under the control of Coastal Command. At that stage of the war, this was an appropriate arrangement but, as the Allied bombing campaign developed, the Commander-in-Chief of Bomber Command, Air Marshal Harris, made strenuous attempts to gain control of the strategic reconnaissance units, but they were to remain under the control of Coastal Command for the duration of the war.

Frank Baylis crewed up with an experienced pilot, Flying Officer Joe Morgan, who had already completed an operational tour on Beauforts, and been a staff pilot flying the Botha. They flew together for the first time on 10 November 1943 when they had a local flight in one of the early Mosquito IV aircraft (W 4066). This was followed by a number of cross-country flights at high level when the main method of navigation was map-reading using a topographical map. It was during one of these flights that Baylis first came across the 'jet stream', although he did not realise it at the time. On a navigation cross-country exercise he turned over Oban to head for the next turning point at Shrewsbury, which was estimated to take fifty-four minutes. Flying over a complete cloud cover the crew were approaching the time to turn when they caught a glimpse of a coastline – a major surprise. A further glimpse gave Baylis a fix over Portland Bill! They had travelled over 100 miles further than expected, and the long flight back to Dyce confirmed that they were flying into a wind with a strength far in excess of the forecast. Little was known of the phenomenon in those early days, but the Mosquito's ability to fly at heights in excess of 30,000 feet meant that they were some of the first aircraft to confront the jet stream problem.

Much of the PR conversion course was devoted to learning high-level photographic techniques with the F 52 cameras mounted vertically as a split pair. Lenses of varying focal length could be fitted depending on the scale of the photograph required. The navigator lay in the nose of the aircraft and used three parallel white lines marked on the optical flat in the nose of the aircraft for sighting. Crew cooperation was essential since photographs were taken at short time intervals based on the height of the aircraft, its ground speed and the type of lens fitted to the camera. Any alterations to the aircraft's heading to maintain the target tracking had to be completed between photographs so that the aircraft was not banking or skidding during the exposure of the film. Pilot errors often resulted in gaps in the photographic coverage. It was also important for the navigator to calculate the correct time intervals between exposures, otherwise the necessary overlap between successive photographs would be insufficient to provide stereoscopic cover – a crucial requirement for the photographic interpreters who had to make precise measurements for their detailed reports. After completing the fifty hours of flying, Frank Baylis and his pilot joined 544 Squadron in January 1944 when the Squadron was equipped with Mosquito PR IX aircraft, one of two Mosquito PR Squadrons based at Benson, the home of the RAF's PR force.

At the time that Frank Baylis and his pilot joined 544 Squadron, the PR Squadrons were heavily involved in obtaining photographs in support of the planned invasion of France, and in constantly monitoring the V-1 rocket launching sites located in northern France. Other sorties continued to be flown in support of the strategic bombing campaign, and a constant watch of the Baltic ports was maintained. Benson's two Mosquito Squadrons covered the whole of Europe with one Squadron concentrating on Germany, and the other on targets in France in Italy. After a month, the squadrons changed allowing the crews to maintain their knowledge of each area. A small detachment was maintained at Leuchars to concentrate on targets in Norway and the Baltic.

The routine of a PR Squadron was very different from other Squadrons. Crew names were kept on a 'ladder' maintained in the operations room, and all the crews gathered after breakfast and were briefed on the weather. The target list was checked and, where the weather was suitable for photography, crews at the top of the 'ladder' were allocated to sorties, and the intelligence officer briefed each individual crew. They then prepared their own routes and flight plan, taking off once the aircraft was ready. On return, the camera magazines were downloaded, sent for processing and interpretation, and the crew name was placed at the bottom of the 'ladder'. The crew had an initial debrief with the Squadron intelligence officer and, on completion, he issued them with an 'egg chit' for an operational meal! Once the photographs had been plotted on a map, a copy was sent to the Squadron, and the crew were debriefed in more detail when results and techniques could be assessed.

Baylis and his pilot flew their first operation on 30 January 1944 when they took MM 231 to photograph targets in central France. Flying above 30,000 feet, but below the condensation trail (contrail) level that would give away the aircraft's position and route, they took photographs of six targets in the Lyons area. Their second operation a few days later almost ended in disaster. Joe Morgan had levelled the aircraft at height over the English Channel and was checking to see if the aircraft was making a contrail, when he announced that he was not feeling well. Shortly afterwards he slumped over the controls and fainted. Baylis turned up the oxygen supply to full, leaned over to grab the flying controls in an attempt to descend the aircraft when he noticed that the pilot's oxygen tube had become disconnected from his face mask. As soon as this was reconnected, the pilot regained consciousness, and the crew were able to divert to Manston where the pilot made a quick recovery. Two days later they flew the sortie again, and successfully photographed targets in southern Germany and eastern France. Over Regensburg they met the USAAF bombers of the XVth Air Force flying out of Italian airfields and this, of course, had stirred up the enemy defences. The box barrage of the flak was awesome, but a timely reminder of the dangers to any aircraft that loitered near a heavily defended target.

Although the Mosquito was a fast aircraft capable of flying at very high level, the PR aircraft were unarmed and only flew in good weather in daylight, ideal conditions for an enemy fighter attack. It was essential, therefore, for the crew to keep a good lookout with the navigator covering the rear section with the pilot flying S-turns every two or three minutes to clear the tail. However, the aircraft was most vulnerable when it was on a photographic run maintaining a constant heading. When the target was a coastline or a stretch of railway, the same heading had to be maintained for long periods, and the pilot in particular, had to maintain a very close

A 544 Squadron Mosquito PR XVI with the D-Day invasion identification stripes. The various camera positions in the belly of the aircraft are clearly visible. (*IWM. CH 14264*)

lookout for enemy fighters as the navigator in the nose was pre-occupied with taking the photographs.

During March and April, Baylis and his pilot were detached to Leuchars when they flew eight operations to Norway and Denmark. In addition to the U-boat bases at Trondheim and Bergen, the German Navy used the ports and deep Norwegian fjords regularly, and these were kept under constant surveillance in order to track shipping and monitor the development of facilities and capabilities. Airfields in both countries were in constant use by the *Luftwaffe*, and these too were photographed on a regular basis. In compiling intelligence reports from photographs, one of the most important features was to visit a target frequently in order to identify any changes that might have occurred. Very often, valuable intelligence was gained when photographs indicated that there had been no changes.

During this period, the intelligence staff had become increasingly interested in the renewed activities at Peenemunde where the V-1 rocket programme had been discovered during mid-1943. The Bomber Command onslaught on Berlin had also been at its height, and this called for regular photographic cover to assess the effectiveness of the bombing. On 11 May, Baylis and his pilot took off in MM 246, equipped with 50-gallon overload fuel tanks, to photograph a series of targets including Peenemunde and Berlin. After skirting the heavily defended Frisian Islands they crossed the coast of southern Denmark to enter the Baltic. After photographing Warnemunde, they headed for Peenemunde at 30,000 feet where they took their photographs before turning south to carry out two runs over Berlin. They then headed for Frankfurt-on-Oder and Halle before landing back at Benson after a six-hour flight. More flights to Berlin followed, but by early June, the main activity had transferred to France in readiness for the Normandy invasion.

The Allies had begun the planning for the Normandy invasion – Operation 'Overlord' – in late 1942, and photographic reconnaissance was one of the most vital means of gathering the necessary intelligence. As the day for the invasion approached, Allied bomber aircraft mounted a concentrated campaign to destroy the radar sites and the rail and road networks in northern France. Photographic reconnaissance was a constant requirement to monitor progress and to identify new targets. Films were processed at Benson, and the negatives forwarded to Medmenham where the photographic interpreters pored over the films before making their assessments and reports. Many photographic prints were made for briefing purposes for distribution to army and navy formations involved in the Normandy landings.

On 3 June, Frank Baylis and his pilot took photographs of towns in central France, and two days later they were photographing the heavily bombed railway marshalling yards at Chartres, Poitiers and Le Mans. Throughout June, they flew numerous sorties over France, and these included keeping a close watch on German naval activities at Marseilles and Bordeaux. It was during this period that they flew their first operational sortie in a Mosquito Mk XVI (MM 354), the first PR variant with a pressurised cabin for high-altitude work.

July and August were spent flying high-level sorties over France obtaining photographs of all the major rail networks leading to the Normandy beachhead. In addition to assessing damage, it was important to identify German reinforcements moving to the battle area, in particular any columns of transport and troops and Tiger tanks being transported on rail flat trucks. The latter task was so important that the Mosquito crews were ordered to take additional risks, and to descend to low level if the weather dictated. On these sorties, the PR aircraft landed at Farnborough to give a quick visual report to the intelligence officers,

A high level photograph of the Saintes marshalling yards taken by Baylis on 2 August 1944. (*Frank Baylis*)

and to have their films processed rapidly in order that the light bombers of the Second Tactical Air Force could be tasked to attack these high priority targets.

Flying steady tracks over targets in unarmed aircraft and in broad daylight could pose considerable risks for the PR crews. During August, the Morgan/ Baylis crew were tasked to photograph the railway system near Lyons. As they approached the city, they saw great columns of billowing smoke to 20,000 feet following an attack by Italy-based USAAF bombers. They decided to skirt the city and resume their photographic run along the railway line to Belfort when Joe Morgan asked his navigator to check the rear before they settled on their long, steady run at 25,000 feet. To his consternation, Baylis saw six or seven Messerschmitt Bf 109s closing on their tail. They immediately abandoned the task, selected full power and full boost and dived for the nearest cloud. They were able to pull away from the German fighters and escape, but it was a timely reminder of the perils of the unarmed PR role.

By September, 544 Squadron had switched to targets over the rest of Europe, and Baylis visited Narvik in northern Norway, which included a refuelling stop at Sumburgh in the Shetlands on both the outbound and return journeys. A few days later he took off in a Mk XVI (MM 303) on one of his longest operational sorties. After refuelling at Coltishall, he set heading for the Baltic to photograph the ports of Danzig, Stettin and on to Königsberg in East Prussia, before turning south over Poland to photograph targets near Warsaw. The aircraft finally landed, with minimum fuel, after a flight of six and a half hours, at San Sevaro in southern Italy where the resident PR Wing processed their photographs. This was one of the most demanding sorties

A low-level oblique photograph of the U-boat pens at Bordeaux taken by Baylis on 28 September 1944. (*Frank Baylis*)

Frank Baylis (left) and his pilot Flight Lieutenant Daniels RCAF just before departing for a sortie over Norway in March 1945. (*Frank Baylis*)

flown by the PR crews. Apart from being at the maximum range of the Mosquito with 100-gallon drop tanks, the crew had to fly 1,200 miles over enemy-held territory. The following day the crew returned to Benson after photographing targets at Genoa, Leghorn and Paris. The operations flown by Baylis to northern Norway and the Mediterranean over these few days provide a graphic illustration of the scale and variety of tasks completed by the PR Squadrons. After two more operations – their thirty-ninth – Baylis's pilot was posted to complete a specialist course, and their close partnership came to an end.

Frank Baylis returned to 8 OTU at Dyce where he was crewed with Canadian Flight Lieutenant 'Danny' Daniels who was new to the PR role. Towards the end of the short course, they were tasked with an operational sortie to photo-graph the Norwegian towns of Molde and Aalesund. They had just completed the run over Aalesund at 27,000 feet when Baylis noticed drops of a black liquid coming from the starboard engine, which soon started to overspeed before catching fire. The extinguisher put the fire out, but the engine could not be feathered, and the propeller started to windmill – the liquid had been hydraulic fluid. Turning for the Shetlands, the aircraft started to lose height due to the excessive drag caused by the windmilling propeller. An emergency radio call was put out, and a Warwick air-sea-rescue aircraft was vectored towards the Mosquito. The aircraft continued to lose height, and had reached 800 feet before Daniels could hold it level and, with both feet on the same rudder pedal, the Mosquito wallowed along for a further 150 miles before the Shetlands came into sight where Daniels executed a perfect single-engine landing. When the engine cowling was removed, most of the engine fell out! Within a few days, Baylis rejoined 544 Squadron with his new pilot just before Christmas 1944, and they started operations immediately.

By January 1945 the Allied armies had entered Germany, and the PR Squadrons were heavily engaged in taking photographs for bomb-damage assessment, but the continuous heavy bombing attacks often created a great deal of smoke making both navigation and photography difficult. A new threat to the high-flying Mosquitoes had emerged, and encounters with the

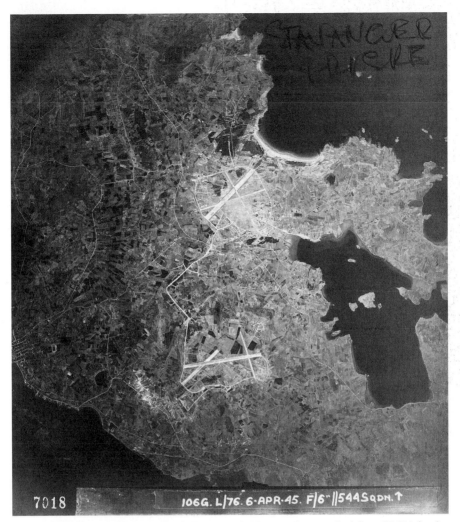

The huge German airfield complex at Stavanger in Norway photographed from 30,000 feet by Baylis on 6 April 1945. (*Frank Baylis*)

jet-propelled Messerschmitt Me 262 and the rocket-powered Me 163 became more common. On 2 March, Baylis took off in MM 273 to photograph Stettin and Dresden before landing in Italy, and four days later he photographed Chemnitz and Mannheim. In addition to photographing the cities attacked by Bomber Command and the USAF Eighth Air Force, the other major task was to continue the hunt for the remaining surface fleet of the German Navy, much of which had taken refuge in the Baltic, and Baylis flew numerous sorties to photograph the ports of Bornholm, Lübeck and Stettin. Despite the late stage of the war, German shipyards were still producing U-boats at Hamburg, Kiel and Cuxhaven, and these ports were visited on a regular basis. On completion, the U-boats moved to operational areas in Denmark and Norway, and these were also photographed almost daily.

By April, the search for escaping U-boats was a priority and, during a fifteen-day period in April, Baylis and his pilot flew seven sorties from Leuchars to Norway photographing every possible haven for the submarines. On 19 April he took off on his final operation when he photographed Innsbruck in Austria, landing after a six-hour flight, his sixty-third operational sortie. His operational hours totalled 300, and it is remarkable that he did not receive a gallantry award for his outstanding and highly successful tour of operations. Shortly after the war, it was announced that the Belgian government had awarded Warrant Officer Frank Baylis the Croix de Guerre. In the meantime, both his pilots had received the Distinguished Flying Cross!

Baylis joined the PR Development Courier Flight at Benson and, at the end of May, he and his pilot delivered a Mosquito PR 34 (RG 186) to Calcutta via Cairo and Karachi. After a year flying Ansons with the RAF Eastleigh Communications Flight at Nairobi, he returned to the PR world and joined 13 Squadron equipped with Mosquito PR 34s at Fayid in Egypt. Over the next eighteen months he flew 500 hours on a wide variety of photographic tasks that took him to Greece, Iraq, Transjordan and Kenya. Many of these areas had been neglected during the war, and maps needed to be updated. At the end of this hectic eighteen-month tour, Frank Baylis was assessed as an 'exceptional' PR navigator, and he was awarded a very well deserved Air Force Medal. There are many who feel that this was very belated recognition for his outstanding service.

On return to England, Baylis joined 540 Squadron at Benson, also equipped with the Mk 34. His first photographic sortie was to fly from Leuchars to photograph the areas around Stavanger and Haugesund in Norway. He could be forgiven for thinking that nothing had changed – except that no one was shooting at him. On 11 September 1949 two Mosquito crews were tasked to fly to Leuchars where they met a scientist from the Atomic Research Establishment based at Aldermaston. Baylis and his pilot, Flying Officer Whitworth-Jones, were selected as one of the crews, and they flew PF 679 to the Scottish airfield where the scientist attached small radiation sensors to the wing. The following morning the two crews took off on separate tracks to fly to their 'prudent limit of endurance', with Baylis heading for a position north-west of the Lofoten Islands, well inside the Arctic Circle. A day later they followed the same routine along a track that took them to the north of Iceland. Later, they discovered that the Soviet Union had exploded a nuclear device in the Russian Arctic region, and their aircraft sensors were collecting air samples for analysis. In the New Year's Honours List two months later, it was announced that the four aircrew had each been awarded the King's Commendation for Valuable Services in the Air.

Six months later, Frank Baylis flew his last sortie in the RAF having completed over 2,000 flying hours, the majority in the Mosquito PR force. He soon joined Hunting Aero Surveys and continued his career as an aerial photographer.

Chapter Nineteen

Artillery Spotter Pilot – Aubrey Young

Aubrey Young was completing his accountancy examinations in London when he received his call-up papers, leading him to enlist in the 9th Battalion (The Buffs) Royal East Kent Regiment in July 1940. After completing his initial infantry training he was sent to the south coast for anti-invasion duties. He transferred to the Royal Artillery, and was soon commissioned as a Second Lieutenant in the Hampshire and Dorset Yeomanry, a field gun artillery regiment. During a gunnery course at Larkhill he attended a lecture outlining the role of the new Air Observation Post (AOP) Squadrons. Learning that they were keen to recruit artillery officers as pilots, and with almost two years' army service without seeing action, he and a colleague volunteered for training as AOP pilots.

In November 1942, he reported to Marshall's Flying School at Cambridge for a twelve-week elementary flying training course on Tiger Moths. The flying instructors were RAF pilots, but all the students were army officers destined for the new AOP Squadrons. Young flew his first solo after ten hours of dual instruction, before completing the ninety-hour course. This was followed by a fifty-hour course at 43 OTU located at the School of Army Co-operation, Old Sarum. The unit was equipped with the Auster I, a development of the Taylorcraft Plus D aircraft. After conversion to the Auster, the course introduced pilots to wireless communication, message dropping, target pinpointing culminating in a series of tactical exercises and live artillery shoots on the nearby Salisbury Plain. An important part of the course was perfecting take-offs and landings from short, rough strips, some little more than 150 yards long.

The basic role of an AOP pilot was to take control of artillery, select targets, pass information to the guns, observe the fall of shot, and then give corrections until the target was destroyed. A small target might require just one gun, but concentrations of troops, armour or vehicles could involve engagement by a battery of guns. The pilot flew at 500 feet to locate and identify targets before giving instructions over the radio to the guns. He then descended to tree-top height until the guns called ready when he climbed back to 500 feet to give the order to fire. After observing the fall of shot, corrections were passed and the target re-engaged. This was a very skilful operation, requiring the pilot to position his aircraft carefully, observe the target and maintain a close watch for any enemy action, including anti-aircraft fire. Exercises were also carried out in classrooms on large exercise tables when tactical situations could be simulated. This whole phase was the core element of the training of an AOP pilot. At the end of the course, Aubrey Young was awarded his army pilot's wings, and posted to 659 Squadron based at Firbeck near Worksop.

Young had barely arrived at Worksop when he was transferred in June 1943 to 657 Squadron, which was at Clifton, near York, and preparing for overseas service in the Middle East. Within two weeks, the Squadron sailed from Glasgow and headed for Algiers. The AOP Squadrons belonged to the RAF, but they came under the operational control of the relevant Royal Artillery formations. All the pilots were officers drawn from the Royal Artillery, and the Army and the RAF provided the other ranks almost equally, with the latter being responsible for the servicing of the aircraft.

On arrival in Algeria, the Squadron was established at Bone, where the aircraft were reassembled before pilots flew area familiarisation flights. Shortly afterwards the Squadron moved to Philippeville, where the Flights dispersed. An AOP Squadron was organised into three Flights of four aircraft plus a Headquarters Flight, and Young was allocated to 'A' Flight. Each pilot had his own aircraft with a dedicated ground crew of one RAF aircraft fitter, who serviced the aircraft, an army wireless technician and an army driver. The pilot also had a three-ton truck and a jeep. This allowed each aircraft within the Flight to act as an independent unit capable of deploying to a landing strip close to an artillery regiment.

Training was the order of the day for a number of weeks after arriving in the theatre, but in early December Aubrey Young and three of his colleagues had an interesting interlude. No 655 AOP Squadron had moved to Italy, but additional aircraft were required as reinforcements, and the four pilots of 657 Squadron were tasked to deliver these aircraft. They set off in their Austers flying at 90 knots heading for Tunis and onwards to the island of Pantellaria. The next stage involved a long sea crossing to Sicily before proceeding to an airstrip on the toe of Italy, and on to Naples for a night stop. After landing on Naples airfield in the dark, Young taxied across the flare path and cut the electricity supply, plunging the airfield into darkness. His colleague, Captain Buchan, was circling in the overhead with little fuel waiting his turn to land, but he made a safe arrival. The following day the four pilots completed the delivery flights by flying to their final destination at the forward airfield at Vasto on the Adriatic Coast. They then found their way back to Algeria.

After a period of intensive training, including artillery shoots on the training ranges at Châteaudun and night flying, the Squadron prepared to move to Italy. The sixteen aircraft departed on 21 February 1944, and followed the route to Vasto flown earlier by the reinforcement aircraft. Severe weather and snow made flying conditions for the tiny Austers very difficult. Young and his fellow pilots had to make many unscheduled intermediate landings before finally arriving at Vasto beach where each

Captain Aubrey Young with his Auster AOP III of 657 Squadron in Italy, June 1944. (*Aubrey Young*)

Flight was allocated to an artillery formation of I Canadian Corps. Young's Flight supported 1st Canadian Army Group Royal Artillery (AGRA), and moved into tented accommodation at Mozzagrona situated by the River Sangro. The airstrip was created along a road covered with Sommerfield track and matting, which eased the problems of the mud after a particularly bad winter.

Conditions were quiet on the Corps front, and the Squadron's jobs were mainly reconnaissance and registering enemy positions. This gave Young and his fellow pilots an opportunity to visit their assigned artillery units and establish a close rapport, an essential ingredient for success in the AOP role. With stalemate all along the Italian front, all eyes were focussed on the key obstacle for the advance to Rome – the Gustav Line dominated by the Benedictine monastery perched 1,500 feet above the town of Cassino. The Germans used the monastery as an observation post, and after two abortive attacks, the Allied advance was stalled until it could be captured. In anticipation of a further major onslaught, the Squadron moved on 8 April to various landing strips near Cassino where Young carried out a number of recce flights during which he encountered intense small-calibre anti-aircraft fire. The slow, low-flying Austers were obvious targets for the enemy guns, and the Squadron lost two pilots in the first few days.

The night of 11/12 May marked the opening of the third battle to capture Cassino and break the Gustav Line with an intensive artillery barrage. Young flew two sorties on the 12th, but the smoke and low cloud made artillery spotting difficult. The Polish attack against the monastery was repulsed, but ground forces crossed the River Liri, and Field Marshal Kesselring, the German Commander-in-Chief, ordered a withdrawal to the next defensive line. Smoke and poor weather continued to hinder artillery spotting, but Young made a number of attempts to engage the German nine-barrel *Nebelwerfer* artillery. Eventually the monastery fell to the Poles on the 18th, and the advance could continue to the Adolf Hitler Line. The Squadron moved forward to newly prepared landing strips, Young managing to 'prang his kite' when the brakes stuck on. He was slightly injured, but was back in the air a few days later carrying out shoots with 138 Field Regiment, including a successful engagement against a *Nebelwerfer*. As the Germans retreated, they had to pull their lethal 88mm guns out of their camouflaged, static positions thus exposing them to air observation. The AOP aircraft also engaged vehicles, tanks, mortars and

The ruins of the abbey at Monte Cassino with the smoke of battle rising from the Liri Valley floor. (*Public Record Office. AIR 23/8567*)

spotted troop concentrations on bridges, roads and fords. With almost total air supremacy over the battlefield, AOP pilots were able to give full attention to their targets without fear of interception. They were also able to abandon their low-level tactics for spotting and operate up to 5,000 feet, above the effective range of the light anti-aircraft fire, and where they could observe a greater area.

On 26 May Young took delivery of his new aircraft and supervised the rigging. That night there was a heavy air raid against the landing strip and three aircraft were burnt out, including Young's new 'Sammie II'. The next few days witnessed some of the fiercest fighting of the Italian campaign, and the Squadron experienced the most arduous period in its history. Pilots were flying two or three times a day in a very hostile environment, and losses occurred. The ground crew worked under the most difficult conditions, sometimes under fire, and a move to new landing grounds became an almost daily requirement. Rome fell on 4 June when Young and his 'A' Flight moved to a field near Tivoli just as the German forces departed. The advance towards Florence continued with Young's Flight constantly on the move in order to stay close to the battle, and near to the artillery units they were tasked to support. Now supporting 1st Royal Horse Artillery (RHA), Young controlled artillery shoots against enemy motor convoys, gun pits and artillery in addition to flying regular reconnaissance sorties. The gunners attached so much importance to AOP that they sent to the Flight's landing ground each day a ground liaison officer equipped with scout car and wireless. He remained in constant touch with his regiment, and this allowed an aircraft to be in the air within a few minutes of support being called for.

Throughout July the advance continued, and Young flew almost every day in support of the advance to Arezzo. By early August the Squadron was operating 10 miles south of Florence engaging guns in the hills to the north of the city, but a rest was on the horizon, and the Squadron was pulled out of the front line. However, the rest was short lived as they were ordered back to the Adriatic coast to support the Canadian Corps in the attack against the Gothic Line. The Squadron established itself near Ancona, and Flights moved forward to advance landing grounds on the banks of the River Metauro on 28 August. The engineers were still preparing the strip and blowing up trees as Young arrived. The fuse had been lit to fell another tree as he started his approach to the strip with the airmen waving frantically to alert him to the danger. Misinterpreting the waves as a welcome, he landed and was a few yards from the tree when it blew up covering his aircraft in earth and small debris, but little damage was done. Three days later, the battle of the Gothic Line started.

For four days, Young was directing fire against bridges, pillboxes and transports before the Canadian infantry and armour broke through the Gothic Line on the 30th. The following day the Germans tried a counter-attack with armour – this was spotted by Captain Barras of 'A' Flight who immediately called down artillery fire on a large concentration of

Young with one of the 88 mm dual-purpose guns he knocked out on the Gothic Line with the 2nd Canadian Medium Artillery on 1 September 1944. (*Aubrey Young*)

tanks. Young took off to continue controlling the guns, and other members of the Flight followed him to keep up the barrage, which halted the counter-attack and forced it to disperse. For the next fourteen days the Flight flew at maximum effort while continuing to move forward to new landing grounds. Royal Navy ships added to the artillery bombardment and Young spent 4 September controlling the guns of HMS *Loyal* against targets near Rimini. The following day he exploded an ammunition dump on Rimini airfield, and then it was back to the bombardment of tanks and 88 mm guns. On the 9th he achieved two direct hits on 88 mm guns, and achieved his 200th operational flying hour during the sortie. For an AOP pilot, this involved very little transit time, since the ALGs were close to the front, and almost all the sorties were flown in contact with the enemy.

Throughout September, the pilots continued to fly at maximum rates with the Canadian artillery pounding the retreating Germans, allowing the key ridge at Coriano to be captured. The ground forces soon broke clear of the mountains and onwards to the plains, and the key city of Rimini soon fell. By the end of the month, the Flight was established on a landing ground north of the city. During this hectic period the Squadron received Auster IV aircraft fitted with a 130 hp Lycoming O-290 engine. Young collected his new aircraft and christened it 'Sammie IV'. The month ended on a high note when it was announced that four pilots had been awarded the Distinguished Flying Cross, and Major General Vokes, GOC 1st Canadian Infantry Division, invited 'C' Flight to wear the Divisional badge on their vehicles and aircraft in recognition of 'the high quality and valuable support given by the Flight'. (See map on page 141)

With the fall of Rimini, access was gained to the plain of Lombardy and the key roads leading to the main industrial centres in the north. With the onset of winter and its inevitable mud and snow, the main axis of attack had to be the roads leading to Bologna and the coastal road to Ravenna. This involved crossing no less than eight rivers making progress slow against a tenacious enemy. Heavy rain created difficult flying conditions from the 200–250 yard narrow airstrips, and the coconut matting laid to provide a solid base was only partially successful. Fortunately, the *Luftwaffe* fighters had long since left Italian skies, so, weather allowing, patrols were flown above the range of the light anti-aircraft fire at 6,000–7,000 feet.

The Canadians were withdrawn from the front line at the end of October and 'A' Flight was assigned to Porter Force, a force consisting of elements of Lieutenant Colonel Porter's 27th Lancers, the Governor General's Horse Guards of Canada, and supporting arms. On their right flank was Popski's Private Army, an organisation that had made its name as a highly irregular, but extremely effective, force in the Long Range Desert Group and commanded by the charismatic Major Popski. This combined force made steady progress towards the River Montone, and the Flight moved to Cervia where they were able to use a narrow road as a landing strip. By mid-November the advance was held up by stubborn German resistance at a strong point at San Appolinare close to the main road leading to Ravenna, and known as the 'sugar factory'.

On 18 November, Aubrey Young had directed 75 mm tank fire against the tall chimney of the factory, which was being used as an observation post. The following morning 1st Royal Horse Artillery intended to mount a determined attack against the factory, and Young was detailed to provide the AOP support for the attack, with the particular object of immediately engaging any hostile batteries that might open up. Part of the attacking force was drawn from the RAF Regiment who were making their first infantry attack. To be in position for

The tower at San Appolinare used as an observation post by the Germans was knocked out by Young and 1st Royal Horse Artillery on 18 November 1944. (*Aubrey Young*)

the com-mencement of the dawn attack, he had to take off from the very
narrow strip in the dark with one of his ground crew holding a torch
at the end of the strip to give him a sense of direction during his take-
off roll. As soon as he arrived over the factory he spotted two groups of
enemy guns engaging the attacking force. He directed fire against them,
and they were silenced, the house in which one of the guns was sited being
set on fire. This discouraged other guns, and the attacking force suffered
no casualties due to enemy shellfire. Young remained in the area flying very
low over suspected enemy positions in an attempt to draw fire so that their
position was disclosed to the infantry. As a result of his success in silencing
the enemy guns, and identifying enemy positions, the infantry were able
to move forward and capture the sugar factory allowing the advance to
continue. Throughout the engagement he had remained at low level, and
been under constant ground fire.

For this gallant action, Captain Aubrey Young was awarded the
Distinguished Flying Cross, the official recommendation concluding:

> Towards the end of his mission, Captain Young flew very low over suspected
> enemy localities in an attempt to draw enemy small arms fire, so that their
> positions should be disclosed. He then flew very low around the Sugar
> Factory and reported that the position was secured and that he could see
> prisoners had been taken. This action was a great encouragement to the men
> of the RAF Regiment for whom this was the first experience of an infantry
> attack. Throughout the mission, Captain Young showed great skill and daring
> and technical ability of a very high order.

After various high-ranking Army officers had recommended the award, Air
Vice-Marshal G.B.A. Baker added in his own handwriting the following
comment: 'This citation refers to one action which involved greater gallantry
than it suggests. I approve an Immediate award of a DFC.'

A week later, Young was involved in a piece of very irregular warfare for an
AOP pilot. Major Popski had become a frequent visitor to the Flight and he
had flown with Young on a number of patrols. The advance of his force across
a key bridge was being disrupted and delayed by a German patrol dug in
with machine-guns and located in farm buildings. Popski hatched a plot to
bomb the haystacks and buildings housing the machine-guns with mortar and
phosphorous bombs. He invited three of the AOP pilots, including Aubrey
Young, to a dinner where he disclosed his plan. The pilots gave it a lukewarm
reception, but agreed to cooperate, and on the following day, a few trial runs
were carried out on the beach when the method appeared to work. The
following morning the weather conditions for the attack were perfect with poor
visibility and a cloud base of 200 feet. The first aircraft took off and delivered
its attack, but the 'bombs' failed to explode. Twenty minutes later, Young and
Popski arrived on the scene, by which time, the German gunners had been
alerted, and they opened fire on the slow-flying Auster. Popski fused the bomb
and tossed it from the cockpit, but the return fire was too hot causing Young
to pull up into the low cloud. He judged when to descend for a second attack

against the farm. More 'bombs' and some grenades were thrown out before Young beat a hasty retreat to the coast to return to the airstrip. Popski was disappointed with the results, but had thoroughly enjoyed another chapter in his unconventional and adventurous war. After receiving a 'rocket' from his superiors, his response was to ask for a private AOP Squadron. Needless to say, his request received a curt and unprintable response.

Early in December the Canadian Division launched a major attack, but the weather and strong resistance from Tiger tanks slowed the advance. The AOP pilots directed fire on to the tanks, but the low cloud base and rain dictated that the pilots had to fly at low level. Anti-aircraft fire was heavy, and on one sortie, Young's aircraft was repeatedly hit, and he was lucky to survive when a piece of shrapnel lodged beneath his seat. Although armour plating had been issued to fit under the pilot's seat, the pilots decided it was too heavy and would adversely affect take-off performance, so it was not fitted to the Austers. The heavy rain and mud seriously hampered the advance, and the availability of AOP support. By the end of the month, the advance had to stop at the River Senio where it remained until the spring.

The stalemate continued throughout the winter but the pilots remained busy against German artillery conducting no less than 475 shoots during January. In the meantime, the artillery of the Italian 'Cremona Gruppe' had joined the Canadian Corps and this provided some interesting

Young with his ground crew and a fellow pilot with his new Auster AOP IV 'Sammie IV' in the mud of an Italian winter. (*Aubrey Young*)

language problems for the pilots. During February, the Canadian Corps was withdrawn from the Italian Front and the long, and highly effective, relationship between 657 Squadron and the Canadian gunners came to an end. However, the Squadron continued to wear the 'Red Patch' emblem of their Canadian colleagues on their aircraft and vehicles.

During the winter stalemate, it was decided to train rear observers for AOP work. Squadrons in France had been carrying them since the Normandy landings, but it had not been necessary in the Italian theatre owing to the lack of fighter opposition. However, it had been decided that all Squadrons should have them and 657 Squadron started to train some, and Young was allocated three Leading Aircraftman drawn from the Squadron's ground crew. On completion of fifteen hours' flying time, and a series of ground lectures, the observers were awarded a pay rise of a shilling a day, and entitled to wear a brevet of a half a wing on their sleeve. Young's observers, LACs Ashby, Davies and Hilton, completed their training on 17 March 1945. This coincided with rumours of a move, which was soon confirmed, and the Squadron started to prepare for a transfer to Holland. On 21 March, Young flew his last operation in Italy when he controlled guns of 142 Field Artillery and of 2 Commando Brigade. By the end of the day, the Squadron had flown its last sortie after operating for exactly a year in Italy, having carried out over 4,000 shoots against the enemy during its part in an advance of over 200 miles.

The Squadron moved to Leghorn by road to join a US Navy landing craft en route to Marseilles before convoying to the Belgian village of Oostmalle, arriving on 7 April. Four days later they moved to the airfield at Gilze Rijen in Holland where they collected sixteen new Auster Vs. The Squadron pilots were delighted to discover that they would, once again, be supporting I Canadian Corps who had also recently arrived from Italy. 'B' Flight of the Squadron was heavily involved in the Canadian advance to clear German pockets of resistance beyond Arnhem to the north, but Young's Flight saw little activity, and this ceased towards the end of April in order that food could be air-dropped and distributed to the starving Dutch people. Aubrey Young had flown his last operational flight after fourteen months of continuous operations.

With the fighting at an end, the Squadron was tasked with communication and liaison flying, which included helping with the location of German convoys and prisoners who had been cut off in Holland. Early in June, it moved into Germany as part of the forces of occupation, and established itself near Magdeburg to operate with 5th British Division in the communications role. The Squadron had been on the move for almost two years, and by September most of the wartime members had left including Aubrey Young who returned to civilian life after a distinguished career as an AOP pilot.

Chapter Twenty

Rocket Typhoon Pilot – Ken Brain

At the outbreak of the Second World War, Cheshire-born Ken Brain was employed as a senior controller at a power station, an appointment that was classed as a 'reserved occupation' thus making him ineligible for military service. The one exception to this rule was to volunteer for flying duties: he duly enrolled as potential aircrew at the Chester recruiting office in June 1941. After a six-month wait he was called to Cardington for a medical before proceeding to the Air Crew Reception Centre at the Lord's cricket ground. After the issue of kit and instruction in the rudiments of drill and saluting, he left for 6 Initial Training Wing at Aberystwyth where he and his colleagues were introduced to the basic flying subjects. On completion of the three-month course he was selected for pilot training and posted to 28 Elementary Flying School at Wolverhampton on 1 July 1942.

Ken Brain had never flown before his first familiarisation flight in a Tiger Moth (T 6271) with his instructor Flight Lieutenant Stocken. After numerous disruptions, he flew solo after fifteen hours, completing the concentrated course in twelve weeks having accumulated eighty hours' flying time. He departed for the Service Flying Training School at the RAF College Cranwell for advanced training on the single-engine Master, gaining his pilot's wings on 16 March 1943. With almost 200 hours on single-engine aircraft he was a natural for fighter aircraft, and he proceeded to 59 OTU at Millfield where he completed the basic fighter course on Hurricane Is before moving to the advanced Squadron to convert to the Typhoon. The course included training flights for all the traditional fighter roles including formation, dog-fighting and air-to-air firing, the latter conducted over the ranges off the coast of Northumberland. Ready to take up his place as a fighter pilot, it came as a shock to him when he was posted to RAF Ossington near Newark, the home of 82 OTU equipped with Wellingtons. He was one of six pilots posted to the newly formed 1685 Bomber (Defence) Training Flight equipped with Tomahawk Is.

The Curtis Tomahawk was a standard fighter with USAAF pursuit (fighter) Squadrons, and an export model was ordered for the French Air Force. None of the French aircraft were delivered before the collapse of

As a Sergeant Pilot, Ken Brain stands by his Tomahawk I, AH 861, of 1685 Bomber (Defence) Flight at Ossington in March 1944. (*Ken Brain*)

France in 1940, and 140 were taken over by the RAF to be added to British contracts. The majority flew in the desert campaigns in North Africa, with others equipping tactical reconnaissance Squadrons in the UK. The Mk I version was used in the training support role, and it was this aircraft that Brain found himself flying at Ossington.

The role of the Bomber Training Flights was to provide targets for the trainee crews flying the Wellingtons. The Tomahawks would intercept the bombers using a wide range of tactics and different attack patterns. The student air gunners had to identify the fighters before giving the appropriate evasion tactics to the pilots while 'engaging' the Tomahawks with their camera guns. The intensive flying rate of the bomber OTUs created considerable demands on the small Flights of target aircraft, and pilots would regularly fly four sorties each day. Brain carried out most of his flights in Tomahawk AH 861 before the Flight was re-equipped with the Hurricane. In the twelve months that he served at Ossington he accumulated over 400 hours flying fighters, experience that stood him in great stead when he joined his first operational fighter Squadron, equipped with the Typhoon Ib.

The Typhoon had been a disappointment as an interceptor fighter, but it excelled as a close-support aircraft. By mid-1944, the majority of Typhoon Squadrons formed part of Second Tactical Air Force (2 TAF). In the months leading up to D-Day in June 1944 the Typhoon Squadrons had been heavily engaged in attacking tactical targets in northern France, but the losses to the murderous flak had been considerable. Replacement pilots were needed urgently, and Brain was an obvious candidate with his considerable experience on single-engine fighters and previous Typhoon experience. He joined 137 Squadron at Manston just before D-Day as a newly commissioned Pilot Officer. On his arrival his Commanding Officer asked him about his experience, and on learning that he had almost 600 hours on fighters he exclaimed 'that makes you one of my most experienced pilots!'

No 137 Squadron had remained part of the Air Defence of Great Britain Command (ADGB) but was equipped with the rocket-firing Typhoon armed with four Hispano 20 mm cannons and eight 3-inch rockets with 60-lb heads. Brain's early flying on the Squadron was devoted to rocket-firing practice from 30-degree dives and strafing with the 20 mm cannons. His first operational sortie on June 16 flying MN 584 was a disappointment. He was tasked to seek out the V-1 'Noball' launching sites in the Pas-de-Calais region, but complete cloud cover caused him to abort. However, he was more successful in the afternoon when he observed that the flak was 'not very accurate going in but pretty hot coming out'.

The Germans launched the first V-1 flying bombs against England on 12 June, and the ADGB Squadrons were soon tasked with 'Anti-Diver' patrols to intercept the new terror weapon. The Typhoon had the speed to engage the V-1s and Brain flew in MN 191 on the Squadron's first patrol

Ken Brain with his Typhoon, JP 504, of 137 Squadron (*Ken Brain*)

on 22 June, with Flight Lieutenant Wood as his leader. They took off at 0745 and were vectored by Hythe Control to intercept a diver flying 10 miles south of Rye at 2,500 feet, which they saw but could not intercept. Almost immediately, another was sighted 12 miles south of Dungeness flying at 3,000 feet on a north-westerly course – Brain dived down firing short bursts of his 20mm cannon from 400 yards aiming just behind the nose. He saw no strikes and, as the diver disappeared under the nose of his Typhoon, he pulled away. On rolling away he saw the V-1 going down, and his leader saw it hit the sea and explode. Twenty minutes later the pair landed to celebrate Brain's, and the Squadron's, first success on the very first patrol carried out by 137 Squadron.

Following his initial success there was more action later in the day. Taking off at 1815 as a pair with Flight Lieutanant Brandreth as leader, the two Typhoons were vectored south-east of Eastbourne by Hythe Control. A diver was sighted at 5,000 feet on a northerly course, and Brain dived in to attack firing short bursts from 600 yards followed by a long burst from astern as he closed, observing strikes on both wings. The diver spiralled down hitting the sea in a great explosion, and so ended an eventful first day of combat.

The following week brought more encounters with the V-1, and the Squadron's score mounted, but Brain's attacks brought no further success until 30 June. With Flight Lieutenant Wood leading, he took off in his Typhoon (MN 169) at 0735 to patrol off Boulogne at 5,000 feet under Swingate Control. Just after arriving on patrol he saw a diver at 3,500 feet on a north-westerly course, and he started firing at 600 yards. After a long burst of cannon fire, the diver caught fire and crashed into the sea. The patrol was resumed and Control informed the Typhoons of another diver crossing the French coast at 4,000 feet. The leader attacked first and, having exhausted his ammunition, was contemplating tipping over the flying bomb with his wing when Brain called him to 'move over'. He fired a short burst from 400 yards causing a fire in the fuselage, and the diver crashed, exploding as it hit the sea. Fifty exciting minutes after taking off, the two Typhoons landed back at Manston.

Ken Brain had flown his first operational sortie of the war just ten days earlier and, in this short period, he had accounted for four of the dreaded flying bombs. Patrols continued throughout July, and the Squadron score mounted steadily, but he was out of luck. Since commencing anti-diver patrols, the Squadron had accounted for thirty with one pilot claiming five, and three other pilots, including Brain, claiming four.

In addition to the anti-diver patrols, the Manston-based rocket-firing Typhoons were tasked with shipping recces searching for E-boats in the English Channel. On 3 August Brain attacked an E-boat with cannon near the island of Schouwen, and the following day a rocket attack against a 2,000-ton coaster brought spectacular success. The coaster was grounded in the East Schelde and the formation leader, Canadian-born Warrant Officer Bill Flett, rolled into a dive attack to fire his eight rockets before pulling up sharply to avoid exploding debris. Brain followed, and saw the

Typhoons have wreaked havoc on the tanks of the German Panzers during their attempt to escape through the Falaise gap. (*Air Historical Branch*)

leader's salvo hit the coaster and 'lift the ship out of the water'. The pair re-attacked with cannon, and the ship blew up. They went on to attack an E-boat when Brain's Typhoon MN 126 was damaged, but he landed safely at Bradwell Bay.

During the build up to D-Day, and the operations that followed, the majority of the Typhoon Squadrons flew in the close support role under the command of 2 TAF. The ground campaign in Normandy had gone well, but the German Army put up stubborn resistance, and by mid-August the Allied momentum had been lost. With air superiority achieved, the Allies poured in more ground attack aircraft and, on 13 August, 137 Squadron flew into B6 airfield at Coulomb near Caen having transferred to 124 Wing of 83 Group in 2 TAF. The Squadron was operational in a few days, and a maximum effort was called for on the 17th when the Typhoon Wings flew over 1,200 close support sorties in the Vimoutiers region. Brain flew his first ground-attack sortie on the following day when his formation attacked a convoy of transports, leaving sixteen 'flamers', six 'smokers' and ten damaged. On a later sortie he attacked a staff car with two pairs of rockets.

Over the next two days, the German Army was routed as the Typhoons roamed in pairs attacking the German armour and motor transports with

Squadron Leader A.R. Sutherland DFC and Major C. Gray man a Visual Control Post (VCP) in Normandy during 1944. (*Air Historical Branch*)

rockets, cannon and bombs. Aircraft losses were high with almost all the Typhoons lost brought down by the murderous light flak. By the 20th the battle around the Falaise Gap was over. The Typhoon Wings continued to provide close support under the control of the Visual Control Posts (VCP) that travelled with the forward elements of the army, but with the Germans in full retreat, interdiction sorties against transports and lines of communications became more frequent. The crossings over the River Seine were attacked and Brain 'pranged' three barges leaving one on fire.

By the end of August the Germans were in full retreat, and the Squadron moved three times in the space of ten days before arriving at B58 just outside Brussels on 6 September. Within two days, the Wing flew its first sortie over Germany when a train was attacked, a target that the Typhoon pilots would soon become very familiar with. With the Allied armies making rapid progress through Belgium and into Holland, the Typhoon Wings were tasked with armed recce sorties into particular areas. Any military target or road, rail or river traffic was attacked, and the Typhoons rarely returned without firing their rockets and cannons. It was dangerous work and, although the *Luftwaffe* rarely appeared, the light flak batteries took a heavy toll.

By mid-September the Allied armies had pressed into Holland. To maintain the momentum of the advance, the ill-fated Operation 'Market', the airborne assault on Nijmegen and Arnhem, was launched. The weather was poor, and the very low cloud seriously curtailed the support that the Typhoon Wings could give. After attacking motor transports Brain recorded in the remarks column of his logbook 'lousy weather'. It is now no more than a matter of conjecture what the outcome of this tragic failure might have been if the Typhoons had been able to engage the enemy.

Within days, 137 Squadron had moved to B78 at Eindhoven where it remained for the next few months. Sadly, the Squadron lost its popular Norwegian Commanding Officer when Squadron Leader Piltingsrud DFC was shot down by a Focke-Wulf 190, the only loss to fighters by the Squadron throughout the whole north-west Europe campaign.

October proved to be a hectic month for the Typhoon Wings, and Ken Brain flew every day on interdiction and armed recce sorties. Once the Nijmegan bridgehead had been secured, a comprehensive programme of railway interdiction was fulfilled, and this involved the cutting of tracks, the destruction of rolling stock and marshalling yards, and the general harrying

Two Typhoons attack a German headquarters. The first has hit the target and the second aircraft has just fired and is visible half way down the smoke trails. (*Air Historical Branch*)

of all movement on railways. These attacks were all carried out as the army moved north through Holland and pressed towards the River Rhine in Germany. Brain 'pranged' the marshalling yards at Goch on 5 October, then it was a repeat performance at Emmerich followed by a similar attack at Wesel. He attacked trains near Utrecht and Barneveld, barges were sunk near Venlo, and gun and observation positions were hit with rockets and cannon near Geldern. Altogether he flew over twenty operations during the month, all in the face of intense light flak.

The attacks during November followed a similar pattern, but by the end of the month, the Typhoons were heading deeper into Germany to attack the railway system. December brought poor weather, and those who had to live in the spartan conditions at Eindhoven, and at the other advanced airfields in early 1945, will long remember the winter of 1944. As the Squadron operational diarist commented, 'Pilots are warm and comfortable in the crew-room so long as they sit between the leaks.' Despite the poor weather, there were some successful days, and the operations flown on 5 December give a clear impression of the activities of a rocket-firing Typhoon Squadron.

During the course of the day, three armed reconnaissance operations, each of six aircraft, were mounted. The first was tasked to the Wesel–Munster area and the formation soon found a locomotive and ten boxcars heading north, which were attacked and damaged. A second train with twenty wagons was attacked a short time later causing more damage, before five 88 mm anti-aircraft guns were silenced with a rocket and cannon attack. Later in the day, the second flight of six aircraft returned to the area, and damaged a locomotive and ten trucks before attacking a factory north of Dinslaken. The flak was intense, and one of the pilots was shot down and taken prisoner. The third flight took off in the late afternoon. A locomotive and five wagons were damaged, two factories were set on fire, and fifty troops were attacked and 'were seen to scatter'. The Typhoon pilots of 2 TAF were some of the busiest in the war.

1 January 1945 saw the final major *Luftwaffe* attack when they launched their audacious Operation *Bodenplatte*, the attack against the Allied airfields. The most severely hit was Eindhoven, the home of 137 Squadron and seven other Typhoon and three Spitfire Squadrons. At 0850, six Typhoons of 137 Squadron had taken off to attack trains. Thirty minutes later the Bf 109s and Fw 190s of *Jagdgeschwader 3* commenced a sustained attack that lasted almost twenty-five minutes. Brain was driving to the airfield from the pilots' accommodation area to prepare for a sortie when he saw the attack start, so he kept well away until the attacking aircraft departed. On arrival at the airfield, he and his colleagues could hardly believe their eyes as burning aircraft littered the area. In the event, over twenty were destroyed on the ground with many more damaged. One of the 137 Squadron pilots was killed as he taxied his aircraft to a dispersal, and the Squadron suffered other casualties. The six aircraft airborne were diverted to other airfields leaving the Squadron with just four serviceable aircraft. Brain was ordered to lead these four remaining aircraft and to fly up and down the bomb

A 137 Squadron Typhoon at Eindhoven in December 1944. The Hurricane 'hack' in the background was destroyed during the *Luftwaffe's* attack on Allied airfields on 1 January 1945. (*Ken Brain*)

line to let the *Luftwaffe* know that the Typhoons were still in business. He and his colleagues were tasked to make numerous radio calls using all the callsigns of the Wing for the benefit of the German radio monitoring posts. He was to remark later that it was the least exciting war operation he flew, but probably one of the most important. The *Luftwaffe* didn't return.

Early January saw the Typhoon Wings extending their operations further into Germany as a prelude to the forthcoming operations to cross the River Rhine. To increase the range of the Typhoons, expendable long-range drop tanks were fitted, and these almost doubled the range of the fighter-bombers. Leading Blue Section on 5 January, Brain attacked and destroyed a locomotive and coaches in the Bremen area, and this brought the Squadron's tally for the day to five. A move further east to B86, a newly built airfield at Helmond, and this allowed the Squadron to range beyond Munster.

The start of February saw some improvement in the weather and on the 8th, the British and Canadian armies launched Operation 'Veritable' to move up to the Rhine prior to the crossing of this final major obstacle. The role for the Tactical Air Forces was to isolate the battlefield, rather than provide close air support, and thus prevent the Germans from bringing up reinforcements. The railway systems remained the prime targets for the Typhoon Wings, and 137 Squadron embarked on almost daily sorties on the 'milk run' to Munster attacking trains when many were destroyed. On 13 February, flying his regular aircraft PD 611, Brain led six aircraft on an armed recce to the Munster area, and four trains were attacked in the space of a few minutes. One locomotive was destroyed, three were damaged, and numerous wagons destroyed. A few days later, he led the Squadron on a similar armed-recce sortie when two locomotives were destroyed with two more damaged.

The combination of rockets and cannons proved lethal against these relatively 'soft' targets, and derailed and destroyed trains littered the north German countryside. The price was high however, as many of the trains had flak carts embedded among the freight wagons creating an intense barrage of anti-aircraft fire. Attacks were carried out across the direction of the train and, after releasing their rockets, the pilots would pull up and turn sharply to increase the deflection angle for the German gunners. Despite these tactics, losses were high. Not surprisingly, the Typhoon Squadrons attracted few volunteers.

Daily attacks against the railway system continued, but 25 February proved to be the last day of Ken Brain's operational flying career. During the morning, his formation had attacked and destroyed two locomotives near Xanten. Just after lunch he took off in PD 611 on his 112th, and final, operation. Wing Commander K. North-Lewis DFC, the Wing Leader, led a twelve-aircraft formation, with Brain leading Blue Section, to attack guns on the edge of a wood at Arcen near Geldern, which were harassing army units. Six salvoes of eight rockets were seen to burst in the target area, and the guns were silenced.

Within days, 137 Squadron was withdrawn from the front line to go to Warmwell in Dorset for an Armament Practice Camp. The aim of these camps was to provide rocket firing practice for the Typhoon Squadrons! It did, of course, allow the Squadrons some rest from the intensive and stressful operational arena. On returning to Helmond, Ken Brain was informed that he was to be rested and posted to 62 OTU at Ouston as an instructor. He had been at the airfield a few days when he received a telegram from his father saying that he had just read in the local newspaper that Ken had been awarded the Distinguished Flying Cross. He told his Commanding Officer who put it in daily orders, and gave him a piece of his own DFC ribbon and told him to 'sew it on, lad'. The official notification arrived shortly afterwards, the citation states:

> This officer has completed many attacks against gun positions, troop concentrations, tanks and trains in support of the army. In spite of intense anti-aircraft opposition Flying Officer Brain's fine leadership has been largely responsible for the successful completion of many operations. Throughout this officer has set an inspiring example to the other members of his Squadron.

Within a few weeks the war in Europe was over, and the need for Typhoon pilots virtually ceased overnight, leaving the instructors without a job. Ken Brain was given a desk job responsible for posting officers, and as soon as an attractive flying appointment became available, he posted himself. He joined 4 Delivery Flight of the 41 Group Ferry Pool at Hutton Cranswick, and for the next eighteen months he ferried almost every type of single-engine fighter to airfields in Britain. He made his first jet flight in a Vampire on 21 February 1946 when his CO gave him a half sheet of paper as a brief, showed him the knobs and switches and declared him 'converted'. Following the brief written instructions, Brain started the aircraft, taxied carefully to the runway, opened the throttle and took off to deliver the aircraft to a fighter Squadron. Shortly afterwards, in the middle of 1946, Ken Brain's distinguished career in the RAF came to an end.

During the 1990s, together with many of his wartime colleagues, he returned to Normandy, Eindhoven and to Helmond. Each was given a commemorative medal as a token of the gratitude of the French and Dutch people who still remembered those who had come to their countries to liberate them fifty years earlier. These pilots were as proud to wear these touching mementoes, as they were their official decorations.

Chapter Twenty-One

Low-Level Fighter Reconnaissance – 'Sandy' Webb

With storm clouds building up over Europe during the mid-1930s, the RAF embarked on what became known as the 'Expansion Scheme'. The rapid construction of permanent airfields, and the introduction of new, modern combat aircraft were long overdue, but would be of little use if there were insufficient men to fly this rapidly expanding air force of more complex aircraft. The Royal Air Force Volunteer Reserve came into existence in July 1936 to provide, *inter alia*, the nucleus of pilots should war eventually be declared. Thus, the 'Citizens Air Force' was born, and the call for volunteers went out with thousands of young men stepping forward to join and learn to fly in their spare time. One of the first was George Francis Herbert Webb, known to all his friends as 'Sandy', who 'signed on' on 3 August 1936.

The 21-year-old Sandy Webb reported to the Desford Flying School near Leicester on 5 August 1936. He was airborne for the first time on the same day when he took off with Flight Lieutenant Howes in a DH 82 Moth (G-ADPC) for a forty-minute familiarisation flight. His formal instruction started two days later followed by two or three flights every day until he completed his first solo on 25 August 1936, just three weeks after 'signing on'. By the end of October, he had completed his training of fifty hours when he was assessed as an above average *ab-initio* pilot. The following spring he returned for an annual refresher course when he flew a further ten hours. Twelve months later he reported to 10 Elementary and Reserve Flying Training School at Yatesbury to complete his advanced training on Harts and Audaxes.

With war imminent, Webb decided to join the Royal Auxiliary Air Force, and was one of many applicants to apply to join the last Squadron to form, 613 (City of Manchester) Squadron. He was successful, and was among the first group to be offered a commission, reporting to the Squadron at Ringway on 13 May. He was commissioned on 1 August and, within three weeks, the Royal Auxiliary Air Force had been 'embodied' into the Royal Air Force. Within a few days he was flying the Hawker Hind.

Hawker Hectors of 613 Squadron in pre-war markings. They were used in action by 613 Squadron during the operations at Dunkirk. (*N. Webb*)

The Squadron flew in the Army Co-operation role, and he was sent to the School of Army Co-operation at Old Sarum to complete specialist role training, flying the Lysander during the course. On his return to the Squadron, it was in the process of converting to the Hawker Hector. Once the Squadron had reached full strength in October, it moved to Odiham where it was located close to major Army units, and intensive training began. Webb's Flight converted to Lysanders in the New Year when photographic reconnaissance became a particularly important role.

Training intensified as the Phoney War came to an end, and the Hectors and Lysanders moved to Hawkinge to provide assistance for the beleaguered British Expeditionary Force (BEF). On 25 May, the all-metal Hector biplanes were tasked with dive-bombing gun positions near Calais, and two days later, Webb and his colleagues in the Lysander Flight dropped supplies to the soldiers stranded in Calais. Webb and his gunner, Leading Aircraftman Bell, carried out two supply-dropping sorties in P 6970. With the completion of the Dunkirk evacuation, the Squadron was withdrawn to Netherthorpe near Sheffield to help train and exercise with the Army. The need for close cooperation in land/air warfare had been graphically illustrated in the recent battles.

For the next few months, 613 Squadron was heavily engaged in all aspects of army cooperation, which included tactical reconnaissance, photography, bombing and gunnery. During this period, the Lysanders were sometimes tasked with supplementing the modest Air-Sea Rescue forces. Webb flew a number of 'Jim Crow' sorties searching for aircrew shot down over the sea before leading the high-speed launches to aircrew located in their dinghies or floating in their Mae West lifejackets. In this way, the Lysanders made a significant contribution to the Battle of Britain.

Early in 1941 there was a rationalisation of the RAF's photographic reconnaissance resources culminating in the establishment of the Photographic Reconnaissance Unit (PRU) whose task was 'to provide long-range strategic photographic reconnaissance and it should not be used for visual reconnaissance'. Meanwhile, 1416 Flight was formed at Hendon in March 1941 in Army Co-operation Command to meet the particular requirements of the GOC-in-C Home Forces in the event of invasion. 'Sandy' Webb, by now an experienced army cooperation and photographic reconnaissance pilot, became one of the Flight's founder members.

Because of its low-level tactical role, the Flight was equipped with six 'G' Type Spitfires. These retained the eight-gun armament of the standard fighter, but carried an additional twenty-nine gallon fuel tank under the pilot's seat. The camera installation was unique. Unable to fit the cameras in the wings due to the gun installation, the PRIG was the first photographic reconnaissance Spitfire to be fitted with an oblique camera. Each aircraft was fitted with one oblique, usually with a fourteen-inch lens, and two 'split' vertically mounted F24 cameras for special photographic tasks. These could be fitted with the four-inch lens or the fourteen-inch lens. This installation allowed the pilot to obtain photographs from immediately below the cloud base, which also provided his sanctuary if attacked. After a short period, the PR1Gs were painted in a very pale shade of pink, which was found to be more effective camouflage.

Webb completed a Spitfire conversion and delivered the Flight's first aircraft (X 4784) from Heston. By May, he was flying regular photographic sorties over England providing mosaics to update the mapping. Many of these sorties were conducted over coastal areas and possible enemy amphibious landing areas. On 17 May he was flying Spitfire X 4784 taking photographs over Dover at 20,000 feet when four Messerschmitt Bf 109 fighters pursued him, and he had to make a hasty retreat. After landing, a bullet was discovered in the port wing necessitating a wing replacement.

The Spitfires of 1417 Flight were in great demand throughout the summer of 1941, and Webb flew no less that sixty hours in July. This also coincided with the arrival of Blenheim IVs to form a separate Flight, and

Sandy Webb at the controls of a Blenheim of 140 Squadron. (*N. Webb*)

Webb completed his conversion to the aircraft in V 5456 during the month. Pilots also had to maintain their skills at air gunnery and the Flight retained some Lysander aircraft as target-towing aircraft. On 17 September, the expanded Flight was re-numbered 140 Squadron with Webb appointed as a Flight Commander. A few days earlier, the Squadron had moved to Benson, which had become established as the main photographic reconnaissance airfield in England, and it commenced operations over northern France.

The first 140 Squadron operational sortie was flown by Webb on 14 September when he took X 4907 to the Cherbourg area to complete an oblique line overlap at 3,000 feet. Operational sorties flown by the Squadron built up rapidly during October with the main targets situated on the French coast. This was the beginning of a continuous survey of the beaches, harbour installations, radar network and transportation routes that the Squadron would monitor for the next three years leading up to D-Day. Photographic reconnaissance is not only about acquiring information, it is equally important to detect changes, and this can only be achieved by returning to targets at frequent intervals. An enemy would appreciate this requirement so defences were always on the alert, and many PR pilots were lost because it was necessary to keep going back to the same targets.

During the first twelve months, the majority of 140 Squadron's sorties were flown at low level with oblique cameras, and pilots soon became very familiar with Le Touquet, Cherbourg, Le Havre, Dieppe and many other Channel ports and beaches. Whenever the weather was suitable these and similar targets were covered. Cloud cover was important for vertical photography. The Spitfires would fly at cloud base and, if intercepted, they would climb and disappear in to cloud. Lack of cloud meant the abandonment of a sortie.

Webb's operational sorties soon mounted, and by February 1942 he had completed over thirty, almost all at low level. On 1 March he was flying R 6910 and the Squadron diary records his sortie profile: 'Flew to Selsey Bill and set course for Cherbourg Peninsula. Crossed coast between Cap Levy and Pointe de Barfleur and flew inland to locate RDF station which was made difficult owing to the inaccurate map. Turned to Le Vicel and spotted target. Made two low-level photo runs. Satisfactory and returned to base.' This laconic statement hides a great deal. Such a sortie needed meticulous briefing and map preparation using the latest intelligence to avoid enemy defences. Flying a single-seat and single-engine Spitfire without escort required great piloting and navigation skills, and after photographing the target a return, almost all over water, was crucial. A bomber sortie was considered successful if the target was bombed and a fighter sortie if it fulfilled its patrol. However, a PR sortie could photograph its target, but unless it returned with the photographs, it was a failure.

The F24 was a relatively old camera and the reconnaissance Squadrons were constantly testing new cameras. In early 1942 the F52 camera was

Aircrew of the Blenheim Flight of 140 Squadron with the CO, Squadron Leader Le Mesurier DSO, DFC, in the centre with Sandy Webb on his left. (*N. Webb*)

introduced. This camera had numerous advantages, including a larger film magazine capable of taking up to 500 exposures, and it provided a larger contact print size giving a better scale for more detailed interpretation. Lenses of 20- and 36-inch focal length were available, and this improved quality further. Electric heating was supplied to the fuselage-mounted cameras to prevent freezing up and the formation of condensation on the lenses. To obtain the necessary detail of some targets, sorties had to be flown at very low level, and this led to the development of the F52 cameras with a five- or eight-inch lens. To compensate for the additional movement due to the speed of the aircraft a moving film strip had to be used, and a further modification enabled the film to move at a compensating speed and was fitted with a focal-plane shutter giving continuous exposures every second. This provided the necessary 60 per cent overlap to create stereoscopic pairs for accurate interpretation by the analysts.

With the new camera fits installed from April 1942, and the introduction of the Spitfire IV, the majority of the Squadron's operations were switched to high level. These were flown at around 25,000 feet, but when condensation trails formed, the Spitfires descended to an altitude where the trails ceased. The majority of targets remained in northern France with an occasional sortie to Dutch ports, and during the month Webb flew fifteen sorties. On one or two he had to abandon the task when *Luftwaffe* fighters started to close in on his aircraft. At this time, the name 'Dieppe' started to appear regularly in the Squadron diary.

On 1 May 1942 the Squadron establishment was increased to ten Spitfires and six Blenheims and the post of Squadron commander upgraded to Wing Commander. The Fight Commanders were also upgraded and Webb was promoted to Squadron Leader. On the 17th he flew another sortie to Dieppe, and on 30 May he took a Spitfire PR IV (AR 234) to photograph the Somme estuary on a series of runs at 28,500 feet. It was his fiftieth operational sortie. He was back the following day completing the task at 32,000 feet. Four more sorties were flown during June, including a daring long-range sortie to the Paris and Rouen areas. Three days later on 26 June it was announced that he had been awarded the Distinguished Flying Cross. The citation captured the brilliance of his work as a photographic reconnaissance pilot:

Flight Lieutenant G.F.H. Webb has carried out 52 operational sorties over enemy territory. Forty-eight of these have been photographic reconnaissance flights completed during the past five months and of these, twenty-two were low level operations in which photographs were taken at heights varying from 300 to 2,000 feet. His results have been of enormous value and his low level obliques, particularly of certain RDF Stations, on the enemy occupied coast have provided a mass of invaluable information…He has always chosen to take on the most daring and difficult operations himself and has been an inspiration to his Flight. Many times during the winter he has taken off and returned with successful results in weather conditions that appeared to be almost impossible for a single-seat aircraft unequipped with radio. In all these operations he has shown the greatest courage and determination in the face of the enemy.

Spitfire PR IG of 140 Squadron. (*N. Webb*)

Throughout the summer of 1942, 140 Squadron was engaged in a special task for GHQ Home Forces carrying out a reconnaissance over a large area of France, and obtaining data regarding beach gradients and lines of communication in connection with the planning for the invasion of the Continent. Webb was heavily involved in this work, and he took photographs of many of the beaches, ports and road networks that would feature heavily later in the war. These sorties were all flown above 30,000 feet. This work was hampered by lack of aircraft, despite the loan of four Spitfires from the PRU. General Paget, GOC-in-C Home Forces, made a personal appeal to the Chief of Air Staff seeking additional aircraft for his only reconnaissance Squadron.

Webb and his fellow Spitfire pilots of 140 Squadron also flew very low-level sorties over Dieppe during the planning period for the operation that took place on 18 August. Detailed models of Dieppe and the defences were made from the photographs taken by the reconnaissance Squadrons and used for briefings. These models were then photographed from the seaward side at a very low angle to represent their appearances at twilight and 750 copies of this silhouette were issued to Flotilla leaders and officers commanding all ships. On the afternoon before the raid, sorties were flown over all the Channel ports but revealed no change in the disposition of shipping or enemy defences. Webb carried out four runs over the Somme estuary followed by a further sortie over Boulogne. On the day of the raid all the forces in the landing craft were supplied with photographs and plans of the beaches from which they would operate.

Although the Dieppe raid was a tragic failure, many lessons were learned. The examples above highlight the indispensable part played by photographic reconnaissance in the planning and preparation for special operations, and it was as a result of these and other experiences that aerial photography and intelligence work was refined and brought to the highest level in undertaking the tasks for the invasion of the Continent. By this time Webb was one of the most experienced tactical reconnaissance and army cooperation pilots in the RAF, and he became increasingly involved in discussions and trials to further improve tactical reconnaissance techniques. Despite this, he managed to continue to fly on operations and conduct many trials in the Squadron's Spitfires and Blenheims. The latter were being used increasingly for night reconnaissance and they paved the way for the time that the Squadron was re-equipped with the Mosquito.

Early in 1943 Webb was rested from operations, but remained with the Squadron, responsible for planning and tasking and for the Squadron's move to Hartford Bridge. He was also heavily involved in the planning of Operation 'Spartan', the largest tactical army/air cooperation exercise held so far in the war. In May 1943 he was promoted to Wing Commander and became the Squadron Commander, but major changes and developments were taking place in the command and control arrangements for land/ air warfare. On 1 June 1943 the Army Co-operation Command was disbanded, and its units were transferred to the new Second Tactical Air Force (2 TAF). Webb's vast knowledge and expertise were now considered to be too valuable to continue operational flying and he was the natural choice for the post of Wing Commander Operations at the newly formed 34 Photographic Reconnaissance Wing with the existing 140 Squadron as a foundation, and soon to be joined by 16 (AC) Squadron. The Wing came under the direct control of 2 TAF working alongside 21st Army Group.

The Dieppe raid had highlighted the value of oblique photographs for planning, and the experience gained, both at Dieppe and from the Desert Air Force, emphasised the need, prior to the invasion, for a fully mobile tactical Air Force organisation to work alongside the Army. Reconnaissance Squadron establishments for equipment and personnel were drawn up to make them completely mobile and self-contained. The Squadrons were supplied with equipment for developing and printing photographs in mobile prime movers or trailers, and teams of interpreters were established that would remain with the Squadrons. Other teams were located at the various Army and Air Force headquarters where second and third-phase interpretation was to be carried out. Webb became a key member of the team tasked with creating such an organisation.

Despite this workload, he still flew regularly to keep himself abreast of techniques, and he converted to the Mosquito IX as soon as the aircraft started to replace the Spitfires of his old Squadron. His first flight took place on 5 September. Two weeks later he flew a 16 Squadron Spitfire IV (EN 386) on a high-level reconnaissance sortie over northern France. He was determined to remain abreast of what he demanded of his pilots. On 12 November he flew his first operational sortie in a Mosquito when he and Flight Sergeant Curzon took MM 240 to obtain low-level photographs of Port de Raz.

At the beginning of 1944 he attended the War Course at the Staff College, returning to 34 Wing at the beginning of March. Within a few days he had flown two more operations, the first in a Mosquito to photograph targets in Normandy from 24,000 feet, and the following day a three-hour sortie in a 16 Squadron Spitfire PR XI (PA 869) photographing river lines and crossing points on the Loire. He was also heavily involved in night photography trials and moving the Wing to Northolt where the Supreme Commander, General Eisenhower, inspected them shortly afterwards. Two weeks later, HM King George visited the Wing.

Throughout the spring of 1944, the Wing was in full operation with their new aircraft engaged in photographing invasion targets and V-1 sites. An exercise had illustrated the need for adequate night reconnaissance, which up to this time was only provided by a Flight of 140 Squadron Mosquitoes. Considerable discussion took place to determine the most suitable aircraft for the task of both night reconnaissance and low-level photography. The Wellington was selected, and 69 Squadron, newly returned from Malta,

A wrecked V-1 'Crossbow' site photographed from very low level. (*Public Record Office. AIR 34/838*)

Ground crew load cameras on a Spitfire PR XI of 16 Squadron. A F52 camear with a 36-inch lens is on the ground. Webb flew with 16 Squadron when he took his spectacular photographs of the battle of Arnhem. (*M. Horsfall*)

joined 34 Wing as a specialist night Squadron. This gave Webb an opportunity to add another aircraft type to his long list, and he flew his first sortie on 25 April. Despite being on a staff appointment, he flew at every opportunity, and on all types, and he logged no less that forty hours in April on six different types including operational sorties over France in the Mosquito and Spitfire.

In May he flew fifty-seven sorties in six types with more operations. He photographed the railways at Dinard from 27,000 feet in a Spitfire. Later in the month, flying a Mosquito, he took low oblique photographs of the railways at Chartres and Angers, and a few days later he was in another Spitfire taking low-level photographs of the gun batteries at Le Tréport.

On the night of the invasion of Normandy, 5 June 1944, the Wellington XIIIs of 69 Squadron flew their first night reconnaissance over Rouen. Early the following morning Group Captain Lousada, Officer Commanding 34 Wing, announced that D-Day had arrived. Shortly afterwards, Webb took off in a 16 Squadron Spitfire XI (PA 929) for a contact patrol with the recently landed 6th Airborne Division east of the River Orne. He then flew to take photographs of Caen for bomb damage assessment when he came under heavy fire from German flak batteries, but he returned with 'some remarkable photographs'. Three days later he took off in very bad weather for another contact patrol with 6th Airborne, and the Squadron diary records, 'His was the only aircraft over the beach-head but it was a highly successful patrol.' On 3 July he flew as second pilot on a 69 Squadron night reconnaissance operation.

Not content with flying reconnaissance operations during his supposed 'rest' tour, Webb embarked on a number of 'dicing' sorties in July leading a pair of Spitfires shooting up river traffic on the Seine, an RDF site at Cap d'Antifer and convoys at Chartres. Throughout this period he was heavily engaged with his primary responsibilities preparing the Wing to move to the Continent, and he made regular trips to the advanced landing grounds established in Normandy. By the end of August, the Wing was established near Bayeux, but moved in rapid succession to Amiens and then B58, Melsbroek just outside Brussels, where it arrived on 8 September.

'Sandy' Webb's operational career as a photographic reconnaissance pilot was coming to an end in September, but not before he flew some low-level sorties during the ill-fated Operation 'Market'. He was appointed

The main dropping zone for Operation 'Market' at Arnhem. A photograph taken by Webb on 17 September 1944. (*Public Record Office. AIR 37/1231*)

to organise and command a reconnaissance detachment of four Spitfire XIs operating from Northolt, and to operate in conjunction with the Headquarters of the 1st Allied Airborne Army during the operations at Arnhem, Nijmegan and Eindhoven. He recruited four experienced tour-expired former members of 140 Squadron who were 'resting'. This detachment flew thirteen sorties whenever the weather allowed. As one would have expected, Webb chose to fly on these operations, and despite very poor weather and heavy anti-aircraft fire, he completed three successful low-level visual and photographic sorties of fourteen landing areas.

On 17 September he took off at 1345 in PL 834 equipped with F24 oblique cameras fitted with 5- and 14-inch lenses. After take-off he crossed the Dutch coast at Schouwen and flew to Dordrecht where he photographed the bridges. He then flew to Arnhem where he arrived as 'a wonderful drop was going on' and he photographed the historic event. He continued to take photographs of the Nijmegen bridges and the DZ at Grave. He flew home via the Air-Sea Rescue launches positioned in the North Sea, landing after a three-hour sortie when he immediately debriefed General Brereton, the US Commander of the 1st Allied Airborne Army.

The following day he took off in the same aircraft to photograph the Arnhem DZs and the on-going battle for the famous bridge taking photographs that have become the hallmark of the operation, and attracted universal acclaim for decades since. He went on to Nijmegen where he came under heavy fire from the flak batteries and, as he arrived at Eindhoven, he watched the gliders of the US 101st Airborne Division land under heavy fire. He landed at Farnborough after a four-hour flight to debrief the Allied commanders.

Some months later it was announced that Queen Wilhelmina of the Netherlands had awarded Webb the Order of the Bronze Lion, a decoration instituted for men who had distinguished themselves in time of war for bravery or leadership in the face of the enemy. Webb's decoration was for:

> Distinguishing himself during operations near Arnhem from 17 to 25
> September 1944 by doing particularly brave deeds and setting in every respect
> a praiseworthy example in very difficult circumstances.

On 30 September an Anson communications aircraft was returning to Northolt from a visit to the Wing when it crashed near Biggin Hill killing the five occupants. These included the CO of 34 Wing Support Unit, the CO of 140 Squadron and two specialist officers. At the time of this tragedy, Webb had been flying operations continuously for three years, and the authorities decided that he needed a rest tour, and he was posted to Northolt to fill the vacancy of CO of 34 Wing Support Unit, a post he held for the next few months.

Three days after returning to England, Group Captain P. Ogilvie, the CO of 34 Wing, wrote the following citation:

The spectacular photograph taken by Webb showing the German armoured vehicles destroyed by soldiers of the 1st Parachute Brigade on the northern end of the Arnhem Bridge. (*IWM. MH 2061*)

This officer has completed thirty successful reconnaissance sorties on Spitfire, Mosquito and Wellington aircraft while holding the appointment of Wing Commander Operations at No 34 Wing. He has consistently chosen dangerous operations, often of an experimental nature, and his enthusiasm and determination has been an inspiration to the whole Wing. I consider that he has set an invaluable example and most strongly recommend the award of the DSO.

For unknown reasons, Air Marshal Sir Arthur Coningham, the Commander-in-Chief of the Second Tactical Air Force, decided to recommend the award of a Bar to the Distinguished Flying Cross, which was approved. Having studied 'Sandy' Webb's operational career in considerable detail, it is difficult to understand why his remarkable exploits did not receive greater recognition.

With the war in Europe drawing to a close, Webb wanted one more tour of operations, and he managed to get himself appointed as Wing Commander Flying of 124 Typhoon Wing based in Holland. He flew his first operation as the number two of a twelve-aircraft armed reconnaissance in the Steinhuder Lake region. The formation was directed to marshalling yards at Leese, and reports claimed that all the rockets hit the target. Later the same day, he led a formation to attack two trains near Soltau. One had steam up and was carrying fifteen tanks, and in spite of 'a terrific barrage of flak', the attack was pressed home leaving two goods trains burning.

As the Allied advance into Germany moved rapidly forward, the Wing was occupying new airfields every few days, but operations continued. The forward air controller directed Webb's formation to 'something big' on 16 April, and twelve Typhoons attacked barracks at Verden near Bremen when it was 'well plastered'. The following day a Hitler Youth Camp near Oldenburg was destroyed. During a period of poor weather, 124 Wing moved to the former *Luftwaffe* permanent airfield at Lübeck. Operations resumed on 24 April when the Wing flew at an intensive rate for the next few days, with Webb leading his Squadrons on many of them. Gun positions and strong points were attacked in support of the advancing armies, and 108 sorties were flown on 26 April. Three days later, Webb led a large formation from 137, 181, and 182 Squadrons against an enemy headquarters 15 miles east of Hamburg. There was a large explosion as the target was left burning with great columns of smoke. During April, the Wing had flown 1,231 sorties on 167 missions destroying large quantities of enemy motor transport, parked aircraft, locomotives and rolling stock for the loss of eleven pilots. On the first day of May, Webb led an attack against a large concentration of motor vehicles near Schwerin heading for Denmark and 128 vehicles and were destroyed.

On 2 May 1945, Wing Commander 'Sandy' Webb DFC and Bar took off in his Typhoon SW 530 at the head of his formation on an armed-reconnaissance mission. North of Lübeck he sighted a train and decided to attack it despite the presence of a flak-truck. Before firing his rockets, he was hit by the anti-aircraft fire. He crashed in flames and was killed. The Germans buried him on the farm where his aircraft fell.

From the first days of the war over five years earlier, 'Sandy' Webb had always 'led from the front'. The day after his tragic death, the Typhoon Wings flew their last sorties of the war.

Bibliography

Extensive use has been made of primary sources held at the Air Historical Branch and at the Public Record Office. Reference was made to many files in the following series, AIR 2,14,26,27,28,29,40,41,50. ADM 1/11105, ADM 207/13 and 30 and WO 208/3303 were also consulted. Other primary sources included aircrew flying logbooks, personal diaries, accounts, private memoirs and many interviews.

Published works

Air Ministry	*Wings of the Pheonix*	(HMSO)
Bingham, V.	*Bristol Beaufighter*	(Airlife, 1994)
Blanchett, C.	*From Hull, Hell and Halifax*	(Midland Counties)
Bowyer, C.	*Beaufighter*	(William Kimber, 1987)
Bowyer, M.	*No 2 Group*	(Faber, 1974)
Bowyer, M.	*The Stirling Story*	(Crecy, 2002)
Carter, N. & C.	*The Distinguished Flying Cross*	(Savannah, 1998)
Chorley, W.R.	*Bomber Command Losses*	(Midland Counties)
Delve, K.	*Source Book of the RAF*	(Airlife, 1994)
Delve, K.	*Vickers Armstrong Wellington*	(Crowood Press, 1998)
Franks, N.	*Hurricanes over the Arakan*	(Patrick Stephens, 1989)
Goulter, C.J.M.	*A Forgotten Offensive*	(Frank Cass, 1995)
Gunby, D.	*Sweeping the Skies*	(Pentland Press, 1995)
Harris, Sir Arthur	*Despatch on War Operations*	(Cass, 1995)
Jefford, C.G.	*Observers and Navigators*	(Airlife, 2001)
Jefford, C.G.	*RAF Squadrons*	(Airlife, 1993)
Jones, W.E.	*Bomber Intelligence*	(Midland Counties, 1983)
Kelly, T.	*Battle for Palembang*	(Robert Hale, 1985)
Lamb, C.	*War in a Stringbag*	(Cassell, 1977)
Leaf, E.	*Above all Unseen*	(Patrick Stephens, 1997)
Lee, Sir David	*Wings in the Sun*	(HMSO, 1989)
Maynard, J.	*Bennett and the Pathfinders*	(Arms and Armour, 1995)
Merrick, K.A.	*Flights of the Forgotten*	(Arms & Armour, 1989)
Middlebrook, M.	*The Berlin Raids*	(Viking, 1988)
Middlebrook &	*Bomber Command War Diaries*	(Viking, 1985)

Everitt Morgan & Shacklady	*Spitfire, The History*	(Key, 1987)
Moyes, P.	*Bomber Squadrons of the RAF*	(Macdonald, 1964)
Moyle, H.	*The Hampden File*	(Air Britain, 1989)
Nesbit, R.C.	*Strike Wings*	(Wm Kimber, 1984)
Nesbit, R.C.	*The Armed Rovers*	(Airlife, 1995)
Onderwater, H.	*Second to None*	(Airlife, 1992)
Pelly-Fry, J.	*Heavenly Days*	(Crecy, 1994)
Probert, H.	*The Forgotten Air Force*	(Brasseys, 1995)
Probert, H.	*Bomber Harris*	(Greenhill Books, 2001)
Rawlings, J.D.R.	*Coastal, Support and Special Squadrons*	(Janes, 1982)
Rawlings, J.D.R.	*Fighter Squadrons*	(Macdonald & Janes, 1978)
Richards, D.	*Hardest Victory*	(Hodder & Stoughton, 1994)
Richards & Saunders	*Royal Air Force 1939–1945*	(HMSO, 1953)
Sharp & Bowyer	*Mosquito*	(Faber & Faber, 1967)
Shores, C.	*2nd Tactical Air Force*	(Osprey, 1970)
Shores, C.	*Dust Clouds in the Middle East*	(Grub Street, 1996)
Shores & Cull	*Air War for Yugoslavia, Greece and Crete*	(Grub Street, 1987)
Shores & Cull	*Bloody Shambles*	(Grub Street, 1992)
Shores & Cull	*Malta. The Hurricane Years*	(Grub Street, 1987)
Shores & Cull	*Malta. The Spitfire Years*	(Grub Street, 1991)
Shores, Ring & Hess	*Fighters over Tunisia*	(Grub Street, 1975)
Smithers, A.J.	*Taranto 1940*	(Leo Cooper, 1995)
Tavender, I.	*The Distinguished Flying Medal*	(Savannah, 2000)
Terraine, J.	*The Right of the Line*	(Hodder & Stoughton, 1985)
Thetford, O.	*Aircraft of the RAF Since 1918*	(Putnam, 1995)
Verity, H.	*We Landed by Moonlight*	(Ian Allan, 1978)
Warner, G.	*The Bristol Blenheim*	(Crecy, 2002)
Webster & Frankland	*The Strategic Air Offensive*	(HMSO, 1961)

Index

Figures in *italic* refer to illustrations.